The police now moved through the apartment and peered into the kitchen. The wall phone next to the microwave oven was off the hook, dangling from the cord. It was smeared red, and bloody prints of bare feet were traced across the tile floor in a crazy-quilt pattern of capricious gore. Many of the prints overlapped each other. The kitchen floor looked like a flight of vampires had danced their way through a macabre blood feast. A few pieces of cutlery, an empty coffee cup, and a half-filled bottle of water on the kitchen counter provided a curiously mundane contrast to all the blood.

As the entry team approached the end of the hallway, the policemen observed the feet of a man who appeared to be lying on the floor inside the master bedroom. Riedl was closest to the bedroom, and he slid his weapon back into its holster. Then, with the corporal covering them, Riedl, the police dog and his handler moved into the bedroom.

The body of a middle-aged man was lying there, facedown on the floor of the doorway . . .

DEADLY WHITE FEMALE

Clifford L. Linedecker

ST. MARTIN'S PAPERBACKS

DEADLY WHITE FEMALE

Copyright © 1994 by Clifford L. Linedecker.

Cover photograph by Don Banks.

ISBN: 0-312-95165-5

Printed in the United States of America

St. Martin's Paperbacks edition/April 1994

10 9 8 7 6 5 4 3 2 1

For Roger
And for those who loved him.

Acknowledgments

The assistance and cooperation of many people have contributed to the creation of this book, and they deserve my thanks.

Special thanks go to Mike Saelens, whose efforts and performance far exceeded the expectations I had when I asked him to gather some of the information and conduct interviews that I wasn't able to complete while I was in the Beltway area doing my research. Mike performed above and beyond the call of duty, and his unique and encyclopedic knowledge of Washington, D.C., northern Virginia, and Maryland were a tremendous help.

Carl Graziano, formerly of Prince Georges County's *Journal* in Hyattsville, deserves a thank-you for providing early background information that made it possible for me to prepare a presentation for the book. Also thanks to *Journal* photographer Lon Slepicka for original photographs and for copies of others made available by law enforcement agencies.

Others who consented to interviews or otherwise provided assistance include former Detective Bill Cowell of the Arlington County Police Department, Prince Georges County Assistant State Attorney General Laura J. Gwinn, Assistant U. S. Attorney Barbara S. Sale, defense attorney Harry J. Trainor, Jr., and attorney Frank Soulier.

Finally, a big thank you goes to my editor, Charles Spicer, for suggesting I write the book.

Contents

DREAMS COME TRUE FOR US WITH PA-
TIENCE—DWM 36 tall attractive warm witty romantic unpretentious ISO petite SDWF with
similar dreams. Kids welcomed with open heart.

In Search Of column
Washingtonian

Her lips were red, her looks were free,
Her locks were yellow as gold:
Her skin was white as leprosy,
The Night-mare Life-In-Death was she,
Who thicks man's blood with cold.

The Ancient Mariner
Samuel Taylor Coleridge

Introduction

If love is a cure for loneliness, it can sometimes be a dangerous solution. Great poets and philosophers have always known that, of course.

England's esteemed late nineteenth century poet laureate Alfred Lord Tennyson touched on some of the fears of love flamed out of control when he wrote in "Maude":

> And most of all would I flee from the cruel madness of love.
> The honey of poison-flowers and all the measureless ill.

In *Romeo and Juliet,* Shakespeare devoted an entire play to what is perhaps the world's most tragic and enduring love story. But he had many other cogent and sensible pronouncements on the subject of love and on its dangers as well.

It was the Bard of Avon who first wrote, in *A Midsummer Night's Dream, "The course of true love never did run smooth."* In the same play he sagely observed:

Love looks not with the eyes, but with the mind.
And therefore is wing'd Cupid painted blind.

Nothing has changed much in the arena of love since
the time of the Bard and of Lord Tennyson, except that
in the modern world we live in, the process of seeking
out romance may be more dangerous than ever before.

Finding, wooing, and winning one's soulmate may be
life's greatest game, and the rewards for success are crucial to happiness because it can affect everything you
do, everything you are, and everything you become. But
the game of love has sobering perils and pitfalls to contend with.

In some societies today marriages are still arranged,
often very successfully. In Western society however, for
the unattached young—or old—there are aspects of the
procedure for finding a mate that seem to make it almost a game of chance, a risky crapshoot that comes up
with snake-eyes on the first toss more often than with
winning sevens. Some, especially the more romantic,
may talk of a role played by kismet, karma, or fate in the
matching of soulmates. But whatever it is, finding "Mr.
Right" or "Miss Right" is a chancy business.

It is, however, an undertaking that at any given time is
dear to the hearts and minds of a large portion of the
American population. According to figures from the
U.S. Census Bureau, in 1992 there were nearly 82 million singles of marriageable age in the country. That
compares with about 67 million in 1980.

Lonely men and women look for romance on the job,
in bars, dance halls, music concerts, churches and tem-
ples, beaches, campgrounds, and in senior citizen centers. They consult psychics and astrologers, or friends
set them up with blind dates. Sometimes they go high-
tech, tying in to electronic chat lines and networks with

personal computers, and share information about likes and dislikes by tapping out messages with their fingers. And some sign up with agencies that film interviews with eligible men and women, then show videotapes of carefully selected prospects to other clients shopping for mates.

With increasing frequency, however, the lovelorn are turning to an old tried-and-true source for partners: the personals columns of newspapers and magazines. Or they leaf through some of the more than twenty-five publications in the country that are now devoted entirely to matching up heterosexual singles.

Census figures disclose there are one hundred women for every eighty-five eligible men in the United States. Surveys conducted in the early 1990s have indicated however that about sixty percent of lonely singles who place personal ads are male.

Roger Wayne Paulson was a lonely man who placed an ad in the personals promising dreams realized, then plunged into a nightmare. The woman he met was everything he was looking for—and more. She was attractive, charming, and intelligent. But she was also a woman of many faces with a complex criminal background that was filled with intrigue and mystery. She became the instrument of Roger's destruction.

Murder in the lovelorn ads isn't a new phenomenon. Far from it! Personals columns have provided the avenue for tragedy since long before Roger Paulson was born. Around the turn of the century, America's most notorious female serial killer, Belle Gunness, advertised in the personals columns of ethnic Norwegian newspapers for rich husbands. Then she murdered the would-be spouses when they showed up at her farm home near La Porte, Indiana, and stole their money, watches, and other valuables.

At about the time the sturdy widow was filling her basement and garden with the bodies of unwary swains in Indiana, a short, potbellied, balding, red-bearded Frenchman was using the lovelorn columns of Paris newspapers to carry out a similarly grisly scam. The victims of Henri Landru, who became known as France's real-life "Bluebeard," were man-hungry middle-aged spinsters and lonely widows. He lured the unsuspecting women to a country cottage, where they were strangled and their flesh rendered in big pots atop a stove before burial. Then he stole their cash, and sold their clothes and furniture to support his family.

But there have been many less notorious predators in more modern times who have prowled through the lovelorn ads to lure murder victims.

In Maine, Dennis R. Larson was sentenced to a fifty-year prison term for murdering his wife of a few weeks by pushing her over the side of a steep eighty-foot cliff at Acadia National Park. Kathy Frost Larson met her husband-to-be only seven weeks before her death in October 1987, after responding to his ad in the personals columns of the *Bangor Daily News*.

Soon after the marriage, Larson took out a $200,000 life-insurance policy on his bride with a double indemnity clause for accidental death. Police suspicions about the husband's role in the fatal plunge were fueled when they learned he collected about $20,000 in insurance on the life of his first wife, who disappeared in 1975. The Great Falls, Montana, native told police his wife, Leslee Reynolds Larson, was washed away by Prickly Pear Creek. Her body was never found.

It seems obvious that seeking romance in the want ads can be a dangerous business today, as it was a century ago. Prison inmates are enthusiastic advertisers and correspondents for the personals, and they place ads in everything from college newspapers and city dailies to the supermarket tabloids.

Nevertheless, every year around the country thousands of couples do find love and satisfying life partners in the want ads. One of my close friends, a middle-aged Indiana journalist, found a wonderful wife through the personals just when he appeared to be mired for life in lonely bachelorhood.

Some especially cautious men and women hedge their bets by seeking out ex-wives and girlfriends, or ex-husbands and boyfriends for private conversations when new relationships begin to show promise of becoming serious. Instead of simply jumping in with both feet and living an illusion of trust with a stranger, others hire private detectives to conduct premarital investigations, or simply snoop into the background of a favorite dating partner. Surprisingly often, the man or woman whose life is being checked out hasn't been totally truthful.

Sometimes handsome actors or beautiful actresses are even sicced on a lover or sweetheart to find out if he or she is the kind who is likely to cheat.

That hardly seems fair, or a very good way to lay the foundation for a loving and trusting relationship. But at the very least, it's sure to provide someone who is shopping for love with some indication of who is really being invited into their life, their home, and their bed.

Cliff Linedecker
1993

Prologue

7:56 P.M.—The woman's voice over the telephone had the sound of desperation, fear, and a hint of disbelief.

"Oh God! Oh God! Oh God!" she moaned as the police dispatcher strained to hear. "Oh my God, I've been shot. He shot me."

Then the low moaning was replaced by a shrill scream: "Don't let me die here!"

The dispatcher was experienced and trained to handle emergencies. Speaking as calmly as she could, she continued prodding the hysterical woman for information. She had to have an address.

"Who shot you?" the dispatcher repeatedly asked. "Where is he now?"

At first the questions seemed only to further agitate the distressed woman, who had dialed 911 only moments before. At last, however, the professionally persistent probing paid off. The woman said she was shot in the arm by her boyfriend.

Still seemingly teetering precariously on the edge of hysteria, she at last gasped out an address at the Powder Mill Apartments on Evans Trail in Beltsville, Maryland.

7:58 P.M.—Another 911 call was registered from the

Powder Mill Apartments. This time a man was on the line. He said he thought there had been a shooting and someone was hurt.

A police squad car and an ambulance from the Calverton Station of the Prince Georges County Fire Department were already on their way, speeding toward the apartment complex about a block away.

Chapter One

Lisa Ann

The classic California girl is supposed to be a long-legged blond beauty who spends her days being pursued by handsome surfers while she frolics in the sun and sand.

Lisa Ann Miller was a California girl, and although she was petite and pretty, she never came close to being a beach bunny. Her childhood was miserable.

She was born in the Contra Costa county-seat town of Martinez at the edge of Suison Bay to Floyd and Glennie L. Hart Miller on July 9, 1962, the same year President Kennedy announced that U.S. military advisers in Vietnam would return fire if fired upon; that John H. Glenn, Jr., became the first American to orbit earth; and Rachel Carson launched the environmental movement with her frightening book, *Silent Spring*.

It was also the summer that the first known victim of the Boston Strangler was found murdered in her home. But Anna Slesers's ghastly slaying occurred nearly four thousand miles across the country from Fremont, California, where Lisa Ann spent most of her abbreviated and unhappy childhood.

On the southeast shore of San Francisco Bay the city

of Fremont is spread along the site of the old Mission San Jose de Guadalupe, which was established by Spanish priests, soldiers, and explorers in 1797. The city as it's known today wasn't formed until 1956, six years before Lisa Ann's birth, when the Alameda County communities of Mission San Jose, Warm Springs, Niles, Irvington, and Centerville joined together into a single municipality.

The new city, which today has a population of around 131,000 people, was named after John C. Fremont, an early soldier, explorer, and mapmaker who played a cardinal role in wresting California from the Spanish and developing it for American settlement.

Lisa Ann's childhood was spent near the natural beauty of the Bay area south and across the Dumbarton Bridge from San Francisco. But it was spoiled and frittered away by the alcoholic rages and violence of her father. Floyd Miller was a mean drunk who flew into rages, broke furniture, and punched the women in the household when he was boozing. That was most of the time.

The family patriarch's disreputable behavior produced the kind of home that breeds human wreckage. Miller's drinking binges and handy violence was typical of behavior that fit a classic recipe for producing children whose tragically battered bodies and egos can predestine them to become losers or failures.

During most of her childhood growing up in the East Bay area, Lisa was squeezed into a double-wide trailer with her parents and four siblings, including a sister, Johnnie Elaine, who was one year older than she. Despite her wretched homelife, Lisa Ann held her own with her classwork at school and developed a taste for serious reading. Before the Millers interrupted their peripatetic wanderings along the East Bay to settle in

Fremont, she attended schools in both the Concord and Pittsburgh communities in Contra Costa County.

Slim, with blue eyes and mouse-brown hair that bleached almost blond in the California sunshine, Lisa Ann was neither ugly nor exceptionally pretty. And although she couldn't by any stretch of the imagination have been considered the most popular girl in school, she seemed to make friends easily enough among both male and female classmates. Her plain appearance apparently didn't create any problems for her as she entered adolescence and began dating.

The dating scene in the Bay Area can be especially exciting and fruitful for teenage girls. Not only do they have access to their male schoolmates, but young sailors and other servicemen are all over the area.

In the 1970s, when Lisa Ann was a teenager in Fremont, the huge Naval Air Base at Moffett Field just across the Dumbarton Bridge at the narrow southern tip of San Francisco Bay was home to thousands of sailors.

A drive of a few more minutes north along the Nimitz Freeway (U.S. 880), however, could carry Lisa or her friends to an inviting clutter of even more Navy bases, including the U.S. Naval Air Station at Alameda, the U.S. Naval Supply Center, and the U.S. Naval Receiving Station at man-made Treasure Island under the San Francisco—Oakland Bay Bridge.

Lisa Ann was sixteen years old when she became pregnant. She forged her parents' permission, and in 1978 married a young enlisted sailor, Steven Rohn. The groom was only a couple of years older than the bride. A son, Steven Franklin Rohn, was born to them on March 24, 1979. The young couple got along well enough together so that on April 22, 1980, Lisa gave birth to their second son, Michael Jack Rohn.

Things weren't going as well back in her parents'

trailer however. Floyd Miller's drinking was raging out of control, and during a violent confrontation in 1980, Johnnie Elaine blasted her father in the stomach with a twelve-gauge shotgun.

Miller was as tough as he was mean, and he survived the terrible injury, although he spent months in a hospital. Police investigators decided that the nineteen-year-old girl shot her father in self-defense, and she was never charged in the case. Floyd Miller lived seven years after the shooting. And by the time he died in a car accident in 1987, his daughter Johnnie Elaine had been dead nearly four years.

Johnnie Elaine hadn't been as resilient, or as lucky, as her father was. She was living with a boyfriend in a southern Oregon commune in 1983 when she was shot to death. The shooting was officially classified by local authorities as an accident, but not everyone who knew Johnnie Elaine believed that. Dark murmurings still persist that the troubled young woman committed suicide, possibly as a final desperate act of guilt over her father's shooting; as the result of years of abuse; or due to some other cause.

Years later *People* magazine would quote Lisa as saying through her lawyer that she was very upset and deeply affected by her older sister's death.

By the time Johnnie Elaine died, Lisa's marriage had crumbled. The star-crossed union began to sour shortly after the birth of her second child. In 1981 she and her husband were living across the country near the world's largest naval base in Norfolk, Virginia, when they were divorced.

Lisa was nineteen years old, and her mother and other family members had moved inland and farther north in California, to the rustic mountain town of Weed near Mount Shasta, at the edge of the heavily forested Cascade Mountain range. With her boys in tow, Lisa made the transcontinental trek back to her home state and enrolled as a student at the College of the Siskiyous in Weed. She was attending the small-town college in Siskiyou County when she met a handsome dark-haired lothario named Raymond Arnold Huberts.

Fate and body chemistry mixed with a mutual desire to feed off each other. When Lisa and Huberts met, they paired up and stuck together as easily and naturally as pollen to a honeybee.

An experienced con man and fast-buck artist who was rapidly approaching his fortieth birthday, Huberts was nearly twice as old as Lisa and had been in and out of trouble with police most of his adult life.

Born in the north Chicago suburb of Winnetka on October 14, 1943, by the time Huberts met the twenty-year-old divorcée, he had drifted around the country trying his slippery hands at a variety of illegal activities.

His most serious run-in with the criminal justice system occurred in Portland, Oregon, where he was convicted of possession of counterfeit currency. He served a term at the federal prison in Terre Haute, Indiana, for the offense. But he also compiled a record of other arrests in Pennsylvania and South Florida, for alleged offenses ranging from willful cruelty to a child to mail fraud.

By 1983, when the one-time midwesterner and the California divorcée teamed up, Huberts was back on the West Coast. Soon after he and Lisa met, they left the isolation of the small towns and forests of Siskiyou County and moved downstate to the San Francisco Bay area where she had spent her childhood. The geographical area was more promising and the timing right for someone with a desire for quick money and few if any scruples about how to cash in.

The South Bay on both sides of the Dumbarton Bridge attracted hundreds of thousands of families and single men and women during the early and mid-1980s. Computers, aerospace, and the military were all big, thriving businesses. Universities, colleges, and private companies poured additional millions of dollars into the local economy in payrolls and purchases for high-tech research.

If Huberts spent any time attempting to find work in the aerospace or computer industries, there is no indication of those efforts in police records. Police accused him of running a call-girl operation.

Lisa didn't have the skills or training to slip into a high-paying job in the sophisticated industrial world of computers or aerospace. But she was eager and willing to cash in on the fast, easy money to be made in the sex trade. Huberts was also quick to recognize a promising opportunity when he saw it.

Lisa had been divorced less than two years when her life began lurching out of control, rapidly plunging into a downward spiral of self-destruction. She wasn't one of those fortunate women who was a natural beauty with cover-girl loveliness. But she was young and sexy and she knew how to make the most of her assets. Bay area police records indicate that soon after her first meeting with Huberts, she went to work with the silver-tongued ex-convict in the dial-a-prostitute business. On-the-job experience provided all the training she needed to become a big money maker.

Since San Francisco's earliest days, through the period of the Gold Rush, up to the present time, trade in commercial sex has always been big business in the Bay area.

During the Gold Rush years, hundreds of boys who were either kidnapped, abandoned by parents, or ran away seeking western adventure, wound up in "peg houses." The boys were forced to sit naked on greased wooden pegs, which dilated their anuses. Pederasts with gold dust in their pockets merely checked out the dimensions of the pegs in order to select the boy they wanted for sex.

When topless dancing first emerged on the American scene, Carol Doda captured the public imagination for her ponderous breasts and nightly on-stage gyrations at a popular San Francisco club.

Before acting out their own tragic Cain and Abel drama, brothers Artie and Jim Mitchell made San Francisco a world center of the pornographic movie business. Headquartering themselves in the O'Farrell Theatre in the city's tenderloin, they began by showing and producing loops and soft-core films. Then they moved on to create the hard-core classic, *Behind the Green Door*. The movie grossed more than $25 million and made a porn superstar out of Marilyn Chambers whose fresh, clean, all-American face once appeared on boxes of Ivory Snow.

The Mitchell brothers' smut empire was already in serious trouble in February 1991 when Jim fatally shot his younger brother, Artie. But the enterprising brothers are hardly missed, if they are missed at all, by the legion of streetwalkers and outcall hookers who keep the sex business thriving in the Bay area.

Throughout San Francisco's history, prostitutes have walked the Tenderloin area around Market and Sixth streets, the Embarcadero, Mission Street, and just about every other major thoroughway and many of the side streets; and worked the crib houses, massage parlors, and escort services. The money in the business is fast, and depending on individual outlook, easy.

Being a successful prostitute can involve much more

than mastering the mere mechanics of various sexual acts. Once they have taken the plunge from naive innocence or busy amateur to calculating professional, prostitutes have historically honed the arts of seduction and thievery.

Prostitutes traditionally associate with other hookers, pimps, thieves, fast-buck artists, and various other rogues and pharisees who exist on the fringes of society. And they instinctively realize, or quickly learn, that it can be easier to steal from one or two clients than to service a dozen.

Cash, credit cards, social security cards, driver's licenses, and other identification documents or valuables can be slipped out of billfolds or pockets when an unwary client is sleeping or has his mind and attention focused on other things. Credit cards can be the most valuable if a thief or a confederate knows how to utilize them for a series of quick purchases. Criminals are quick to update their techniques when trouble develops, and credit card thieves are no different.

For a while hookers or their accomplices usually took billfolds and everything in them, or simply cleaned out the credit cards. But that was easily noticed by the owners and led to too much trouble, so some of the more professional thieves developed a safer system. They began replacing the victim's cards with others that were "burned out." The substitutes were pilfered earlier and used by the thieves to run up large balances that were likely to show up soon on "hot sheets" that list forged and stolen cards.

Professional credit card swindlers often buy or swap for cards stolen by prostitutes of both sexes, as well as by pickpockets, burglars, petty thieves who rifle the mail, and other small-time criminals who feed on the darker edges of society. That was the element of society that the young mother from the Bay area moved into after meeting Huberts.

Lisa was twenty years old, and, with her blue eyes, blond hair, the right cosmetics and tight skirts, was an overnight success as a whore. Once she stepped firmly into the tawdry neon world of the sex trade, the cash began rolling in. Any innocence that might have survived her earlier life was quickly plundered by her new profession.

In November, a few months after her twenty-first birthday, police moved in. Lisa was picked up and accused of prostitution. The next day, authorities removed her boys from her home in Fremont. Police said the children, three and four years old, were left alone for at least twenty-four hours without adult care or supervision.

Lisa's mother, Glennie, eventually wound up with custody of the boys, and a few years later they were living with her in Yreka, some four hundred miles north of San Francisco and about fifteen miles from the Oregon state line.

Vice squad cops in a string of East Bay communities became familiar with the hardworking young hooker. Over a period of a few weeks, she compiled an impressive rap sheet that listed arrests in Hayward, Alameda, and Berkeley.

She became familiar with the routine of arrest, the photographs and fingerprints taken during the booking process; with courtroom proceedings, such as probable cause hearings; with procedures governing bail, and with the legal justice system's commitment to protecting the constitutional rights of the accused.

She knew of the Miranda warning, the 1966 U.S. Supreme Court requirement that suspects in police custody must be advised they have a right to refuse to talk, that any statements they make may be used as evidence against them, and that they have the right to have an attorney present.

But listening to the warning read in a real-life situation is different than hearing a Kojak, a Columbo, or some other television sleuth rattle it off to a hangdog suspect. It's a miserable and frightening experience, and you can't dismiss it by flicking off the tube.

Call girls are generally among the most sophisticated, better protected hookers. Some of them are tutored by lawyers about what they can or cannot say to prospective clients, in order to avoid arrests by undercover vice cops. The smart girls don't talk about money for sex, but leave that up to the customer. And when police officers bring the subject up, they often set themselves up for accusations of entrapment, which leads to the dismissal of any charges.

But if there was any hint of glamour tied to the sordid world of the outcall prostitution business for Lisa, it had turned sour and was proven to be false. There was nothing glamorous about being rounded up and hauled into police stations and temporary lockups with streetwalkers, pushers, pill poppers, crackheads, and assorted lunatics who were periodically swept off the most misery-brushed streets of Alameda County.

Lisa's enthusiasm for working as a laborer in the Bay area prostitution trade quickly began to fade after her brushes with police. Huberts was also beginning to consider a change of geography and occupation. He had logged his own vice arrests in Palo Alto, Alameda, and Hayward.

Speaking to journalists through her lawyer years later, Lisa claimed she regretted her venture into the commercial sex trade, but explained that she was very young and dazzled by the money.

Authorities never pursued either prostitution or abuse charges against her for the back-to-back alleged incidents involving her professional activities and parenting lapse. In fact, neither she nor Huberts were ever convicted on any of the vice charges.

In the early spring of 1986 Lisa and Huberts left the grubby hopes and pathetic realities of the prostitution business behind them. They headed across the country for a new beginning in the East.

Chapter Two

Roger

Roger Wayne Paulson's childhood and youth was about as different from Lisa Ann's as it could be.

Roger was a military brat. He grew up in a Navy family with a pair of loving parents from Minnesota and three older siblings.

World War II was raging in 1944 and the tide had begun to turn in favor of the Allied forces when Leonard Paulson turned seventeen and headed for the local recruiting office to join the Navy.

He liked military life, especially the Navy, and remained in the service after the end of the war to build his career and raise his family. His wife Joyce was also from Minnesota and quickly slipped into the routine of Navy life as she moved from base to base with him.

Despite their traveling, all the Paulson's children were born in the United States. A son, Gary, is the oldest. Then, spaced about a year apart, a daughter, Gwenn, and another boy, whom they named David, joined the family.

At last, on a Wednesday, November 26, 1953, about three years after David's birth, Roger was born in Washington, D.C. It was almost exactly four months after the war in Korea officially ended, and a few days before Hugh Hefner published the first issue of *Playboy*, featuring a nude calendar photograph of Marilyn Monroe.

Astrologically, Roger was born under the sign of Sagittarius, the archer. His element was fire, his planet Jupiter; based on his sign, his nature could be expected to be just, mature, and proper; and he would presumably have such faith in human nature that it could border at times on the dangerously naive. Sagittarian men are also more likely to be considered more attractive to others for their sincerity and generosity of spirit than their physical appearance.

According to some people who believe that the stars do indeed have some control of behavior and destiny, his most promising and successful romantic matches would be with women born under the signs of Aries (March 21 to April 19) and Leo (July 23 to August 22). Lisa's sign was Cancer, the crab (June 22 to July 22), neither the best nor the worst potential mate for a Sagittarian male. Cancerian women are often said to be cuddly lovers, but they can also be clinging and reluctant to let go of spoiled relationships.

Like his older siblings, as Roger grew up he became used to spending a year or two at a school, then moving away with the rest of the family to begin classes somewhere else. Usually there was a whole new set of friends to make, but he was resilient and learned to deal with the unique socialization demands of being a military child. And it helped to know that most or many of the other children he met were in the same situation.

Despite the necessary uprooting and starting over in new locations, there is a certain stability to life in the military and as military dependents. Years after Leonard Paulson's retirement, his wife recalled that the ground rules were always the same for her children while they were being raised. "No matter whether you were living in Timbuktu or Athens, our home life didn't change that much. It was very stable."

The Paulsons were never stationed in the West African nation of Mali or in Greece, however. Instead, they settled on or around several Navy bases in the continental United States, but they also spent two years in Guam and six years in Hawaii. They arrived on the main island of Oahu on August 20, 1959, the last day that Hawaii was officially a United States territory. The next day the islands became the nation's fiftieth state. Roger was five years old.

His father was sharpening his skills in communications and had been busy moving up the ranks. For a while in Hawaii he was stationed aboard a destroyer based at Pearl Harbor. Then, in 1962 after sixteen years service, he moved up from the enlisted ranks and was commissioned as an officer.

Along with the commission, Leonard Paulson was given a new assignment to a communications station a few miles from Pearl Harbor. The station was near Schofield Barracks, the huge Army base in the north-central area of the island that was made famous by James Jones in the blockbuster book and 1953 Oscar-winning movie, *From Here to Eternity*.

The baby of the Paulson family was a solidly built boy, who made friends easily and involved himself with many of the traditional activities of childhood. He loved model trains, and spent hours by himself or with friends fashioning intricate layouts of miniature track and constructing bridges, buildings, and other accessories from professional kits.

And like other family members, he loved cats and kittens. Many military families agreed that cats were much easier to care for and move with than dogs. Most of the time while the Paulson children were growing up, there was at least one cat in the house.

Roger was an easy child to raise. He loved jokes, laughed easily, and was generally undemanding, although like anyone else there were times when he was riled and his temper flared. The outbursts of temperament usually subsided as quickly as they emerged, and soon he was the same easygoing boy he had been before. He was raised to have a strong sense of what was right and wrong.

He was a slightly above average student in school, developing an early fondness for music and learning to play bass guitar. But he never played or marched with the school band, and didn't participate in many extra-curricular activities, which wasn't all that unusual for the child of a military family.

Instead, from the time Roger was sixteen he worked at part-time jobs after class and during summer vacations to earn his own spending money and pay for the old car he drove. Although he wasn't a tinkerer who liked to bury his head under the hood of a car for hours and tear a motor apart, several of his jobs were at gas stations and with businesses that sold tires and accessories.

During his early teenage years, Roger paid more attention to his jobs, cars, and music than to girls. He and a few buddies even formed their own band. When they broke up or when the family moved, he got together with other musicians to form new groups.

He didn't date a lot, but when he did become interested in a girlfriend, he was a one-woman man. He pursued that girl and that girl only. He preferred going steady to playing the field.

By the time Roger began his senior year in high school, his father was stationed in Washington, D.C., and the family was living in suburban Maryland. He graduated from high school in Wheaton in 1971, about a year before Leonard Paulson retired from the Navy as a lieutenant commander. After high school, Roger attended a semester at Montgomery Junior College in Rockville, Maryland, before dropping out. He didn't want to put up with all the required courses.

On November 10, 1973, about a year after his father left the Navy, Roger married his high school sweetheart, Ruth Ann Pensmith. The young couple had been living in Titusville on Florida's southeast coast across the NASA Causeway from Cape Canaveral and the John F. Kennedy Space Center, but they returned to Maryland for the nuptials.

They obtained their marriage license in Montgomery County and stood up before family and friends at the Millian Memorial United Methodist Church in Rockville. The church pastor, Reverend Raymond J. Purnell, performed the ceremony. Both the bride and the groom were nineteen.

Roger's parents left the Washington area after retirement and settled in Charleston, South Carolina. But Roger didn't like the low country or the sprawling shipyards and naval bases, despite the critical role they played pouring an annual payroll of $1 billion or more into the economy of the old southern port city. Although his brothers and sister settled in the Palmetto state, he and his wife stayed behind in the Beltway communities of Maryland.

Nevertheless, he remained close to his family. He visited his parents and siblings regularly, and wrote often. His letters home were chatty, upbeat, and were decorated with cartoons or happy-face drawings he sketched in the margins. His oldest brother, Gary, had liked guns since childhood, and Roger sometimes went shooting with him during visits in South Carolina. Eventually, Roger began acquiring a few collector guns of his own, including a rusty 1909 Argentine Mauser 30.06 caliber rifle, and a 1912 bolt-action that appeared to have been manufactured in Germany.

In Maryland he worked at a series of jobs selling tires or in other retail activities during the day and practiced or played gigs with various bands at night and on weekends. He finally joined up with three other instrumentalists and two girl singers, to form a group named Pearl.

Curiously, the name of the precious gem had cropped up in Roger's life before, when his father's ship was home-ported at Pearl Harbor. Appropriately perhaps, the name of the community of some 20,000 at the northern tip of the harbor's mid loch is Pearl City.

Pearl had its own agent who took care of bookings and handled other business matters. And the band played popular dance music and light rock at local clubs in the Beltway communities.

Roger and Ruth Ann were married about nine years before their son, Christopher Wesley, was born on August 7, 1981. Roger left Pearl soon after Christopher's birth. He loved his music. But he was thrilled to be a father, and wanted to spend his free time after regular working hours with his wife and son.

The couple bought their own home on Sandy Court in the tiny Washington suburb of Kensington, Maryland, a convenient five-minute drive from Wheaton to the north and the Capital Beltway to the south.

Roger had drifted into the carpeting business as a salesman and estimator when his world began collapsing. The marriage was breaking up, and on September 1, 1989, Roger and his wife reached a mutual agreement to a legal parting. A statement of voluntary separation was filed with the Montgomery County Circuit Court in Rockville.

The catchall phrase of legal separation and divorce, "irreconcilable differences," was cited as the grounds for the act. The formal legal statement included terms of a property settlement, child support, and custody arrangements. Both parents agreed that the best interests and welfare of Christopher was their paramount concern in working out the pact.

The agreement called for them to share joint legal custody of Christopher, although the boy's mother would have primary physical custody.

According to the carefully spelled out terms, Roger's son could visit with him every other weekend from five P.M., Friday, until seven-thirty P.M. Sunday. The visitations would be extended until seven P.M. on Mondays that were legal holidays. He was also permitted two-week visitations with Christopher during the summer school breaks, visits during spring vacation, and would share time on other holidays, to be set up according to an alternating schedule.

School authorities were notified to send copies of report cards, evaluations, and other communications concerning Christopher to both parents.

Initial child support payments were set for Roger at $300 per month, with the amount to be adjusted according to state guidelines after the couple's house was sold. Ruth Ann was to continue health insurance coverage for their son, which she already carried on a family policy. Costs of the boy's college education were to be shared equally by both parents so long as he was a full-time student under the age of twenty-three and carried at least a 2.0 grade average. There was no alimony.

Ruth Ann and Christopher were allowed to live in the house until it could be sold, and Roger was to help pay for the upkeep. After the sale was final, proceeds would be equally distributed between the two after payments on the notes for a 1988 Chevrolet and a 1985 Chrysler. Ruth Ann was to get the Chevy and Roger the Chrysler.

At the time the house was sold, Roger's wife would be required to pay him more than $3400, which was half the value of contributions she made during their marriage to the Montgomery County government's pension plan. She had a good job with the director of the county's Department of Housing and Community Development, and worked in the tidy tenth-floor office of a modern apartment building just a block from the courthouse in Rockville.

Most of the furnishings in the couple's home were allotted to Ruth Ann. But Roger got the dining room furniture, furniture from a middle bedroom, stereo equipment, a thirteen-inch television, tools, gardening equipment, hobby items, presents his family had given to them, and photographic equipment.

Suddenly, after nearly sixteen years of marriage, he was on his own, and he took the breakup of his family hard.

He was so depressed that he checked himself into a psychiatric hospital for treatment of fatigue. He wasn't treated in Maryland, but selected a hospital in Virginia where the likelihood of his employer learning he was a patient would be greatly reduced. The counseling and treatment apparently helped, and he remained there only five days.

But it had been a long time since he lived the bachelor life, and he hardly knew what to do with himself when he wasn't working at his job with Floor Concepts, a carpeting company in Beltsville. He lived for a while after the separation at an apartment in the town of Laurel near the horse-racing track, then moved a few miles south to a ground-floor, two-bedroom rental unit at the Powder Mill Apartments at 11346 Evans Trail in Beltsville to be closer to his job. The two-story yellow brick buildings in the complex were constructed with basement apartments, as well as those on and above ground level.

When Roger left his home in Montgomery County to live in the Prince Georges County communities of Laurel, then Beltsville, it was like moving from day to night. Although both counties share in the economically energizing scatter of federal agencies and facilities that spill over from Washington, D.C., into the suburban communities, they are about as different as they can be.

Montgomery County is upscale, wealthy, and mostly white. Much of Prince Georges County is economically depressed, local government services are severely overtaxed, and the population is heavily blue collar and about forty percent black.

When Roger moved into Apartment 102, he took two cats along with him. In mid-June 1991, about the time of the summer solstice, he adopted another pet, a black and white kitten. He named her Jellybean. He also kept a few colorful and exotic fish in a large aquarium that stretched along the foot of his bed. The aquarium and the fish were a constant source of intrigue for the cats, but he managed to keep his pets safely separated and prevent accidents. Roger was a man who was hungry for affection and loved pets and children.

Living the bachelor life, he spent more time with his photography hobby, bought new lenses and other advanced equipment, read photography magazines and signed up for classes to hone his skills both behind the lens and in the darkroom. And he got himself an official-looking card that advised it was a press pass for an amateur photographer.

At about that time, he began confiding to a few close friends and acquaintances about his military service in Vietnam. He framed a Purple Heart and a Silver Star, and placed them in a prominent location on a shelf in his apartment. The Silver Star is the nation's second highest military award for bravery, and the Purple Heart is awarded to members of the Armed Forces who are wounded in action against the enemy.

The friends he told war stories to weren't aware that he not only hadn't served in Vietnam, but was never in any branch of the military service. He was ten years old in August 1964 when Congress passed the Tonkin Gulf Resolution and the United States stepped irrevocably into the Vietnam War.

As the United States began pouring thousands of troops into Southeast Asia, Roger was busy with his model railroading and with his classes in elementary, junior high, and high school. And he was a nineteen-year-old junior college student in January 1973 when the administration of President Richard F. Nixon at last engineered a ceasefire that ended U.S. participation in the hostilities.

And despite his years as a musician playing pickup clubs and dance halls where young people congregated to drink, play, and scout out potential boyfriends or girl-friends, he had never been good at the flirtatious skirmishing and give and take of the romance game. He hadn't logged in much dating experience before he was married.

Now as a beefy two-hundred-pound-plus, bespectacled, prematurely balding, about-to-be divorced father of a nine-year-old son, his romantic prospects appeared to be even less promising. He had never had much luck picking up girls or women.

The drastic change in Roger's life had left him hurt

and lonesome. When he was with friends sharing a pizza or at an outdoor cookout, he might drink a can or two of Bud. But when he was hurting, he was more likely to settle down with his trains, fuss over his pets, turn on the TV and watch the Redskins, or spend the day with Christopher.

He wasn't a man who hit the bars to try and drink his pain away—or to meet women. So he placed an ad in the personals columns of the October 1990 issue of the *Washingtonian*.

The *Washingtonian* is similar to many of the slick up-scale magazines published in other large cities around the country, and the October edition was the twenty-fifth anniversary edition. The feature story, emblazoned across the front page, was "Secrets." Five subheadlines promised to tell the reader about: "Places You Can't Go," "Things They Never Tell You," "People Who Keep Secrets," "The City's Greatest Mysteries," and "25 Secrets You Can Use."

In retrospect, the subject of the lead story would later appear ominously prophetic.

Under a column labeled "In Search Of," Roger's personal was sandwiched between a couple of ads placed by female divorcées; one urging lonely males not to give up on chances of finding love once again; and the other listing herself in boldface type more simply as a DWF— divorced white female—and pointing out she was a writer who loved books, art, and films.

Roger's ad, containing only the barest punctuation, appeared among more than forty others on page 304 of the magazine, extended barely five lines, and advised:

DREAMS COME TRUE FOR US WITH PA-TIENCE—DWM 36 tall attractive warm witty ro-mantic unpretentious ISO [in search of] petite

SDWF [single or divorced white female] with similar dreams. Kids welcomed with open heart.

The number of his ad at the *Washingtonian* concluded the appeal. Unlike many other advertisers, he didn't request photographs and didn't rule out smokers, drinkers, or readers from outside his own immediate area.

According to sociologists and others who have examined the phenomena of personal ads, Roger was typical of many advertisers. Studies show that nationwide the number of males placing ads outnumber females about three-to-two, although there are broad regional differences where populations of one gender greatly exceed the other for one reason or another. And people typically turn to the ads after the breakup of a marriage or other close traditional long-term love connection.

When Roger placed his ad in the *Washingtonian*, he had determined to place his hopes and vulnerabilities on the line and his trust in a stranger. He couldn't have been more anxious or ready to establish a new romantic relationship. He was desperate to find his personal "Miss Right," the someone new who would fulfill and change his life.

Chapter Three

Capital Crimes

If William Lee Cowell had been an actor, he might have been cast in Hollywood as a tough, no-nonsense cop who liked his work and was good at it.

He wasn't an actor, however. Police work was the profession he chose as his real-life role when he was a young man looking forward to accepting an honorable discharge from the Marine Corps.

In 1961 Cowell was living in rural Schuyler County, Missouri, some 160 miles northeast of Kansas City and a few minutes drive from the Iowa state line, when he was inducted in the military. He trained at Camp Le-Jeune, North Carolina, as a rifleman—a job and designation known in the blunt slang of the military as a "grunt."

Cowell missed serving in Vietnam by a hair. American involvement in the fighting in Southeast Asia was just beginning to build up when he became eligible for reassignment. Regulations stipulated that Marines had to have at least one year left to serve before they could be assigned to Vietnam. Cowell had eight months to go, and he was sent to the Marine Corps Development and

Educational Command at Quantico, Virginia, to complete his tour of active service.

N. W. Cowell had served for ten years as Schuyler County sheriff, and his son William had been attracted to police work since he was a boy. There was never really much question in his mind that he would some day follow his father into law enforcement. He liked the responsibility, discipline, and authority that went with the territory. He was also attracted to the trappings that went with the profession, such as guns, fast cars, and, depending on the agency and the assignment, motorcycles.

The young Marine, however, didn't plan to return to Schuyler County to try his hand at police work. The area around the nation's capital, including northern Virginia, seemed to offer far better opportunities for an ambitious rookie lawman than the hardscrabble ranching, farm, and coal mining country of the Show Me State where he came from.

Located along the west bank of the Potomac River south of Washington, D.C., Quantico is a swift one-hour drive or less up Interstate 95 to the Beltway. A few months before he was scheduled for discharge, Cowell wrote to the Washington Metropolitan Police Department, the Arlington County Police Department and to the Virginia State Police headquarters in Richmond to inquire about job opportunities.

He got offers from all three police agencies to take their tests, but he had already personally checked out the Arlington County Police Department and made up his mind. As soon as he set eyes on a veteran spit-and-polish Arlington County motorcycle officer, who kept his boots and his bike gleaming, he knew in an instant he had found the job he was looking for. The officer and his equipment looked as if they could have been lifted straight out of a recruiting ad.

Motorcycle officers with the Arlington County Police Department rode Harley-Davidson 74's, and piloting one of the big bikes along the streets and highways was exactly what Cowell had in mind. But other people also had their eyes on the same job. And rookies, regardless of how eager they might be to climb on a Harley, had to pay their dues first. Cowell handily passed the entrance examination and was sworn in as an Arlington County Police Department officer. But he wasn't assigned to motors. Like other rookies, after completing training at the police academy, he wound up on regular patrol duty.

Simply familiarizing himself with the area that the Arlington County police have responsibility for patrolling was no easy overnight task.

Unlike the system of local government in most states, Virginia has more than one hundred independent counties with no incorporated cities or towns, and independent cities with no county government. In northern Virginia alone, there are seven counties and ten independent towns and cities, each with its own police, fire rescue, school, and judicial systems. Arlington County is one of those.

Consequently, the Arlington County Police Department has primary responsibility for keeping the peace in roughly twenty-five square miles of commercial and residential properties, rustic and historic areas, back roads and superhighways.

Located just outside the west loop of the Beltway surrounding the U.S. capital, the county is home to the famous Arlington National Cemetery, where the eternal flame flares at the grave of assassinated President John F. Kennedy, and where the Tomb of the Unknowns and the burial plots of thousands of military veterans are located.

Arlington County is also home to the massive Pentagon, the U.S. military's national headquarters building, which covers more than 3.7 million square feet of one-time swampland, and provides office space for more than 23,000 military and civilian employees. Cowell was just beginning his career during the Vietnam War when hundreds of peace marchers surrounded the building and unsuccessfully attempted to levitate it, using only love, a chanted mantra, and the power of their minds.

As an Arlington County police officer, however, Cowell didn't share any responsibilities for helping patrol, protect, or perform any other law enforcement functions at the national cemetery or at other federal parks, preserves, and monuments. That is the job of the approximate five hundred members of the National Park Service police.

Cowell spent his first seven years on the department as a uniform officer performing routine police duties, patrolling from one end of the county to the other before he was finally transferred to Motors.

Then he was at last able to climb into the unique togs worn by motorcycle officers: tightly tapered dark blue pants that hugged the skin; crisply pressed blue uniform shirt; shiny, tall black leather boots; light blue helmet with dark navy-blue trim and goggles. The insignia, a white-winged red wheel pierced by a yellow arrow, was sewn onto the right sleeve of the jackets during the winter as the Motorcycle Squad symbol. During the warm weather of summer, a metal replica of the symbol was pinned onto his shirt.

In Motors, Cowell experienced the heady masculine thrill of reporting on duty, kicking over his Harley and listening to the hardy rumble of the engine as it roared into life, before riding off to patrol the roads and high-ways. The 74's were painted white and generously trimmed with chrome. They were the biggest, most pow-erful motorcycles manufactured at that time, and their noisy, authoritative presence on a street or highway was impossible for motorists to miss.

As "Motor 51," Cowell arrested drunk drivers, wrote out tickets for speeders, directed traffic, and escorted funerals and dignitaries for seven satisfying years, until he was promoted out of the squad in 1975. Years later he was still explaining he didn't leave Motors and begin wearing a coat and tie by choice.

The promotion didn't change his love for motorcy-cles, but after his move to white collar, he did his riding on his own time. During his early years on the depart-ment, he also qualified as a pilot of single and twin-engine airplanes, but flying wasn't part of his new job either.

Moving into investigative police work after nearly a decade and a half with the department, Cowell found himself almost a rookie again. He learned the investiga-tion business from the ground up, handling general assignment cases that included everything from shoplift-ing, hit-and-run accidents, various robberies and as-saults, to bad checks.

In 1978 Police Chief William K. Stover formed the Arlington County Police Department's first White Col-lar Unit of the Major Crimes Division. Cowell was the first man picked for the squad.

White-collar crime investigators don't share the glam-our and drama that goes with the territory staked out by their colleagues in homicide. There is no tracking down and collaring drive-by shooters, spousal murderers, and serial killers; and none of the heady excitement of SWAT team sharpshooters who bust down doors and trade shots with heavily armed narcotics dealers, desperate lunatics, and terrorists.

Cowell learned nevertheless that investigating white-collar crimes involving thefts or swindles that focus on banks, savings and loans, or Fortune 500 corporations and other businesses has its rewards.

He liked the challenge of his new job. He quickly recognized it for what it was: an ongoing contest of wits, a quiet game of patience and paperwork, while pitted against confidence men and conniving women who lived by their cunning and spent other people's money.

On the street and at his desk in a rabbit's warren of partitioned cavities on the noisy third floor of the Arlington Police Department building, he began learning the secrets of the trade. The cubicles were open at the top, and the hubbub of ringing telephones, shouted questions, and slamming file drawers from neighboring spaces were constant companions.

Cowell and his colleagues might have been settled into the set for a segment of the old *Barney Miller* television series, except for the cubicles, which offered the barest sliver of privacy for telephone conversations, occasional face-to-face conversations with victims, and dealing with the mounds of paperwork that accompanied every case.

At schools, seminars, and on-the-job, Cowell learned to examine and identify questionable documents used in forgeries and other white-collar crime. He studied for a week at the White Collar Crime School at the FBI Academy in nearby Quantico, and also with Fred Webb, an expert and instructor in handwriting analysis at the Bureau of Forensic Science for the State of Virginia. Among the lessons and techniques Cowell learned from Webb was the proper and best manner of taking handwriting exemplars—or typical specimens for comparisons.

He learned how to identify tracings of signatures made by holding handwriting samples against light boxes or under glass coffee tables, then shining a flashlight upward to enable reproduction of the faint silhouettes that show through on a check or document. And he learned to spot handwriting simulations; studying a signature or other sample, then reproducing as accurately as possible the distinctive curves, loops, and penpoint pressures of the original writer.

Documents considered by most people to be merely part of their mundane personal and business life, such as bank deposit slips, driver's license, car title, social security card, passport, and routine applications for such things as utility hookups, took on a new significance for Cowell. He used his eyes and mind with all the careful discrimination and attention to detail of an Apache scout studying the tracks of a lone Pawnee warrior. But the tracks he followed left paper and electronic trails.

He studied the intricacies of individual script, and tuned in to the fine differences of handwriting, comparing the pressures used in producing one example of a signature against another. He learned to look for different inks used in completing different parts of documents, for example, to determine if they were filled out at different times; compared the impressions made by typewriter keys; and was taught to protect the chain of custody while preserving the integrity of collected evidence so that it would stand up in court.

While Cowell sharpened his skills in the intricacies of white-collar crime, he rounded up quick-change tricksters who bilked shopkeepers and clerks of ten dollars, twenty dollars, or more with fast talk and a rapid series of bewildering cash transactions; arrested embezzlers for juggling books; and probed a dizzying array of crimes that people could think up using bad paper, cash, checks, financial records—and credit cards.

While he was putting in his first decade as an Arlington County Police officer, credit cards were virtually becoming a second currency for millions of adult American consumers.

Since sweeping onto the world scene in the 1960s, credit cards revolutionized the way consumers, retailers, banks, and other businesses handled financial transactions. And by the mid-1980s when Lisa Ann (Miller) Rohn and Raymond Arnold Huberts were changing their personal geography and restructuring their criminal activities to take advantage of the plastic money revolution, approximately 8000 banks and other companies in the United States were issuing or renewing about 500,000 million credit cards every year.

Major corporations and banks issue plastic money with names such as American Express, Carte Blanche, Diners Club, Discover, MasterCard, and Visa, which can be used to pay for everything from veterinary bills or a dozen roses, to meals, hotel rooms, and international airfare. Other cards are issued by oil companies and department stores.

As the use of credit cards burgeoned rapidly, so did the abuses. (Banks that were mailing unsolicited flurries of credit cards to customers, for one example, began discovering accounts established in the names of cats, dogs, birds, and other family pets.) Foggy Bottom legislators reacted by passing the Truth in Lending Act, establishing identity requirements for card holders, halving maximum liability from $100 to $50, and halting the practice of issuing unsolicited cards.

The Truth in Lending Act was a timely and important

law, but it didn't stop the army of schemers, swindlers, and scalawags from devising ways to use credit cards to steal other people's money. Some of the scams were stupidly crude and obvious, and often involved amateur crooks or people who merely had trouble managing their money and spent more than they could pay off.

But others were crafty and ingeniously slick. Members of the fast-buck crowd found almost as many ways to steal and misuse credit cards, and the vital names and numbers they were imprinted with, as there were different kinds of plastic money.

Some thieves learned to fish around in the garbage and trash outside restaurants, motels, medical clinics, and other business places for discarded receipts and other papers with credit card numbers and other information. It was easy for the scavengers, who are often referred to by their colleagues and investigators as "Dumpster divers," to follow up by copying the information or applying for new cards.

"Shoulder surfers" have a different but effective system. They merely peek over the shoulder of someone using a card, memorize or jot down the numbers and other information, and use it to order merchandise by telephone.

Employees at some businesses where cards were accepted for goods or services developed a system of thievery known as "double banging." The scheme is worked by inserting the card into the imprinting machine along with two, three, or more blank credit invoices. Then the card is returned to the customer for a signature. The thief fills the blank invoices in later for the same amounts of money accepted from cash sales, and sticks the currency in his or her pocket.

Other employees, working cash registers, learned to ring up sales and return a card that has been stolen and overused to the customer. Most customers don't study the names on their cards when they're returned after a purchase. They merely stuff them back into a billfold or purse. The card-switch scam is a slightly different variation of the technique so often used by nimble-fingered hookers and their accomplices with unwary Johns.

Some imaginative thieves slip stolen credit cards that have become "hot" because of overuse into embossing machines and strike over an easily altered number, such as changing a 3 to an 8 or a 5 to a 6. The new number provides a new card with a new line of credit, to be used as rapidly as possible.

A similar, slightly cruder ploy to alter a hot card into a usable card requires shaving off a number with a razor blade and pasting on a substitute number. White-collar thieves tend to be inventive, and variations or new ways to cheat with credit cards are constantly being devised.

But the major scams are almost always structured around stolen cards, and skillful or experienced thieves know that the way to avoid arrest is to use them quickly, then replace them with others more recently acquired. According to the Federal Trade Commission, most financial losses from credit card thievery occurs within forty-eight hours after a card is stolen. Speed and frequent changes of location are the keys to success.

By early November 1986, when Cowell answered a telephone call from a senior fraud investigator for the Dominion Bank, people in the credit card industry were estimating that $100 million annually was being lost through various forms of credit card fraud. (Since that time, annual losses have continued to swell to more than a half-billion dollars.)

By the mid-1980s, however, Cowell had learned most of the tricks of the trade and figured out a few imaginative maneuvers of his own for combatting the thievery.

And he had listened disbelievingly as distraught men spun wild stories about how their credit cards were lost, before finally breaking down and telling the truth: They had gone into Washington looking for action, and picked up a hooker who either stole the cards by herself or was helped by a strong-arm pimp.

At that time, Dominion was one of the leading financial institutions in the Washington, D.C., area, and investigator David Garrett was disturbed about the pattern of a busy scatter of credit card applications the bank had been receiving. The applications for Visa and MasterCards carried a variety of male and female names, but they all had a single common denominator: each one carried the same address at Apartment 353, Columbia Pike, in Arlington.

Garrett was a former detective with the Washington Metropolitan Police Department before moving to the private business sector, and Cowell had known him for years. The civilian investigator said he uncovered the shady credit card dealings after checking out a complaint in a letter that was forwarded to him by colleagues at the bank. Dominion had issued a credit card after receiving an application in the mail, then sent a follow-up letter to the customer. But the card went to one address and the letter to another—which was obtained from computers.

A couple of days later Dominion heard from the man who received the follow-up letter. He had never applied for or received a credit card from the bank. His name and other information on the application were correct, except for the Columbia Pike address. Garrett responded to the alarm bell by checking recent records of newly issued credit cards and turned up a flurry of suspicious transactions.

The banking sleuth's preliminary investigation dis-

closed that frequently the names on applications for suspect cards were those of real people. Personal data such
as birth dates, social security numbers, and other information were also often legitimate. But the addresses
and telephone numbers didn't match up. There were
other inconsistencies as well.

Cowell told Garrett he would check out the situation
and see what he could dig up. Later that day he rode the
elevator down from his paper-cluttered third-floor cubicle, slid into the seat of his plain car and drove to 2520
Columbia Pike for a look around.

It was the address of a sign company, answering service, and private mail drop called the Arlington Post
Office Box Company. Lee Ann Lake, the owner-opera-
tor was immediately cooperative when the thick-set
plainclothes officer began asking questions about private mailbox 353. She said she had been wondering
when someone would drop by with questions. A blizzard
of credit cards in a variety of names were being mailed
to the box.

The box was rented almost exactly two months earlier, on September 11, by a dowdy woman who gave her
name as P. Ward. Only the initial was provided for the
first name, Ms. Lake said. The owner further described
the customer as white, appearing to be about thirty-five
years old, about five feet two to four inches, 100 to 110
pounds, and with light brown hair. Ms. Lake said there
was nothing especially noticeable about her customer's
clothing. She looked like a frump.

The mystery woman paid eighty dollars cash to rent
the box for three months, and that was the last she was
seen by the company owner or by any of her employees.
The customer was never noticed at the business during
normal working hours, but the mail from that box was
collected almost daily. It was easy enough to do, since

the outer lobby and individual drop boxes could be opened after regular working hours by anyone with a proper key.

As Cowell continued his investigation, he learned that Dominion wasn't the only bank fielding applications listing the Columbia Pike mail drop as an address—not by a long shot. Virtually every major bank in the northern Virginia and Washington metropolitan areas, and many from other nearby states, were contacted for credit cards by one or more people with access to Box 353. Most of them had responded by mailing cards.

As soon as the cards were in the hands of the applicants, they were used at area Automatic Teller Machines (ATMs) at banks and other outlets in the area, to withdraw cash advances. Depending on the limits established by individual banks, withdrawals of $100, $200, and occasionally as much as $500 were made each time the cards were used.

Credit card tricksters often use them to make series of purchases, then resell whatever they have bought for a fraction of the value to individuals or to a professional fence. Frequently, they carry shopping lists when they buy, so they can fill orders already supplied by clients who are unconcerned about where their merchandise comes from and how it was obtained.

If they're experienced, or working with an organized group of professionals, they will be careful to keep the value of individual purchases modest in order to avoid undue attention or security checks. They are also often equipped with additional identification, such as driver's licenses or social security cards, with names that match those on the cards.

Regardless of how careful the crooked shoppers are, however, that system has its risks. A single telephone call from an efficient or suspicious clerk checking out a sale, or a number that appears to have been altered, can often identify a card as stolen or forged. And every credit card merchant is provided with updated booklets listing the numbers of cards that have been stolen, grossly exceed purchase limits, or are otherwise suspicious.

Whoever was responsible for the new series of credit card thievery in Arlington County knew exactly what they were doing. They weren't in the business of accumulating merchandise that had to be fenced or otherwise converted to currency. They dealt almost exclusively in plastic and cash.

Audacious and sophisticated, they worked fast and efficiently, grabbing what they could with a card, then discarding it and replacing it with another to repeat the process. After the cards were used to extract the cash limits from ATMs, they were sometimes used to buy a carton or two of cigarettes or for other modest purchases. But the thieves were always careful to keep purchases below the so-called "floor limit," the amount established by various financial institutions, which can be charged without attracting undue attention such as a telephone check on balances or stolen card reports. Floor limits commonly range between $25 and $50.

Although Cowell had no way of knowing for certain at the time how many people might be involved in the operation, a loose suspect-profile gradually began to shape up. Cameras mounted at some of the ATMs had captured photographs of at least one man and one woman making withdrawals. Sometimes the man was photographed, sometimes the woman, and on some occasions they were both shown in the pictures.

The male was white, dark-haired with a mustache, and appeared to be about forty years old. The woman was white, about five feet three or four inches tall, with light brown or blond hair extending five or six inches below her shoulders. Her features were plain, and in the photos she appeared either to be wearing no makeup or very little. The couple often made four and five withdrawals a day. On good days they could take in $2000 or more—tax-free.

A credit card scam of major proportions was obviously under way. Cowell had investigated larger operations, but they involved carefully structured, sophisticated bands of criminals, such as members of a Nigerian crime organization that is notorious in American police circles for their skill at carrying out white-collar crime.

The Nigerian gangsters are worldly wise and smooth, silver-tongued maestros of the fast-buck game. Although violence isn't unknown in their world, the Nigerian approach to organized crime generally lacks the crude savagery of the drug-trafficking Jamaican Posse, or the homegrown Crips and Bloods. They don't operate by blasting the life out of a half-dozen unsuspecting people with Uzis or AK-47's in drive-by street-corner shootings. They steal their money in a more gentlemanly way, working their new-wave shell games with fast talk, plastic, high-tech electronics and paper.

At various times the wily West Africans have been linked to and arrested for money laundering, credit card fraud, and various other imaginatively sophisticated bunco games. Their thievery is so effective and widespread in the United States and other western nations that results of one American banking investigation indicated it was the third-largest source of Nigeria's hard currency. In Nigeria, members of the crime cartel are referred to as 419's or 419 gangs, after a section of the old colonial penal code dealing with deceptive financial practices.

The Nigerians are unique among some of the ethnic gangs that have supplemented or are replacing the old Italian and Sicilian Mafia on the nation's organized crime scene. The Nigerian crooks specialize in everything from get-rich-quick schemes centering around phony multimillion-dollar oil pipeline deals, to shrewd swindles carried out with checks, credit cards, and computers that take advantage of the new financial age. They are highly organized, and according to investigators, were even trained for a while at a Los Angeles church in various methods of organized financial mischief.

One of their more ingenious rip-offs is a highly complicated scheme worked by establishing phony businesses, obtaining merchant credit card accounts, claiming to have sold nonexistent merchandise, and convincing banks to transfer deposits to their statements. But they are constantly coming up with new ruses; reshaping and updating some of the older methods of financial finagling.

Organized Nigerian gangsters looted hundreds of thousands of dollars while working the Washington, D.C., and northern Virginia area, as they did many other large urban areas of the country. But several gang members were involved in the operation by the Nigerians. Cowell had never seen an ongoing credit card flimflam carried off by only two people that was so extensive.

The center of the action was the mail drop at the Arlington Post Office Box Company, smack in the middle of Cowell's territory. But other areas were also being worked by the male-female team, and Cowell got in touch with fraud investigators from several police agencies in northern Virginia, Maryland, and with the U.S. Secret Service.

The Arlington County Police detective also telephoned Assistant Commonwealth Attorney Frank G. Soulier, then dropped by his office for a talk. Cowell reviewed the facts of the investigation up to that point, and the Commonwealth attorney agreed that it was time to begin an around-the-clock surveillance of the private postal drop to see who was picking up the mail.

Early Thursday evening, October 30, when employees of the Arlington Post Office Box Company left their jobs for the day, Cowell's partner, Detective James Griswold, staked out the lobby. The two men had been partners since shortly after the White Collar Unit was formed. When the workload became too much for Cowell to handle by himself, he asked for help, and specifically requested Griswold as his partner. It was a partnership that worked.

At the mail drop, Griswold kept a close watch on Box 353 throughout the night. By seven o'clock Halloween morning, when employees began showing up for work, not a single person had shown up to collect mail from any of the boxes.

The all-night vigil was a disappointment for Cowell and his partner. The Arlington County Police Department wasn't a small organization, and employed approximately 290 sworn officers and scores of civilian employees at that time. But the uniform officers, plainclothesmen, and detectives were spread out handling everything from traffic control to family fights, drunks, and investigation of homicides. Like most law enforcement agencies, the department didn't have financial resources and manpower to spare. Senior police administrators decided they were simply too short of both to maintain a watch on the drop box around the clock until someone was caught picking up the mail. The stakeout was called off for Halloween night.

Sometime after six o'clock that evening and seven o'clock the following morning, the mail was picked up from Box 353.

The credit card scam wasn't the only case Cowell and Griswold were working, and the time they had available to spend on the investigation was severely limited. Periodically for three days, while pursuing other cases during their normal working hours, they drove around to the Arlington Post Office Box Company to check out the mail drop.

It was a futile effort. Cowell pointed out to his superiors that whoever was picking up the mail had established a pattern from the beginning of emptying the drop box after normal working hours. And there was no indication that was likely to change. Senior police department officials were convinced. They authorized Cowell and Griswold to establish the around-the-clock stakeout the detective partners were convinced was necessary to make a collar.

Cowell had another talk with the company owner at 2520 Columbia Pike, and obtained permission to stake out the drop box from the inside offices. Then he began devising his trap.

Advances in electronics, chemistry, psychology, and a variety of other fields of expertise have revolutionized many aspects of modern police work and detection from what it was only a few years ago. In this exciting new age of computers, police are equipped with sophisticated equipment and techniques that would have boggled the mind of a Dick Tracy only a quarter of a century ago.

State-of-the-art infrared cameras and heat-sensitive devices are used to ferret out buried or hidden bodies; new techniques in chemistry match DNA with criminal suspects through blood, sperm, and other body fluids; complex psychological profiles are worked out by teams of experts in human behavior to track serial killers; and an amazing $75,000 device that's about the size of a microwave oven and is named the Ionscan can signal the presence of drugs or explosives in less than four seconds.

Cowell set his trap with a fistful of dental floss and an old coffee can full of pennies.

The onetime country boy from the gently sloping hills and flatlands of northern Missouri jury-rigged a makeshift alarm system. Working carefully and deliberately with his stubby, nicotine-stained fingers, he kneaded together several strands of dental floss and taped one end around a pack of letters inside Box 358. Then he looped the other end around the can of pennies, before finally balancing the completed booby trap on the edge of a table. Then Cowell, or whichever of his colleagues happened to be on the stakeout at the time, settled down inside the office space to wait. It was as simple as sitting in a duck blind; and it required even more patience. They waited several days and nights.

At last the jury-rigged booby trap paid off. It was about seven o'clock on the late fall morning of November 11, and the sun hadn't yet chased away the damp chill and gloom outside. Detective James Andresakas was nearing the end of a weary vigil manning the lonely stakeout.

A few minutes before preparing to leave, he heard the outer door open. The sound of footsteps signaled that someone was entering the lobby. Moments later the faint clink of a key being inserted into a lock could be heard, then there was a tug on the package of letters. The coffee can toppled off the table, spilling the clatter of pennies onto the floor.

Andresakas lifted himself quietly from his chair, slid to his feet, and hurried out of the office into the lobby.

A middle-aged man with salt-and-pepper hair and a mustache, wearing a light-colored sport coat and sweater, was kneeling in front of Box 353. His hands were full of mail, and other letters were scattered in an unruly pile on the floor by his feet.

Andresakas advised the surprised stranger that he was under arrest, and used a hand radio to alert uniform officers who were outside a short distance away in a patrol car.

Although it's a truism that lasers, computers, and advances in chemistry are making it more difficult for criminals to escape detection and capture, the new technology is far from a be-all, end-all solution to the challenges and puzzles of police work. There is no substitute for the tried and true schemes devised by human imagination and ingenuity. The dental floss and penny trap had worked like a charm.

Searching the prisoner, the arresting officers found a wallet inside the breast pocket of his sport jacket. A set of keys that fit the outer door and the lock to Box 353 were taken from his trouser pocket.

A Virginia driver's license was inside the wallet, made out in the name of Ralph Edward Parrish. Issued April 24, 1986, the license included a social security number, and listed the driver's date of birth as April 5, 1934.

There was also a nondriver photo identification card in the wallet carrying the name of Jeff Ross Johnson. Issued the previous June in Washington, D.C., the ID card listed a social security number, gave a date of birth of June 6, 1952, and included an address in the 300 block of R Street, NW, in Washington, D.C.

If the suspect was Parrish, the man whose name was typed in on the driver's license, and the date of birth was correct, he was a youthful-appearing fifty-two years old. If he was Jeff Johnson, and the ID card carried his correct birthdate, he was a prematurely aged thirty-four-year-old with a lot of mileage on him. There was a spread of nearly two decades between the two dates of birth, and the man Andresakas had taken into custody looked as if his true age might be somewhere in the middle.

The prisoner behaved like someone who had been arrested a few times before, and was acutely aware of his legal rights. He didn't try to run or break away when he was confronted by Andresakas. But he also flatly refused to help sort out the perplexing question of his identity.

Cowell summed up the confrontation to a newspaper reporter years later by saying, in his gruff sandpaper voice, that the suspect "wouldn't tell us the time of day."

The uncommunicative mystery man was handcuffed and helped into the backseat of the squad car, then driven to the police building for another attempt at conducting an interview and for booking.

A brown 1979 Chevrolet four-door Nova sedan he had driven to the private mail drop was confiscated and taken to the police department's auto pound. Police later learned the suspect had bought the car in Arlington the previous April, reputedly for his daughter, Doreen D. Breslin. The car carried Virginia license plates. After obtaining a search warrant, evidence technicians combed through the car and confiscated a large stack of mail. The letters had been sent to a variety of addresses.

The suspect wasn't any more communicative at police headquarters than he was when the detectives attempted to talk to him at the mail drop. He had barely sat down in the furnished but spartan interview room when he began to gasp and grab at his throat and chest as if he couldn't breathe and was having a heart attack.

Cowell was aware that if someone wanted to escape custody, it would presumably be easier to accomplish from a hospital than from a building filled with a hundred or so law enforcement officers. He wasn't impressed, and patiently waited until the show was over. It only took a minute or two for the suspect to realize he wasn't going to be rushed to a hospital before he made a seemingly miraculous recovery. He began breathing normally again, sat up in his chair and glared sullenly at the detective.

But the suspect still wasn't talking, and behaved as if he still believed in the old-fashioned values of never cooperating with police or ratting on a friend. He continued to rebuff every attempt to get him to answer questions. Then he demanded to talk with an attorney, slamming the door for good on any further efforts at interrogation.

Cowell walked him to the elevator and rode downstairs with him to the first floor where Arlington County Sheriff's Department officers led him through the booking routine. In Arlington County, sheriff's deputies have separate duties from members of the police department. Sheriff's officers are responsible for booking prisoners, operating the jail, providing court security, and for civil processes such as serving papers. Their uniforms are dark brown, instead of the blue worn by police.

While Cowell stood by, the suspect's height, weight, color of hair and eyes, were recorded; he was checked for tattoos or scars; photographed and fingerprinted. Then he was locked in a holding cell in the booking area, held on preliminary charges of credit card fraud and credit card forgery.

The detective had an advantage over his colleagues in

some other police departments across the country. The FBI headquarters were just across the Potomac in Washington, about an hour's drive away. He sent one of his colleagues off to hand carry copies of the stubborn prisoner's fingerprint cards to the J. Edgar Hoover Building in the capital city with a request that the FBI give high priority to checking them out by computer against the millions of prints on file.

Although the Arlington County Police Department has its own fingerprint experts and computers to help keep tab on local criminals, nothing would be on file to make a matchup if he had never been arrested there. The FBI was different; their computers and cards carried prints of criminals and of hundreds of thousands of noncriminals from all fifty states and the District of Columbia. If the suspect had ever been arrested anywhere in the country, his prints were likely to be somewhere in the Bureau's files.

Despite rapid and ongoing advances in high-tech crime-fighting techniques, even the FBI has difficulty at times keeping up with the awesome task of processing all the fingerprint cards and requests they receive from police departments and other agencies or private businesses. Every day more than 35,000 fingerprint cards are received by the FBI for processing. More than half of them, about 20,000, are the prints of criminals.

It requires an average of seven days for employees in the Bureau's fingerprint division to process a print card forwarded there by businesses, schools, and other non–law enforcement entities for background checks. Prints tied to suspected criminals or criminal cases are given priority, and when checks are requested, the work is carried out by computer.

Even then, technicians can miss making the right matchup because hundreds of thousands of prints collected by the fingerprint division haven't been entered into the computer. They're filed on cards and stuck away in row after row of file cabinets that take up some 300,000 square feet on the upper floors of the building.

The collection, inside the computers and inside the cabinets, represents about seventy years of efforts by the Bureau and local and state law enforcement agencies. The FBI began converting more than seventeen million prints in its files into digital form in 1976 to speed up the matching process by computer. Millions of additional prints have been collected and computerized, both by the FBI and state and local law enforcement agencies, since that time.

Some of the computer fingerprint identification systems used by law enforcement agencies are faster and more efficient than others. In some jurisdictions, even where equipment is only a year or two old, computer searches are slow and untrustworthy. It can take up to six seconds to check one fingerprint, and even then the electronic scan might overlook a print that is less than perfect. Other computers, like those used by the FBI, can check out more than 600 prints per second, and they routinely match up the characteristics of imperfect prints.

But digging the right matchup out of the cabinets is a different story. It can take days, or weeks, or they may never be found because they have been misfiled or clerks simply aren't looking in the right place. And matching prints may never be in either the card files or in the computers in the first place.

Before computers, fingerprint identification was never the super crime fighter that it was cracked up to be. There were simply too many prints, and too few clerks and technicians to dig through files and carry out time-consuming visual studies looking for matching loops and whorls.

One San Francisco detective worked off and on for six years trying to match a fingerprint that evidence technicians found at a murder scene. Then computers were introduced into the process, and after a six-minute electronic search, he turned up the matching print and solved the case.

Despite the difficulties and drawbacks that still exist, the FBI manages to identify about 29,000 criminal suspects and fugitives every year by matching their fingerprints with those already entered into the computers or the card files.

The explosion in forensic technology is leading to improvements in investigative techniques by large and small police departments all over the country. A few years ago evidence technicians in Orange County, California, began carrying portable lasers along with them to help search out and highlight fingerprints at crime scenes. But the FBI, with its greater financial and other resources, has managed to stay in the vanguard both in technological and psychological forensics.

The prints that Cowell was hoping to match with those of his suspect were in the FBI's fingerprint identification computer system. And less than an hour after the fingerprint card was carried to the Bureau's fingerprint division offices, he learned the name, age, and an array of additional helpful information about the taciturn suspect.

He was Raymond Arnold Huberts, a forty-three-year-old veteran criminal with a lengthy rap sheet for financial crimes and suspected crimes involving pandering or prostitution. The next morning the handcuffed suspect was walked to a third-floor courtroom of the courthouse, which is attached to the police building, where he was arraigned under his real name and where he attempted to get his secured bond of $100,000 reduced. The request was denied by a General District Court judge, and the prisoner was returned to the police building. This time, with the classification process completed and his arraignment out of the way, he was locked in with the general population of the Arlington County Adult Detention Center, located on the fourth and fifth floors.

As lead investigator in the case, Cowell was anxious to establish the real name of the suspect as soon as possible and obtain information about the identity and whereabouts of the suspected female accomplice. He wanted to take her into custody before she became suspicious and fled the area.

But Cowell and his colleagues had other things going for them to make up for the prisoner's refusal to cooperate in identifying the suspected female accomplice. Detectives had obtained a search warrant for the car Huberts was driving, and evidence technicians confiscated a thick stack of letters, which were added to the rapidly burgeoning store of information about the suspect.

Some of the mail carried the address of a condominium in Washington, D.C. Along with other information previously developed in the investigation, the letters helped Cowell zero in on the apartment at 490 M Street SW, as the suspect's probable temporary home and headquarters. The address was in an upscale area of the city, on the waterfront looking out over the Potomac River.

The other addresses collected from the letters included businesses listed as answering services and maildrop centers in Arlington, Vienna, and Falls Church, Virginia; Silver Spring, Maryland; Washington; and

Scottsdale, Arizona. The male-female team of slicksters were cagey and took precautions to eliminate risks. They didn't stick with any single mail drop for more than a few weeks, and much of their mail was forwarded back and forth from one box to the other.

Despite the desire of Cowell and his colleagues to get to Huberts's sidekick before she fled the area, Arlington County Police couldn't simply drive across the Virginia state line into the District of Columbia and pounce on anyone who might be in the M Street apartment. The business of law enforcement doesn't work that way. The white-collar crime squad from Arlington would be outside their geographical jurisdiction, and needed officers from the Metropolitan Police Department to accompany them.

Cowell drafted an affidavit to obtain a search warrant for the condominium apartment in Washington, then contacted the Metropolitan Police Department headquarters for assistance. He was told that no one was available to help obtain and serve the warrant. It was Veteran's Day, and although there were approximately five thousand officers in the Metropolitan Police Department, no one was available to help. They were busy directing traffic and or were involved with other functions tied to their normal law enforcement duties.

The experienced Arlington County policeman wasn't all that surprised at the response to his request for assistance. He knew that his colleagues with the Metropolitan Police had been slow to respond to other requests for help in the past. Either senior officers couldn't be located to provide authorization, or other reasons were given for dragging their feet. Pleading a manpower shortage because of busy Veteran's Day responsibilities was as good an excuse as any for shunting the neighboring lawmen aside.

It was frustrating, especially because when all the various law enforcement agencies headquartered in Washington, D.C., are considered, there are more police per capita there than in any other community in the country. Of course, they also have a wide variety of functions.

In addition to the Metropolitan Police, there is the Capitol Police Force; National Park Service; Executive Protection Service; U.S. Customs Service; U.S. Drug Enforcement Agency; Bureau of Alcohol, Tobacco and Firearms; federal marshals; special investigators with the Internal Revenue Service; the FBI and the Secret Service. With all those law enforcement agencies on his doorstep, there were other avenues Cowell could explore for help.

The Arlington detective had already wasted more valuable time than he could afford, when he gave up on the Metropolitan Police and telephoned a friend who was a senior investigator in the fraud unit with the Secret Service. Agent James P. Gaughran knew a lot about credit card scams, and he was a dedicated law enforcement officer who was respected by his colleagues with other agencies.

Even though Cowell contacted him at his home, Gaughran immediately swung into action. A short time later a federal search warrant was issued by a federal magistrate for the M Street apartment. With the help of his friend in the Secret Service, Cowell had executed a neat end run around the foot-dragging Metropolitan Police.

The Secret Service agent accompanied Cowell and a team of plainclothesmen and evidence technicians from Arlington to the M Street apartment. The lawmen obtained a key from the manager of the complex and let themselves inside W-808. The two-bedroom condominium apartment subleased by Huberts was almost empty of furniture, except for a couch, a single chair, and a mirror. It was quickly clear that if a female partner shared the apartment with Huberts, she had left and taken any clothing or other personal possessions with her.

As evidence technicians fanned through the rooms and began dusting door and window frames, kitchen cabinets, sinks, and other surfaces that were likely to yield fingerprints, it was obvious that the fugitive scam artist cleaned up before she left. The apartment was spick-and-span. Virtually every surface likely to have been touched by a hand or finger was wiped clean.

Whoever was responsible for the cleanup had done a near professional job, but it wasn't perfect. A single latent fingerprint was lifted from the bottom of the toilet seat.

Latent prints, in the special parlance of police and the courtroom, are those that are found at the scene of a crime or suspected crime. And they aren't usually found on dead bodies, clothing, purses, or other soft or irregular surfaces. Flat, hard, surfaces on objects like car doors, walls, tables—and bathrooms, with their inviting porcelain and their toilet seats—can be some of the most productive places for evidence technicians to look.

Unfortunately, latent prints lifted from even the best surfaces are often imperfect. There may be only a fragment, a tiny portion of a thumb, or a smudged, barely visible silhouette of an index finger. Until a few years ago those prints were virtually useless for identifying a suspect until they were already caught and his or her finger markings could be examined for matchups with the fragments already in hand. New automated print-search systems available to many police departments around the country, however, are rapidly changing all that. Fragments are frequently all that are needed to

make fingerprint matchups—before suspects are col-
lared.

But the lone fingerprint found on the toilet seat in the
condominium on M Street was excellent. When Cowell
left the apartment, he drove the fingerprint straight to
the J. Edgar Hoover Building.

Cowell didn't have to ask for directions. He had been
to the Bureau's fingerprint division before for help,
many times. Several times he hand-carried fingerprints
of Nigerians nabbed or locked up in connection with
some bank, credit card, or check fraud. Invariably, when
the prints were matched, they came back with a different name than the one being used by the suspect.

The FBI maintains civilian technicians in the offices
around the clock, and Cowell had gone there for help at
various times at such unlikely hours as two or three A.M.
The technicians offer while-you-wait service to police
agencies who hand carry prints to the office. There was
no paperwork for the Arlington County policeman to fill
out. He merely handed the print over to a technician,
then settled down in a chair, selected a couple of golfing
and sports magazines from a stack on a low table and
leafed through them while he waited. It was as casual as
the waiting room in the office of a doctor or dentist.

Less than two hours later the FBI computers had
electronically matched the whorls, loops, and ridges
with a fingerprint belonging to Lisa Ann Rohn. She was
identified as a California-born white female, twenty-
four years old, weighing about 125 pounds, five feet
three inches tall, with blond or light brown hair.

Another police computer check was run on her police
record, and printed out an impressive list of arrests. The
rap sheet showed arrests in Alameda, California, in
mid-November 1983 on charges of disorderly conduct,
prostitution, vehicle theft, cruelty to a child, and con-

tributing to the delinquency of a minor. Other entries on the rap sheet included an arrest in Hayward, California, in January 1985, on a prostitution charge; an arrest in Alameda the following June on charges of prostitution and living in a house of ill-fame; and charges in Berkeley of prostitution and living in a house of ill-fame. There were no convictions.

Even though the vice charges filed against her in Berkeley were dropped for lack of evidence, Cowell contacted police there and asked for a mug shot of the suspected fugitive scam artist. Police in the college town were more cooperative than their colleagues in the nation's capital. They responded promptly with a mug shot taken of Lisa when she was arrested and booked there about eighteen months earlier.

Police mug shots don't flatter the subjects, and Lisa's was no exception. But it wasn't that bad either. Photographed staring directly into the camera, the flat planes of her rectangular face were framed by a seemingly unruly shock of light hair that was pulled away from her forehead and curled down past her shoulders.

Cowell arranged for Lisa's name and description to be entered into the National Crime Information Center computers as a fugitive from justice. The massive FBI-operated data base contained records of nearly fifteen million arrests reported by various law enforcement agencies across the nation.

The investigation was mushrooming, and Cowell quickly became aware that the case was bigger than he had previously suspected. The couple had kept the U.S. Postal Service busy delivering hundreds of applications and credit cards throughout the country.

Banks in Virginia, Maryland, Delaware, New York, Massachusetts, California, Illinois, Ohio, Arkansas, and South Dakota had received requests for MasterCards and Visas. One application was even directed to Bloomingdale's in New York City, but the request was denied. Many of the banks also turned down the applications. Others, however, responded with new cards and generous lines of credit that were quickly put to use at area ATMs.

The sheer number of applications processed by the hardworking fast-buck artists seemed to ensure success for the wide-ranging money-making operation. A bank in Sioux Falls, South Dakota, eventually sent a bill for $1390 to one of the aliases at the M Street address. A bill from Buffalo, New York, was sent to the drop box on Columbia Pike for $968. But some others were for piddling amounts as small as ten, eleven, and eighteen dollars.

It was an exciting world of plastic and electronics that spelled out financial success for the industrious male-female team. They worked hard at the business. During approximately seven months of operating their scam in the northern Virginia, Washington, D.C., and Maryland area, Cowell estimated they may have taken in as much as $500,000. And it was almost all cash!

Cowell wanted Lisa Ann Rohn, and he was determined not to permit her to slip out of his grasp. He had copies of her Berkeley mug shot reproduced, added a description, sixty some aliases she was believed to have used, and put everything on wanted posters. The posters were circulated to financial institutions and police departments throughout the Washington metropolitan area. Others were provided to the press, and Lisa's photograph along with her vital statistics and information about the crimes she was suspected of appeared on various television channels in the area.

The flyers advised that she was suspected of credit card fraud, conspiracy to commit credit card fraud and theft, and was wanted on felony warrants held by the Arlington County Police Department. The addresses of nine private mail drops and answering services that she and Huberts, identified as a suspect and her coconspirator, rented, also appeared on the notices.

The fraud investigator collected additional photos of both suspects taken by bank cameras as they made withdrawals at ATMs. Huberts was easily recognizable as the man in the photos. But changes in Lisa's appearance were startling, and at first glance the ATM pictures hardly appeared to be of the same woman. She looked especially frumpy in one picture, showing her wearing glasses. None of the photos, even those without glasses, looked much like the young woman in the Berkeley Police Department mug shot.

Lisa could be a chameleon when she wished to be. An ability to drastically alter her appearance often went along with the territory for people who chose to make their living as scam artists. Close scrutiny of the ATM photos, however, disclosed the same basic features as those of the young woman who had been arrested on vice charges in Berkeley.

Cowell assembled another package of photos and information. Then he had an alert sent out over the National Law Enforcement Telecommunications System network to forgery and fraud units in police departments across the country. Special attention was directed to units in Washington; Los Angeles, Oakland, and Alameda County, California; Scottsdale, Arizona; and Palm Beach, Florida.

The teletype message included descriptions of the suspected fast-buck artists as well as details of Huberts's arrest and the identification he was carrying on him at the time. Lisa was described as having a lengthy arrest record in Alameda County for prostitution offenses, and the alert advised that felony warrants for her arrest were on file in Arlington. Copies of her photos and latent fingerprints were available on request, it was noted.

The alert also advised: "To date our investigation reveals suspect with a female accomplice arrived our area April of 1986. Since their arrival suspects opened eleven private post office boxes (mail drops) with corresponding answering services. Approximately 200 Visa/MasterCard credit cards have been applied for and received by these two suspects using 97 fictitious names, male and female."

The aliases represented a flavorful goulash of Anglo Saxon and ethnic names that were unlikely to draw attention. Lisa chose names like Doreen D. Breslin, Sylvia Jensen, Shannon Cook, Natalie Avery, Cindy Anderson, Pamela J. Ward, Sara Kennedy, Robin D. Goldberg, Dall Nzovatieka, and Jessica Zquadie. A few of the aliases were equipped with references to Ph.D.'s or medical degrees. The names, Dr. Mary V. Anderson, Dr. Melissa J. Frazer, and Dr. Terry McDermot were examples.

Most of the names were those of real people, some living, some dead. The scam artists used almost any identification they could find. And there was an almost limitless number of locations to seek out such documents and information, for people who knew where to look.

White-collar criminals sometimes go through trash bins behind banks, hospitals, hotels, restaurants, and apartments to collect credit card numbers, names, and addresses. Scrutiny of careless discards from accounting firms can sometimes turn up social security numbers, W-2's, and other valuable tax forms.

Complete new identities can be established by examining headstones in cemeteries for the names of infants or other young children. The secret is in selecting a child of the same sex, born at about the same time as the person wishing to take on that identity. Then a visit or letter to a county or to a state bureau of vital statistics, in many instances, can produce a copy of the child's birth certificate. Applicants can claim they need it to replace another that has been lost or somehow accidentally destroyed, or use some other excuse.

County and state bureaucrats are becoming increasingly cautious about such requests, but the flim-flam—with occasional mutations and improvements—still works as often as not. And birth certificates can be the key to obtaining driver's licenses, social security cards, and other documents important to establishing a new identity. In turn, those documents can be used to help set up bank accounts, register as a college student, or to obtain jobs.

Veteran criminals know that establishing a false identity is as easy as visiting a graveyard, or rifling through a trash can. It's the kind of basic lesson that is learned on the streets or in jails and prisons, where idle convicts spend much of their time passing on tricks of the trade.

Lisa knew it was important to choose aliases like she selected her clothes, hairstyle, and cosmetics. The focus was on avoiding attention. In her business it was better to look like a plain brown peafowl than a splendid peacock. But there was no denying that at times a nonexistent degree could also be a help making the right impression.

Cowell touched all the proper bases in throwing the net out for the young fugitive. But he was facing the kind of challenge that could take years to resolve, if ever. Lisa had apparently learned valuable lessons from her more experienced criminal mentor during their years together about avoiding notice and evading attention.

Her experience as a credit card scamp had taught her how to change names and appearance. And her labor as a California call girl had sharpened her skills in the art of luring and manipulating men.

Lisa Ann Rohn was well-equipped to escape detection and survive on her own. She dropped out of sight as easily and effectively as a daylight-stalked will-o'-the-wisp.

Chapter Four

A Fugitive

When Huberts's fast-moving female partner went on the run after he was nabbed by the White Collar Unit, she didn't scamper far.

Although she never returned to the M Street apartment and scrupulously avoided the mail drops known to the police, she remained in the Washington metropolitan area.

After nearly a year of working the credit card scam in Maryland and northern Virginia, she knew her way around the Beltway communities. And remaining in the area would keep her close to Huberts, so that despite his troubles with the criminal justice system, they could remain in touch.

With her lover's capture, Lisa was abruptly cut loose to succeed or to fail according to her own abilities and talents. But she was bright and cunning, and had learned a lot during the previous four years. She was well-prepared for the challenge.

She didn't have to cross the country and return to the West Coast in order to avoid the manhunt launched by Cowell. Lisa Ann Rohn simply ceased to exist. She vanished, without leaving so much as a Cheshire cat's smile behind.

Several other women emerged in her place. They had names like Doreen R. Davenport, or Dr. Doreen R. Davenport; Stacy Linda Miller, and Lisa's dead sister, Johnnie Elaine Miller. As a fugitive, she continued to collect phony identification, including a District of Columbia driver's license issued in the name of Carol Anne Harris, and other documents.

No one ever managed to piece together a comprehensive map or exact chronology of her movements during the roughly half decade she was a fugitive. Most of the time she succeeded in avoiding attention from the wrong people, even though Cowell knew she was still in the area. The White Collar Unit had uncovered other fish to fry after Lisa went on the run, but the case was kept alive and efforts to capture the fugitive were never abandoned.

As Cowell continued to track the trail of paper and plastic left behind while Lisa and Huberts were busy looting ATM machines in the area, he learned she had been working in the accounting office for a major chain motel. She and her partner apparently utilized a mix of names of the living, the dead, and the nonexistent, along with other information such as addresses and social security numbers.

Cowell was active in the International Association of Credit Card Investigators, which is composed of police officers and civilians who head or work in security operations for major department store chains and various banks and other financial institutions. The association sponsored seminars and training sessions for its membership, which includes investigators from throughout much of the western world.

The Mid-Atlantic Chapter, which covered Arlington,

met every six weeks, providing members opportunities to swap information about cases they were investigating. At the first meeting after Huberts's arrest, Cowell informed other members about the investigation and the search for Lisa. And he continued to keep them informed at subsequent meetings.

He also gave copies of her mug shots to area newspapers and television stations, with information about her suspected criminal activities. Reports filtered in from time to time that she was believed to have been seen using an ATM or was thought to be the woman who had bounced a bad check.

All the reports came from out of the county or out-of-state, and police from the appropriate jurisdictions were notified and asked for help. But making a withdrawal from an ATM takes only a couple of minutes, and bad checks that are accepted by merchants don't show up until long after the suspect has made his or her getaway.

A couple of times Cowell's colleagues in Virginia, Maryland, and Washington missed Lisa or the person believed to be her by no more than ten or twenty minutes. At other times they apparently missed their fugitive by a day or two. But she always stayed just a few minutes, a few hours, a few days, or a few miles ahead of them.

Shifting hairstyles and wigs, addresses, names and identities, as easily as a dust devil changes direction, Lisa kept on the move. She was a tantalizing but frustratingly elusive target while she skipped from one cookie cutter Beltway community to another, adopting and shedding names and identities as casually as other people change blouses or shirts.

If any money was salted away from the hundreds of thousands of dollars law enforcement authorities believed was stolen during the approximate seven-month credit card crime spree in the Washington area preceding Huberts's arrest, it might have provided a handy nest egg for her when cash was especially short.

Lisa lied, schemed, and manipulated when she had to in order to survive. Most of the time she worked at a series of low-paying jobs that provided the kind of cover she needed while lying low. But the mere act of shuttling between the District of Columbia, Maryland, and Virginia put her at risk of being charged with the federal offense of crossing a state line to avoid prosecution.

Huberts, meanwhile, had hired his own lawyer and was cutting himself a deal on a plea agreement. On March 17, 1987, he pleaded guilty to two counts of credit card fraud and three counts of theft using credit cards. In exchange for the guilty pleas, authorities agreed he would not be prosecuted for offenses prior to his arrest on November 11, and similar charges against him would be dropped in the neighboring communities of Fairfax, Alexandria, and Falls Church, Virginia, and in Washington, D.C.

Huberts wound up with sentences of two years in prison on each of the surviving felony charges, for a total of ten years. Five years of supervised probation to begin after his release from custody, and a total of $3000 in fines, were also ordered. One year of incarceration was suspended on each of the counts, however, so it appeared Huberts faced a total of five years in custody. But the American criminal justice system doesn't work like that.

Huberts never managed to raise the high bail established after his arrest, and he was given credit off his sentence for time already served behind bars while awaiting resolution of his case. By taking advantage of additional reduction of the sentence in return for good behavior while in custody, Huberts was expected to be able to cut his time actually served behind bars to about two years.

On April Fools Day he was transported from the detention center in Arlington to the Powhatan Reception Center a few miles below Richmond for classification and permanent assignment to a prison.

Several weeks later corrections officers drove him to the Staunton Correctional Center, a medium security prison west of the Blue Ridge Mountains in the picturesque Shenandoah Valley. Its location there provides employment for hundreds of local men and women, but community leaders are more likely to boast that their town was the birthplace of Woodrow Wilson than to promote the grim prison. The name of the twenty-eighth President of the United States is memorialized by the Woodrow Wilson State Hospital a few miles from Staunton in nearby Fishersville.

On June 14, 1987, Lisa married her second husband, a forty-seven-year-old man from Ecuador named Luis Arnoldo Martinez.

The bride was still living a lie, using the name Stacy Linda Miller on June 2 when she applied at the Circuit Court Clerk's office in Montgomery County for the marriage license. Her age was listed on the document as twenty-seven, her birthday as November 11, 1959, and her place of birth as Oregon. Both she and the groom, who stipulated on the document he had been divorced in 1985, listed Rockville in Montgomery County as their residence. No street address was given.

The rites were performed by the Reverend D. Robert Chance, pastor of the Georgia Avenue Christian Church in Wheaton, Maryland, a few miles north of the Capital Beltway.

Although there was no mention of it on the marriage license, which indicated the bride was single, she was also pregnant. But like so many events and details connected to the adult lives of Lisa and of Huberts, it seemed that almost nothing could be taken for granted and that no documents they had anything to do with could be accepted at face value. That was especially true when such vital human statistics as names, and dates and places of birth were involved. The facts tended to warp and change, to become obscure or get lost.

That was the case with information surrounding the birth of the daughter born to Lisa sometime late in 1987, and of a second girl born two years later. Even the state the girls were born in became a matter of contention, which, along with the matter of exact dates of birth, eventually tangled Huberts in a legal mess that involved criminal charges in the federal courts and civil proceedings in West Virginia.

On October 31, a few weeks after Lisa became a mother for the third time, Huberts was paroled from prison on a detainer. He was assigned to the Hope Village Community Treatment Center to begin a period of mental health counseling. Nevertheless, barely seven months after sentencing—far short of the two years he had been expected to serve—Huberts was once more out of prison.

A little more than a year later he was released from federal parole and left the treatment center to begin his five-year term of supervised probation. He was free to rejoin the civilian population and live on his own, as long as he regularly checked in with a federal parole officer and kept him or her up-to-date on his whereabouts and activities.

Cowell didn't even know of the change in Huberts's custody status, so there was no follow-up to see if Lisa was seeing her old boyfriend. There is no system set up for the routine notification of police to keep them apprised on the release from custody of criminals or on their movement between jails and prisons. And except in rare cases, detectives seldom make special efforts to keep track of their former quarry after convictions. There are always new investigations to demand their attention.

By the time Huberts began serving his probation, Martinez had apparently dropped out of Lisa's life or was about to. But despite Martinez's absence and the fact that Lisa had given birth to two daughters, she didn't resume her relationship with the man she accompanied across the country a half decade earlier. They split up, apparently for good.

While Huberts was paying off his debt to society, other major changes were occurring in his domestic affairs. There was a new woman in his life: Christine Adamczyk, an employee of the U.S. State Department, who worked with the Agency for International Development.

On May 25, 1990, Lisa filed an affidavit in Arlington County, renouncing her custody of her daughters in favor of Huberts, who turned out to be the natural father, and Ms. Adamczyk. She used her maiden name, Lisa Ann Miller, on the document, and said it was her desire to have the girls adopted by them.

According to the "petition for adoption," the children had lived in "the joint home of Raymond Arnold Huberts and Christine Adamczyk" since Christmas Eve, 1989, when they were placed there by their natural mother, Lisa Ann Miller. The couple listed an Arlington address in the 2000 block of North Smythe street in adoption papers which they filed for the girls. Lisa's current address was listed in the petition as an Arlington post office box number.

On July 14, Ms. Adamczyk's formal adoption of the

girls became final. According to documents filed with the U.S. District Court for the District of Columbia, Huberts and Adamczyk were married the following month. In November the balance of Huberts's probation was commuted to unsupervised status so he could join his wife in El Salvador, where she was stationed as a health worker.

The couple were still living in San Salvador, the Central American nation's capital city, when petitions were filed on their behalf in West Virginia to obtain delayed birth certificates for their daughters. The State Registrator of Vital Statistics refused to issue the certificates, claiming he wasn't provided with proper documentary evidence. But on May 15, 1991, a circuit court judge in Kanawha County, West Virginia, granted the request and ordered the registrator to issue the documents.

Despite the West Virginia judge's ruling, Huberts and his bride wound up in serious trouble with federal authorities over the circumstances surrounding the birth of the girls.

According to their birth records in West Virginia, Ariel Huberts was born on September 28, 1987, in Pendleton County. The younger girl was named Dolores, after her father's sister, and her new West Virginia birth certificate indicated she was born on September 10, 1989, in Randolph County. Pendleton and Randolph counties are in mountain country and adjoin each other on opposite sides of the Monongahela National Forest about twenty miles from the Virginia border.

The West Virginia birthdates and birthplaces, as well as the names Ariel and Dolores, were also listed in the document Lisa signed consenting to the adoption, even though it was only two weeks short of a year before the court ordered the birth certificates issued.

But according to federal grand jury indictments returned in the U.S. District Court in the District of Columbia against Huberts and his wife for alleged passport fraud, the sisters were born with different names, on different dates, and in a different state.

Huberts and his wife were accused of using bogus birth information to obtain passports for the girls. It was claimed in the two-count indictment that Huberts and Ms. Adamczyk knowingly gave false birthdates and names for the girls and stated they were born in West Virginia, when in fact they were both born in Montgomery County, Maryland. The true birthdate of the oldest girl, identified in court documents as Litha Victoria Martinez, was said to be July 28, 1987. Her younger sister, identified as Jennifer Lynn Parker, was reportedly born August 2, 1989.

Warrants for Huberts's arrest were issued by the federal court in Washington, D.C., on the charges of passport fraud, and another was issued by the U.S. District Court in Alexandria, Virginia, accusing him of violating his probation. The United States State Department followed up by revoking his passport, and he was ordered to leave El Salvador and return to the United States.

Agents from the State Department were waiting in April 1992 when he arrived in Miami, and took him into custody. He was temporarily locked in the Miami Correctional Center and held on $20,000 bond until he could be transported to the Washington area. In court documents he indicated he had three children. His employment status was listed as "homemaker," and his source of income as his wife.

His forty-year-old wife was permitted to remain free on her own recognizance. She lived with a sister in Oshkosh, Wisconsin, for a while after returning from Central America.

Near the end of May, after nearly two months behind

bars, Huberts posted bail and was released from custody. After a finding that the birth certificates for the two girls were valid, the charges tied to the accusations of passport fraud against Huberts and his wife were also dismissed. The charge of violation of probation, based on the accusations of passport fraud, was also dropped.

Long before that, Lisa's fortunes had taken a calamitous turn for the worse and she wound up in more serious trouble than she had ever been in during her tumultuous life.

A few weeks after Lisa signed away custody of her girls, a woman talked herself into a job as a nanny in Silver Spring. The young woman explained she needed work because her husband had recently been killed in an accident. She said her name was Stacy Linda Miller.

Chapter Five

Dreams

DREAMS COME TRUE FOR US WITH PA-
TIENCE—DWM 36 tall attractive warm witty romantic unpretentious ISO petite SDWF with
similar dreams. Kids welcomed with open heart.

Lisa was using an Arlington address and the name of
her dead sister, Johnnie Elaine Miller, in late October
when she picked up the twenty-fifth anniversary edition
of the *Washingtonian* and turned to the classified ad section at the back of the magazine.

Flipping past ads offering fantasy phone calls, leather
lingerie and latex clothes, nannies for hire and toilet
training kits, she began scanning the personals listed in
the magazine's "In Search Of" columns.

Seeking romance through the want ads is nothing
new, but in the past decade or so the practice had become an increasingly popular way for lonely men and
women to meet each other. The system has many advantages for the lovelorn, over more traditional methods employed on America's singles scene of meeting in
barrooms and in dance halls.

Would-be romantics without the craft and cunning to

survive and prevail amid the hunting frenzy of a pickup bar can save both time and money by advertising, and careful reading of the ads can quickly narrow the dating pool to people who have the qualities that are being sought. Advertisers sometimes exaggerate or understate their own characteristics, but they can be brutally frank about those they are looking for in others. Casually cruel remarks like "no fatties," "no shrimps," "no drinkers," and "no dopeheads," aren't uncommon. Advertisers often demand photographs.

And despite the burgeoning popularity of New Age electronics into the game of seeking romance with strangers by computer networking and video dating, many people prefer the more tried-and-true methods that rely on the printed page.

Many lonely men and women who could never handle a new flirtation via the electronic chat of a personal computer and have given up on blind dates and psychics, are more comfortable setting down their qualifications and desires with pen and paper. Consequently, the *Washingtonian*'s lovelorn ads were an important part of the metropolitan area's lively and exciting singles scene.

In that issue of the *Washingtonian,* there were more than five hundred personals; a curious, eclectic scattering of pleas from John and Jane Does seeking everything from marriage or mixed-gender afternoon quickies, to males and females looking for same-sex lovers, and lonely people with herpes and romance on their minds.

Advertisers identified themselves as white, black, Asian, Oriental, Hispanic, Jewish, Christian, Catholic, married, widowed, divorced, single, smokers, nonsmokers, outdoorsy, athletic, golfers, Redskins fans, and as liberals. Certain key words and abbreviations such as "generous," "full figured" or "rubenesque," and "adventurous" repeatedly cropped up.

An inordinate number of the advertisers described themselves as professionals; lawyers, doctors, engineers, college instructors, and writers. The *Washingtonian*'s "In Search Of" ads were definitely upscale, and reflected its location in the nation's capital. In other respects, however, they weren't that much different from similar personals that appear in other publications around the country.

They were from lonely people so desperate for companionship and romance they could hardly wait to begin living an illusion of trust with a stranger.

Some of the ads were wildly romantic and imaginative; some slightly kinky, with references to dominance, bondage, and chain gangs. One woman advised she was a NASA executive and former exotic dancer. A woman lawyer needed an escort for her firm's Christmas party; and a man who phlegmatically described himself as a single, tall, white male, was looking for a female wrestling enthusiast.

Most of the ads were less exotic, sometimes not even mildly flirtatious, and quickly got to the point. The advertiser was lonely and wanted to meet a sweetheart or companion. About midway through the list of personals, Lisa spotted an ad on page 304 of the magazine that caught her attention. It was sandwiched between those of two divorced women. One woman, in her fifties, was looking for another chance to love again. The other woman was a writer in her thirties, who said she loved books, art, and films.

The personal Lisa was interested in was from an advertiser identifying himself as a divorced, white male looking for a woman who was warm and unpretentious.

Dreams could come true for those who were patient, he wrote.

A few days after the magazine was sent to subscribers and began appearing on newsstands, Lisa mailed a reply to Roger's personal. She used her sister's name, and a post office box address in Arlington.

Roger responded with a long letter of his own. For the lonely man who had written about dreams coming true, it was the beginning of a seemingly innocent and rewarding relationship that would end as a nightmare.

The couple continued writing back and forth throughout the remainder of October and early the next month before finally meeting for the first time on November 9 for a Friday night date. They met at a restaurant, and Roger treated her to dinner. She was petite and pretty, with curly blond hair and warm blue eyes. Roger was captivated, and they had their second date a couple of days later.

On November 21, just short of two weeks after Roger's first date with Lisa, his divorce became final. It seemed the timing of his relationship with a new girlfriend couldn't have been better. Their dates quickly became a regular affair, with the couple getting together once or twice a week for dinner, drinks, or outings.

Roger was a pleasurable companion. He wasn't movie-star handsome, but he wasn't unattractive either. Tall, slightly chunky, with a hairline that was beginning to slink back from his expanding forehead, he had a personality that leaped out at his companions in animated bursts of humor and enthusiasm. He was charming and funny. He loved to clown, but he wasn't a practical joker who looked for laughs by being cruel to others. He was one of those people who seemed to remember every joke he ever heard. And if he wasn't able to dredge up the proper joke for the occasion from his memory, he manufactured his own.

He was a ray of sunshine. But he could also be a warm puppy, and there were times when his own barely submerged vulnerabilities surged to the surface. Roger was willing to give much, but he wanted a lot of love and fidelity in return.

He never visited his new girlfriend in Arlington, but gave her his telephone number so she could call him. And he continued writing to the post office box and talking with her when she telephoned. Her letters and conversations were chatty, witty, and bright, and it must have seemed to Roger that he was one of the luckiest men in the world.

Shortly before Christmas she told him she had moved into a basement apartment in the Takoma Park area of Silver Spring. On Christmas day he drove to the Silver Spring apartment to pick her up, and they shared a holiday dinner with his mother and father.

Johnnie Elaine, as she was still known and introduced, was on her best behavior. She was friendly and chatted comfortably with her boyfriend's parents. The Paulson's spent several days with their son, and saw his girlfriend two or three times during the visit. She seemed to be a pleasant companion for Roger.

Her job in Silver Spring lasted longer than some she had held, but as the new year approached, the nanny was ready once more to change professions. When she applied for a job as a receptionist with Rosenbloom and Associates, a certified public accounting firm on the twelfth floor of an office building in Bethesda, Maryland, she once more used her dead sister's name. It was one of Lisa's favorites.

On January 9, 1991, Lisa was interviewed for the position by Catherine M. Fowler, the office manager. Ms.

Fowler was favorably impressed by the polite, neatly groomed applicant. Her manner wasn't aggressive, but she behaved as if she was comfortably confident and at ease.

The woman filled out a job application, listing a home address on North Fairfax Street in Arlington. She provided the name of Dr. Doreen R. Davenport, Ph.D., as her most recent employer and professional reference. Her handwriting was neat and legible, and when she spoke, her voice was audible and had a good tone to it.

She also completed a battery of tests including exams to determine the extent of her typing and spelling skills. She performed well on the tests, and when she walked out of the CPA offices, it appeared she had an excellent opportunity of being picked for the job if the professional reference she provided stood up.

Later that afternoon, Ms. Fowler telephoned the number listed on the application for the reference. The woman who answered the telephone identified herself as Dr. Davenport and said she was very pleased with the work performance of Johnnie Elaine Miller and was sorry to lose her. Ms. Fowler had no way of knowing about the subterfuge: the woman she had the telephone conversation with was the same woman interviewed in her office a short time earlier. Dr. Doreen Davenport and Johnnie Elaine Miller were aliases used by Lisa Ann Rohn.

The applicant named Pandick Press, Incorporated, in New York City as another reference, but didn't provide a telephone number or complete address. Ms. Fowler didn't bother trying to contact anyone there. After completing her interviews with several applicants, she talked things over with her boss, Jeffrey Rosenbloom, and recommended hiring Johnnie Elaine. He concurred.

Johnnie Elaine Miller got the job and settled down to

work at a desk behind a small partition in the reception area. The position paid $18,000 a year. That was considerably less than she had been used to earning during her high-flying years with Huberts. But she was a fugitive and had to keep a low profile until the heat was off. The receptionist position was just the kind of job she needed to blend in with other men and women in the workaday world and avoid attention. It was comfortably unobtrusive and exactly what she was looking for.

The new receptionist kept busy at her new job answering the telephone, greeting clients, typing, and filing a comforting blur of documents filled with tax, social security numbers, and other intriguing personal and professional information. There was no indication from later investigations that she had helped herself to any of the data to create new identities. It seemed she already had established more aliases than she could use in a lifetime of thievery.

But Lisa had been on the run, juggling jobs and identities for almost five years, and it was exhausting. She was tired. Her breakup with Huberts appeared to be permanent; Martinez had dropped out of the picture; and she was unencumbered by any of her four children. Roger appeared to offer a new beginning, or at the very least a welcome respite from the runaway roller-coaster ride her life had turned into.

Lisa had learned many things during the near decade since her divorce from Steven Rohn, and some of the skills she was best at were pleasing and capturing the interest of men.

She and Roger strolled the red-brick pathways and modern walks of Baltimore's revitalized Inner Harbor, in the shadow of historic Fort McHenry, which withstood an assault by the British in 1814 that inspired Francis Scott Key to write "The Star Spangled Banner."

They dined at sidewalk cafés and seafood restaurants on fresh lobster, clams, oysters, or crabcakes from crabs pulled only a few hours earlier out of traps barely five miles down the Patapsco River in Chesapeake Bay; window-shopped at the quaint or funky stores; and lingered in the plaza between the pair of two-story glass structures that house the Harborplace mall to peer at jugglers, clowns, and other street performers.

They watched water taxis skimming along the surface of the Patapsco, busy as bugs while they shuttled tourists and other riders to picturesque schooners waiting to weigh anchor and sail away on day trips to Chesapeake Bay. The sweethearts visited the National Aquarium and its adjunct, the Marine Mammal Pavilion, and the Baltimore Zoo. Chris accompanied them on some of the outings, on days when he was visiting with his father.

Some of the best times were the simplest; like the long, serious talks; sharing the first cup of coffee of the morning; and strolls they took together to a sparkling little creek near Roger's apartment. Like lovers everywhere, it seemed to him that everything, from inanimate objects to emotions and the senses, were brighter, more acute and intense.

He even flirted with one of his pretty companion's bad habits, and filled out an application for a membership at the aquarium for "Mrs. Elaine Paulson." On an application for membership in the zoo, he used both the names Roger Paulson and Elaine Miller. They were family memberships.

The heavy slate-gray gloom of winter was lifting, and visitors to outdoor displays at the zoo were swapping heavy parkas and overcoats for sweaters and light jackets when the charmingly seductive woman Roger knew as Johnnie Elaine Miller moved in to share his apartment with him and his three cats. He was so caught up in the ecstasy of new love, it hardly seemed believable they had been strangers less than six months earlier. Roger had plunged headlong and completely into the romance. It was his style.

His girlfriend didn't have much to move. There was some clothing, grooming items, a few plants, a couple of boxes of books, some luggage, a briefcase, and a pathetically thin scatter of other personal treasures. She and Roger slid most of the material into the large walk-in closet at the narrow end of the master bedroom, a hall closet, and another closet in the extra bedroom. A few items were temporarily left on the floor of the hallway. She parked her 1982 Ford in front of the building next to his.

It was late March, a time of brisk breezes and fresh beginnings. Outdoor temperatures were rapidly easing into the high fifties, buds were starting to swell on the capital's famous cherry trees, and the area was blooming with life. It seemed to be a good time for both of them to plant some serious emotional roots.

Johnnie Elaine and Roger talked of the possibilities of getting married some day. Then he bought a $7000 engagement ring.

The apartment was roomy, with two bedrooms, a den, a full bathroom, half bathroom, living room, dining room, and a kitchen. Roger and his girlfriend shared the master bedroom, and the other was designated for Chris during his weekend visits.

Roger should have been happy. But he was troubled. Johnnie Elaine had met his parents and his son, but he had never met anyone in her family. In fact, he didn't know much about her at all. She drove away to work in the mornings and returned at night. But in many disturbing ways she was a woman of mystery, and he was never quite comfortable. There were little glitches in their relationship he was uneasy with.

He hadn't forgotten about a disturbing incident that occurred a few nights before she moved in with him. She telephoned him at the apartment and, during the conversation, mentioned that she was calling from home. But background noise made it sound to Roger like she was calling from a restaurant or a bar. After they completed their talk, he got into his Honda Accord and drove by her apartment. Her car wasn't in its usual parking place, or anywhere else nearby where he could find it.

Roger returned home and telephoned the woman he knew as the landlady of the apartment, to ask about Johnnie Elaine.

The older woman didn't know a Johnnie Elaine Miller. Another young woman whom she knew as Doreen Davenport lived in the apartment, the landlady told him.

Shaken and angry, Roger confronted his girlfriend and demanded to know why she was identifying herself to the landlady by one name and to him by another. Johnnie Elaine tried to explain, and Roger eventually dropped the subject. But he didn't forget, and suspicions about the mysterious woman in his life continued to pester him.

Roger believed in the old attributes of honesty and fidelity. But he was jealous, and he worried that his girlfriend might be slipping behind his back and seeing someone else. She had been living with him for almost a month when the mystery began to unravel.

According to the story he later recounted to law enforcement and court authorities and to his Lisa, he was home alone early Wednesday morning on April 24 when he began rearranging the apartment and putting some

of her things away. They had temporarily left some of
her belongings on the floor of the apartment until they
could find a place for them.

Since moving in with him, she had been getting up
early so she could leave for work about six A.M. The
early-bird start was designed to beat the heavy rush-
hour traffic that snarled highways in and around the
Beltway communities on workdays. Lisa was an efficient
employee, and she was prompt.

Roger was also in the habit of showing up early at his
own job, but it was only a few minutes after seven A.M.,
and there was still plenty of time. The apartment was
just a few blocks from his work. Sipping occasionally at
a half-full cup of lukewarm coffee while he worked,
Roger shifted things around in the walk-in closet of the
master bedroom so his girlfriend's books and other material could be stored there, out of the way.

He decided that a closet shelf was roomy enough to
hold a large wooden sewing box kit, a small travel game
pack, and a briefcase she had brought with her. But as
he was lifting the briefcase onto the shelf, it slipped, hit
him on the head and tumbled to the floor along with the
sewing box, game pack, and some other items.

As everything clattered to the floor, the lid of the
briefcase popped open and a cache of driver's licenses,
other documents, and a couple of wigs spilled out.
There was a flood of identification. Most of the material
was driver's licenses. Although the licenses, ID cards,
and other material carried different names and addresses, and there were various differences in appear-
ances, it was obvious to Roger that the photographs
were all of the same two people—a man and a woman.

Although her appearance in each of the photos varied
from slightly different to significantly altered, there
were enough resemblances to remove any doubt. They

were photos of the woman he knew as Johnnie Elaine
Miller. Her name appeared on a Virginia identification
card and on a California driver license that carried a
Berkeley address. Another California driver's license
was made out to Barbara A. Huening and carried a
photo that, except for the glasses, was almost a twin of
the picture on Johnnie Elaine's license. A Virginia
driver's license had a photo of his roommate with yet
another name, Cindy A. Talbot.

A Washington, D.C., identification card made out to
Carrol Anne Harris carried a photo of a woman with a
shock of long, red, curly hair. The photograph of a
pretty, smiling blonde with the name Johnalee Erma
Smitter appeared on a Washington, D.C. driver's license. Another Washington license carried a different
photograph and the name Sheena Joyce Fror. A social
security card carried the name Shauna Joy William.

And there were other documents, including a California birth certificate, wage and tax statements, a Sears
card, a Mobil credit card, a card for the Armed Forces
Benefit Association Alliance, a Smithsonian Institute
card, a card for an insurance company pharmaceutical
plan, club memberships, a public library card, and a fishing license. There were documents from Washington,
D.C., Virginia, Maryland, California, Illinois, Oregon,
and Massachusetts.

Roger's cooling cup of coffee was forgotten as he be-
wilderedly sifted through dozens of documents, including a distressing collection of IDs for the man. Roger
had no idea who the stranger was or what his relationship was with the woman he knew as Johnnie Elaine
Miller.

But there was no question that something was seriously wrong and his roommate was involved in something illegal. And he couldn't see any point in

confronting her about his shocking discovery. He had challenged her about one false name before, and gotten an unsatisfactory response. He was in love with Johnnie Elaine and he knew he deserved some straight talk from her, but she could be difficult to pin down about facts involving her life and background. It was time for a serious sorting out and some honest answers.

Scooping up the spilled documents, Roger shoved them back inside the briefcase, pulled the closet door shut, and wriggled into his suit coat. Then he headed outside the apartment to his car, with the briefcase swinging from his hand. A few minutes later he was driving almost directly south, to the FBI offices on Corporate Drive in Landover.

Roger showed the collection of identification documents to Special Agents David M. Zacur and Patrick A. Patterson and to several of their FBI colleagues. He also briefly traced his relationship with the woman he knew as Johnnie Elaine Miller, and told them that she worked at Rosenbloom and Associates in Bethesda.

He said he was afraid she was involved in something illegal and thought he might be in personal danger. The FBI agents agreed there were indications someone had been breaking some laws.

Zacur went before U.S. Magistrate Judge James E. Kenkel to request a federal warrant for the arrest of the suspect for possession of fraudulent identification documents. In an affidavit prepared for the hearing, the FBI agent listed thirteen different names with various pieces of identification he said were included in the documents found in the briefcase. Judge Kenkel issued the warrant, and a few minutes later five FBI agents drove to Bethesda to take Lisa into custody.

It was a few minutes after four P.M. when the FBI team arrived at the office building on Wisconsin Avenue and rode an elevator to the twelfth floor. One of the FBI men stationed himself outside the CPA office, three others stopped in the main office area, and Agent Steven P. Stowe walked up to the reception desk. A woman was filling out some papers there.

"Good afternoon. How are you doing?" the agent said. "I'd like to speak to Johnnie Elaine Miller." Stowe didn't offer his name or identify himself as being an FBI agent.

Lisa had learned a lot during her days on the street and her days as a fugitive. Instinct, experience, intelligence, whatever it was, something enabled her to size up the situation immediately. She was a quick read, and she obviously knew that she didn't want anything to do with the clean-cut stranger with the short hair and the conservative business suit.

There wasn't the slightest hesitation or indication in her voice that anything was wrong as she returned the greeting and explained that Johnnie Elaine was working in a back office. "I'll be glad to go get her for you," she said, smiling.

But Stowe also knew his way around. Assigned to the Hyattsville resident agency of the FBI's Baltimore division, he had already served more than seven years with the Bureau. And he had taken a good look at an ID photograph of the woman named on the arrest warrant. The blue-eyed blonde he was talking to was a dead ringer for the woman in the photo.

She was already on her feet, had reached for her purse and was turning to walk toward the back rooms when Stowe stopped her.

"I'm sorry, I am not going to allow you to take your purse with you," he said.

"I was just going to stop back by the bathroom on my

way back," she explained, with a slight nod toward the back rooms.

Stowe was adamant. "You still won't be able to take your purse with you," he insisted.

Lisa didn't ask who the stranger was or why he believed he had a right to tell her whether or not she could take her purse with her to the back rooms.

"Okay," she conceded. It was time to end the cat-and-mouse game.

She began walking toward the back rooms, with Stowe a few steps behind her. Presumably she was going to point out Johnnie Elaine Miller to him.

But as she turned a corner and entered a hallway out of sight of the other agents waiting in the outer office, she began walking faster. Then she broke into a run. Stowe dashed after her.

Alerted by the staccato clatter of her heels on the hallway floor, one of the other agents yelled to his colleagues that she was making a run for it. He hurtled around the reception desk and along the hallway, followed by the others.

A phalanx of strange men in business suits chasing the receptionist through the offices wasn't something that occurred at Rosenbloom and Associates under normal circumstances. But things were happening so quickly that other employees didn't have time enough to do anything but watch.

Lisa was making the run of her life, and she circled around a couple of cubicles and headed for an exit door that led into the twelfth-floor hallway where the elevators and stairs were located. She clawed at the handle of the door and was pulling it open when Stowe caught up with her. The agent slammed the door shut and grabbed Lisa by one arm.

"You're under arrest!," he blurted out. "I'm with the FBI!"

Lisa responded with screams, curses, and a frenzied effort to break away. She flailed at Stowe with her hands and nails, and he tried to circle around behind her while still holding on.

"How did you catch up with me? How did you find me?" she screeched. She continued kicking, struggling and screaming as the other agents moved in to support their colleague. Stowe's wrist was cut by his own watchband when she apparently hit it with one of her hands during the scuffle. And his nose was slashed. The struggle was so fast and furious, Stowe couldn't tell if the injury was caused by her glasses, fingernails, or a fist.

"Don't resist! You're going to hurt yourself," the FBI men warned. But she fought until they managed to pull her arms behind her back and slip a pair of handcuffs on her wrists. Then, with an agent on either side of her, they led her back past the astonished CPA firm employees and out of the office to the elevators in the hallway.

She had calmed down and was cooperating as they led her outside the building, with an agent on each side holding her arms. Stowe was walking immediately behind the prisoner, according to established procedure, when she suddenly made another desperate break for freedom. Still handcuffed, she lurched forward then back, kicking and swinging with her feet before she was subdued and quieted down once more.

The prisoner had apparently at last had enough of fighting, and submitted to the booking procedure without any further fuss. She followed directions, standing sullenly before a backdrop split with horizontal lines to measure her height while a photographer snapped a mug shot, patiently permitting a technician to roll each finger and thumb on an ink pad then transfer the print to a cardboard form, and then quietly submitted to the other routine processes. Her purse and other personal items were taken from her and logged in, then filed as the prisoner's property. A set of keys she had for the apartment in Beltsville were eventually turned over to Roger by FBI agents.

After booking, Lisa was lodged temporarily in the Prince Georges County Detention Center in Upper Marlboro. Four days later she was arraigned at the Hyattsville Magistrate Center. Then she was driven north and locked up in the women's section of the Baltimore City Detention Center. The oppressive jail smells of disinfectant, insufficiently masked odors of stale urine and body sweat, the yelling, moans, cries, and the thump of heavy metal doors being slammed shut, closed around her.

When her fingerprints were run through police computers for comparison with others, authorities confirmed her real identity. She was Lisa Ann Rohn, a former accused prostitute from California, who was wanted on warrants from Arlington County, Virginia, as a suspect in a major credit card fraud and theft operation.

An FBI agent telephoned the Arlington Police Department to talk with Detective Bill Cowell in the White Collar Unit of the Major Crimes Division. They had good news for him. It appeared the five-year search for Lisa Ann Rohn was over.

Chapter Six

Nightmares

Roger was torn between anger, disappointment, and love.

His relationship with the charming woman he met through the *Washingtonian*'s lovelorn columns could hardly be turning out worse. He offered her dreams realized, and she responded with the nightmare revelation that her entire adult life was a lie.

The woman he wanted to marry, settle down and build a new life with, was a fraud, a cheat, and a thief. Everything about her was false. Law enforcement authorities had told him her real name, and he knew that the true identity of his roommate was Lisa Ann Rohn.

The details surrounding her arrest only added to the nastiness; her attempts to flee and her struggle with the FBI agents. And if that weren't bad enough, there was the matter of what authorities were referring to as her "getaway bag."

Roger and FBI investigators had turned up several other curious or downright sinister items while searching through belongings she left at his apartment. There were wigs, rubber gloves, a bag containing a .45 caliber Star automatic with a loaded magazine clip, three boxes of cartridges, and $3300. The all-cash cache could provide a handy nest egg for someone who had to make a fast getaway.

Despite these discoveries, and his own disappointment, Roger cared too much for Lisa to give up on the bright, promising new world he had dreamed of. When an FBI agent talked to him about going before a grand jury, Roger begged off. He said he simply couldn't bring himself to be a witness against his girlfriend. It was finally agreed that he could skip the grand jury proceeding, but he was advised he had to testify if the case went to trial.

Roger realized Lisa had a debt to pay to society before the slate was wiped clean and they could begin rebuilding a new relationship based on love and honesty. When he made his first visit with her at the grim, stone Baltimore City Jail, he talked about that and reassured her that he loved her.

The old jail is a separate building directly across the street from the Maryland State Penitentiary, where one of its most infamous prisoners is expected to live out his life. The name of Willie Horton, a rapist and murderer, became virtually a household word during the 1988 presidential election campaign.

Inmates in the twin institutions are subject to most of the same security measures. They share the same careful logs of their movement and activities, daylong regimentation, cell lockdowns at night, and bed checks.

The visiting rules at the jail were strict. Like other visitors, Roger had to pass through metal detectors when he moved into the interior of the jail, where he was immediately assaulted by the forlorn sounds of confinement and the sharp, acrid blast of antiseptic. Watched closely by guards in efforts to prevent the passing of weapons, drugs, money or other contraband, inmates and their guests were permitted to kiss briefly at the beginning of visits. Then they could sit across from each other at a table and talk until the visit ended and a good-bye kiss was permitted.

It was a miserable ordeal for Roger. He had lived a straight and narrow life, and never even collected a traffic ticket. Exposure to the oppressive security and restrictions of the jail was nothing like the relatively easy regimen and rules governing Navy families living in military housing or traveling back and forth between the base and the civilian world.

Nevertheless, he visited Lisa every week. Faithfully, on visiting day for female inmates, he climbed into his Accord, pulled out of the parking lot, and drove onto the Interstate-95 Calverton exchange about a block from his apartment. Then he followed I-95 almost due north for the forty-five-minute drive past a steady lineup of exits leading to the clutter of small suburban towns and into Baltimore.

Several blocks after entering the city, he drove past the site of Oriole Park in Camden Yards, where the new stadium for the city's American League baseball team was under construction, before turning north off Russell Street and continuing on to the dismal 150-year-old prison at Madison Street and Greenmount Avenue.

Between visits, Roger and Lisa exchanged telephone calls and letters. Like other jails and prisons, inmates could place calls to people outside, but friends and relatives couldn't telephone them. Beltsville was outside the Baltimore dialing area, so Lisa had to call Roger collect. After a few calls, he gave her his telephone calling card number to use because it was cheaper. Once she had the charge card number, corrections officers permitted her to use a special telephone reserved for direct calls. On some days she made two or three.

But, regardless of how hard he tried to fight it, jealousy, suspicions, and resentment welled up in him. In their telephone conversations and in his letters, he fretted and complained about his resentments. Lisa was unhappy because Roger had taken her briefcase and the flood of IDs to the FBI. And she hated jail, the mass-produced food, the regimentation, claustrophobia, and the curious hollow loneliness of being surrounded by strangers.

In some ways they appeared stuck with each other. Roger was still desperately lonely and in need of love, but he was resentful and suspicious. Lisa was locked up with few or no close family ties and had to depend on Roger for emotional support, as well as for such everyday material needs as grooming and other personal items.

In Roger's letters to Lisa and in their telephone conversations, they chatted about their relationship, about her legal difficulties and the upcoming trial, and about various mundane matters. He handwrote some of the letters, which were often six or seven pages long or longer, and talked of his love for her and of his fears and doubts. Other letters were typed, but almost all of them betrayed his seesaw emotions, which crazily whipsawed from depression and fear to hope and romance.

He vowed to wait for her, regardless of how long she might have to spend behind bars as a result of possible convictions on the charges pending against her in the federal court in Baltimore and in Arlington County. Even if he had to wait two years or more, he would wait. And he would continue to keep her clothes and other personal effects until she was released, he reassured her.

Differences develop that lead most lovers to quarrel at times. But Roger and Lisa had more than their fair share of problems and of quarrels, while their affair stumbled along, deteriorating into a disturbing love-hate relationship.

As soon as Cowell learned of Lisa's arrest, he filed a detainer on her. He mailed a certified copy of his warrants to the federal court in Baltimore, which was placed in her file jacket. If everything went well and the documents weren't lost or misfiled by some careless clerk or court aide, the detainer would follow Lisa wherever she moved within the criminal justice and corrections systems until she was finally turned over to authorities from Arlington.

Regardless of whatever plans Cowell had for her in Arlington, Lisa wanted out of the Baltimore jail.

Soon after her arrest, Roger advised authorities he would agree to supervise Lisa if she was put into his custody, and to report any violations of court-ordered conditions of her release. He agreed to permit modification of his telephone service so that she could be electronically monitored while she was in his custody.

Electronic monitoring was a relatively new technique for keeping track of prisoners or certain classifications of parolees while permitting them to live in their own home, in group homes, and sometimes to work and commute to and from outside jobs. It was begun in Palm Beach County, Florida, in 1984 as an experiment, and within five or six years the house arrest system had spread to more than two-thirds of America's states.

Although there are differences in the system in various jurisdictions, the technique basically calls for an electronic band to be locked around the ankle or wrist of the person being monitored. The bracelets or anklets then transmit the whereabouts of the individual to a computer around-the-clock.

Most monitoring is set up so that the computer automatically places random telephone calls to the person under house arrest throughout the day or night. Some systems use state-of-the-art video telephones, so that not only voice checks can be made, but visual checks as well. Some of the sophisticated surveillance computer-telephone hookups even conduct long-distance Breathalyzer tests on drunken drivers or other prisoners ordered to stay away from alcohol.

But it is a system that has been mired in continuing controversy since its inception. It doesn't always work the way it is supposed to, and a small percentage of criminals under house arrest find ways to abuse and beat the system.

Advocates point out that electronic monitoring can trim huge amounts of money from the costs of housing nonviolent offenders in correctional institutions. They claim it helps relieve overcrowding of the nation's bursting-at-the-seam jails and prisons where inmate populations doubled from about a half million in 1980 to roughly one million a decade later.

But critics say the house arrest system often leads to disappointment and tragedy. They cite cases where people being electronically monitored have slipped off the locked anklets, otherwise crossed up the signals, or simply ignored them and left their house or apartment to commit crimes.

In late May 1990 several months before Roger placed his ad in the *Washingtonian*, a nineteen-year-old armed robber was shot to death by an off-duty policeman during a gunfight at a seafood restaurant in Winston Salem, North Carolina. The dead gunman, Elrico Eugene Stewart, was wearing the electronic anklet he was fitted with about six weeks earlier when he was placed on house arrest and electronic surveillance after his conviction for a burglary. Stewart had a part-time job as a janitor and had advised a monitoring supervisor he was going to work.

The previous month another inmate on an electronic ball and chain was involved in a murder in nearby Greensboro after cutting off the band around his ankle.

Many other abuses of electronic monitoring have been reported in such widespread areas of the country as Houston, Chicago, and Charleston. Four murders had been blamed on house arrest prisoners in Florida's Broward County by the time Lisa and Roger first met. Broward is the closest southern neighbor to Palm Beach County where electronic monitoring was first tried out.

Despite the problems with electronic monitoring, however, in some respects Lisa appeared to be a good candidate for the house arrest surveillance system. She had never been convicted of a crime, or even accused of committing a violent act. Her roommate also wanted her back home and was willing to take responsibility for helping to monitor her behavior.

According to the proposal, Roger also agreed to put up the $7000 engagement ring and his 1991 Honda as security. If Lisa was released to his custody and fled, Roger would lose the ring and his car, which was worth about $15,000 and was totally paid for.

Stephen Smith, a Pretrial Services officer who interviewed Lisa, recommended she be released instead of being kept in the jail. But he pointed out that the Volunteers of America, which provided housing for some defendants awaiting trial, would not accept her because of the other charges pending against her.

Pretrial Services authorities recommended that if she was released, however, she should be prohibited from possession of firearms, excessive use of alcohol, or use of any narcotics and controlled substances, and put under the agency's supervision.

Represented by an Assistant Federal Public Defender, Lisa appeared in court six days after her arrest for a detention hearing. The suggestions for her release, and arguments against letting her out of jail prior to trial, were spelled out at the proceeding before a U.S. Magistrate.

Although initial court reaction to the request appeared to be positive, eventually, when all was said and done, Lisa remained in jail. There was no release, with or without electronic monitoring. Despite the setback, Lisa and Roger continued talking about raising bail. He hadn't been able to build up a big bank account on a base annual salary of $31,000, even though that was supplemented by expenses, profit sharing, and a year-end bonus. But he was still willing to put up the ring and his Honda as collateral if he could just cut through the bewildering bureaucracy of the legal justice system and the different jurisdictions with an interest in Lisa's future.

During talks with Barbara Slaymaker Sale, the Assistant U.S. Attorney in Baltimore who was heading Lisa's prosecution on the federal charges, Roger repeated his intentions to wait for his girlfriend and his hopes to win her freedom. The prosecutor was counting on him to appear as one of her key witnesses, and they talked several times.

It was difficult for Roger to control his emotions while Lisa and the case against her was being discussed. Repeatedly, although he fought against it, the anger, pain and sense of betrayal welled up and he would have trouble continuing to talk. Sometimes big tears welled in his eyes, oozed over his cheeks and ran down his face. He had been raised to respect and obey the law, and there was no question in his mind that he was doing the right thing. He insisted that once she had served her sentence or sentences and cleared the record, they could get on with building happy lives together.

A Connecticut native who earned her law degree at George Washington University in the District of Columbia and clerked for a federal court judge in Baltimore before moving on to the U.S. Attorney's staff there, Sale was caught between the cold demands of strict professionalism, and her natural human concern and sympathy for the guileless, distraught man.

"I just wanted to tell him, 'Roger, why don't you look somewhere else,' " she recalled years later. "But she was the light of his life. I felt very sorry for him. He was a nice guy, a very lonely man."

Advising people how to handle their love lives was a job for psychologists, clergy, and others trained in counseling, however. Such things weren't within the purview of federal prosecutors, so Sale stuck to the business at hand.

Lisa was charged with the federal offense, described in typical tongue-twisting legalese as "knowingly possessing five or more pieces of false identification when possession is in or affects interstate or foreign commerce, and with intent to use them unlawfully."

The offense carried a maximum possible penalty of up to five-years in prison, a fine up to $25,000, or both, and Sale was determined to obtain a conviction. The briefcase Roger delivered to the FBI contained identification with more than twenty-five different names. And there were from two to twelve forms of identification for each of them.

It was a fascinating case for the Assistant U.S. Attorney, and some of the most intriguing aspects were the mysteries that still surrounded the defendant. Even after the investigation was wrapped up, there were still so many things that weren't known about her. But Sale wouldn't learn anything directly from the defendant. Lisa wasn't talking.

She was represented by Michael Thomas Citara-Manis, a skilled, hardworking lawyer from the Federal Public Defender's office in Baltimore. She didn't plan to testify in her defense, so there would be no opportunities for the prosecutor to cross-examine her on the witness stand or to take pretrial depositions. If any mysteries were cleared up during the proceeding, the solutions would come from other sources.

Lisa's anticipated trial was still several weeks from beginning when Roger bought a Springfield assault rifle. The SAR-48 had a twenty-two-inch barrel and was capable of firing twenty-round clips. Three weeks later he bought a .22 caliber Ruger Mark II automatic target pistol.

On July 16, 1991, Lisa hurried through the early morning routine at the jail, dressed in civilian clothes and was driven the several blocks south through central Baltimore to the Clarence Mitchell Federal Courthouse on the city's Inner Harbor, a couple of blocks from the site of the new baseball park, for her trial.

There was no rush for seats in the spectators' section of the United District Court for the District of Maryland before Senior Judge Herbert F. Murray called the proceedings to order. Except for the defendant, court officers, and members of the jury pool, the courtroom was empty. Lisa's trial didn't promise to be much different from most of the others among the weary parade of routine cases that passed in and out of the federal courts every weekday.

Despite the prosecutor's enthusiasm and intrigue with the case, it wasn't the kind of high-profile proceeding that attracts either courtroom groupies who prefer the real-life drama of murder trials, scandalous divorces, or other cases that are regularly tried in the federal and local courts to television soap opera. There wasn't a single news reporter in the courtroom from the *Baltimore Sun*, the *Prince Georges County Journal* in Hyattsville, a few miles from Roger's home, or from any of the area radio and television stations.

Shortly before the trial began, Roger confided to an FBI agent that he was in fear for his life. He babbled about being in danger either from people whom he knew or from others unknown to him. His conversation was disjointed and erratic, as if he was wilting under the pressure of his anticipated court appearance to testify against his girlfriend. While Lisa was in jail, Roger changed the locks on his apartment doors.

Scheduled witnesses in the trial weren't permitted to observe the proceedings inside the courtroom until after their testimony was completed. But Roger and Cowell chatted in the hallway and in anterooms during the humdrum workings of pretrial conferences and jury selection while waiting for testimony to begin.

For a man who played such an important role in the defendant's arrest and was expected to be a key prosecution witness, Roger carried on a curious conversation with the veteran police officer. He pointed out how beautiful he believed Lisa was, boasted about her lovemaking, and reiterated his plans to marry her after the trial was over and everything quieted down.

Cowell shared some of the prosecutor's emotions about the big friendly man and the naive talk about a future with the defendant. Roger appeared to have all the innocence of a teddy bear, and he was more vulnerable. Months later the gruff detective recalled Roger as "a broken-hearted, big, chubby, roly-poly type of guy who wouldn't step on an ant." The detective was more outspoken than the prosecutor was about his personal feelings concerning the defendant. Cowell cautioned Roger that Lisa was a coldhearted, calculating woman.

But Roger was unconvinced. He was sure that he knew another, softer, sweeter side of Lisa that the burly detective couldn't see. And he said so.

Selection of a twelve-member jury and opening statements took up most of the first day. At last, on July 17, the prosecutor called Catherine Fowler as the trial's opening witness.

Responding to questioning from Sale, the CPA office manager traced the job interview she conducted with the defendant, and Lisa's eventual hiring. She explained she was responsible for advertising for office help, conducting interviews, and making recommendations to her boss.

The witness confirmed that the woman she had known as Johnnie Miller signed the job application with that name. The application, along with a copy of an employee withholding allowance certificate, or W-4 form made out for Johnnie Elaine Miller, were placed into evidence. Both documents had been filled out by the defendant, who supplied the social security number for the W-4.

Then it was Roger's turn to testify. Speaking audibly in a firm voice, and frequently shifting his eyes from the prosecutor to his girlfriend, seated a few feet away at the defendant's table, the witness moved through the routine information about his name, address, job, and marital status.

He told about placing his personal in the October *Washingtonian,* about the exchange of letters with a woman who said her name was Johnnie Elaine Miller, and about their first face-to-face meeting on a dinner date. And he recounted the story about her moving in, his discovery of the cache of bogus IDs, and turning the material over to the FBI in Landover.

The prosecutor asked if heard from his girlfriend after her arrest.

"Yes, she called me about twenty-four hours later, or possibly forty-eight hours later," he said. "I am not sure of the exact time frame. No more than two days later."

"And what did you say to her?" the prosecutor continued.

"I asked her what was going on; if she was all right; and if she needed me to make any phone calls for her," he replied.

When Lisa asked him if anyone had been at their apartment, he told her FBI agents were there and had taken two briefcases, the witness testified. He couldn't remember the defendant's exact words in response to the news.

Roger squirmed in his chair, shifting his eyes from his girlfriend to the jury, then back to the prosecutor. "But she voiced displeasure," he said.

Rules of evidence didn't permit Sale to ask the witness about the contents of the second briefcase. According to procedure governing testimony, the cash, pistol, and other items in the kit investigators referred to as a "getaway bag" were not considered relevant to the inquiry. And the jury may have been prejudiced against the defendant if they learned of the sinister contents.

Roger said that within a couple of days after his girlfriend's arrest, he was beginning to piece together a fairly accurate picture of who she was and what she had been up to. Investigators passed on several details about her background to him. Lisa provided some information, but quickly tired of the dreary business, and he backed off pestering her.

"I pretty much stopped asking technical questions because she wouldn't answer them," he explained.

The prosecutor passed her witness to the defense for cross-examination. CitaraManis moved quickly through a few preliminary questions. Then he asked Roger to describe his relationship with Lisa.

"Beautiful!" Roger replied.

"Would you say you got very close?"

"Definitely!"

"Did you love Ms. Rohn?" CitaraManis continued.

Roger drew in a big breath and filled his chest with air before answering. "Definitely!" he repeated at last, peering past the lawyer to look at Lisa.

"Did you plan to get married?"

Roger continued to look at the defendant. His reply was delivered in a firm voice, without any apparent doubts or reserve. "Yes!" he said.

A few minutes later Roger concluded his testimony and was followed to the witness stand by Patterson.

Responding to the prosecutor's questions, the FBI agent testified about Roger's early morning appearance at the office in Landover with the briefcase. He said Roger claimed he suspected he was in danger and that the woman he was living with might have been using "a different name. He was concerned that the person was involved in—" CitaraManis cut the witness off with an objection, which the court sustained. The prosecutor began again.

"Without saying what Mr. Paulson said to you— please don't say what Mr. Paulson said to you—did he bring the documents to you for you to examine?" she asked.

Patterson confirmed that Roger brought the briefcase to the office, that it was opened and the documents examined. Sale used the testimony to enter several of the documents taken from a large plastic envelope into evidence. They included:

- A Washington, D.C. driver's license made out in the name of Sheena Joyce Fror.
- A Washington, D.C., driver's license and a W-2 wage and tax statement for 1986, both carrying the name of Carol Anne Harris.
- A social security card made out to Shauna Joy William.
- Eleven pieces of identification carrying the name Cindy Ann Talbot. They included a birth certificate from San Jose, California, a laminated employe ID card for Dennison Manufacturing Company in Framingham, Massachusetts, with the same date of birth and a social security number, two golden membership cards from the New Otani Club, a laminated social security card, a Sears card, a Virginia driver's license with an Arlington address, a Virginia photo ID for the driver's license, a W-2 wage and tax statement for 1988, and two Most cards for the Maximum Savings Bank.
- Additional identification documents taken from a second plastic envelope were also entered as evidence. All were made out to Dorene R. Davenport or variations of that name. They included a birth certificate from Contra Costa County, California; a Virginia driver's license ID, a Smithsonian Institute card, and various other documents.
- A third envelope yielded a fistful of identification in the name of Johnnie Elaine Miller or variations of that name. They included a birth certificate; two Virginia driver's licenses and a California driver's license with a Berkeley address; an employe ID card from Cullinet Software, Incorporated, West-

wood, Massachusetts; a student ID card for Mount Hood Community College in Oregon; two New Otani membership cards; and an application for a District of Columbia sports fishing license.

- Additional documents were fished out of envelopes carrying identification for Doreen Donna Breslin and variations of that name; Lisa Ann Miller, Lisa R. Miller, Lisa Rohn Miller, Stacy L. Miller, Stacy Linda Miller; Mary Elizabeth Baker, Shauna Joy Eror, Johnalee Erma Smitter, Mary Lynn Reynolds, Barbara Huening, and variations of that name.

- The membership cards from the National Aquarium and Baltimore Zoo that Lisa obtained while she was dating Roger were among the documents. Others included a library card from the District of Columbia, a gasoline credit card, voter registration cards from Chicago and from Clackamas, Oregon, a Playboy Club International key card (made out to Lisa Rohn Miller), and a Republican National Committee Sustaining Membership Card for 1984.

The state had produced an impressive collection of evidence that provided a graphic lesson for the jury of how easy it is to assemble the documents necessary for establishing a false identity. Driver's licenses and other identification documents had been produced in thirteen different names.

But when the prosecutor began to move toward introducing identification used by the defendant's former male confederate, CitaraManis quickly objected. They weren't relative to the proceedings, he claimed. As jurists quietly looked on just out of earshot, the Assistant Federal Public Defender and the deputy prosecutor huddled with the judge at a bench conference.

"Judge, these are the identifications, apparently, of Mr. Huberts, the gentleman in Virginia who was charged and convicted and served some time. I don't see where these are relevant to these proceedings since basically they are someone else's identifications," CitaraManis argued.

The prosecutor responded that the identification documents all appeared to be tied to the same person. A witness was waiting outside, ready to testify that the man whose photos were shown on the IDs was Huberts, who was arrested in 1986 in Arlington. Cowell was the prospective witness.

Continuing, Sale explained that the witness was also prepared to testify about a warrant obtained for Lisa after Huberts's arrest. "We submit it's relevant to show —that it goes to the motive for her flight," the prosecutor added. "She is fleeing from the offenses that she committed with this gentleman, and the two of them are tied in inextricably together."

The Assistant Federal Public Defender continued to argue against Sale's move. Although the fact the warrant was issued might be relevant, other circumstances leading up to the move were not, he said. "And the fact that this gentleman was prosecuted, and I think for that to come into evidence, is extremely prejudicial to my client if that's what the government intends to use this other witness for," he declared.

He also complained he hadn't been previously informed of the direction the prosecution appeared to be about to take in the testimony of witnesses.

Sale persisted. "We can discuss whether this is a surprise or not," she said. "This evidence shows that Ms. Rohn was keeping not only spare identifications for herself to use as needed, but was also keeping the identification for her boyfriend. . . ." The prosecutor said she would show Lisa was a fugitive on the run from a charge in Arlington and that she intended to use the false identification documents unlawfully.

The debate dragged on. Although the jury wasn't privy to the particulars, the lengthy bench conference was a good example of the hard-fought jousting over legal fine points that occurs during and preliminary to every trial. Attorneys cross swords over who can testify, what witnesses can be asked, how complete their responses can be, what physical evidence is permissible, questions of prejudice and myriad other matters that might appear to a layman—or to a juror—to be wastefully time-consuming and hair-splitting wars of words focused on unimportant details.

But a judge's conclusions when dealing with such matters can mean the difference between verdicts finding different degrees of guilt, or not guilty, and to critical decisions during the appeals process in higher courts.

Judge Murray ruled that the material appeared to have relevance to the defendant's intent. The prosecutor and the defense attorney agreed to discuss limits on the testimony of the witness waiting outside.

A few minutes later FBI agent Patterson's testimony was resumed and the additional identification documents were accepted by the court as evidence. CitaraManis objected again and the motion was overruled.

Agent Stowe followed his colleague on the witness stand and recounted details of the defendant's arrest. A woman juror moved a hand to her mouth and arched her eyebrows as if in surprise when Stowe described the struggle with the defendant at the side door.

During cross-examination about the chase through the office and the struggle between Lisa and the FBI agents, CitaraManis asked how many agents were holding her before she was handcuffed. Stowe said there were two or three.

"This would have held her down on the ground?" CitaraManis continued.

Stowe had testified in trials before. He wasn't about to help create an image of three or four feisty FBI men knocking or wrestling the woman—who was seated demurely at the defense table, quietly watching and listening—to the floor of the office.

"Not on the ground. No!" he replied.

"Up against the wall?"

"I don't recall whether it was actually physically against the wall or not," the witness responded.

CitaraManis dug in. "Okay! Did you push her up against the wall or against the door?"

"I don't know, I really don't know. It happened very rapidly, and she was fighting very hard," the witness replied. "So, I am really not sure."

The lawyer asked if he used a fair degree of force restraining her.

"I circled around her like that, to keep her hands from flailing at me," the witness replied, motioning with his own hands. "And she still managed to cut my nose and my wrist. Actually, the wrist came from the watchband. She hit the watchband."

CitaraManis asked a few more questions about the struggle in the office, and the second flare-up just outside the building. Then he asked if it would be accurate to say that as a result of the force that was used, was it possible Lisa was injured and incapacitated?

"That would not be a fair statement," Stowe replied.

The FBI agent's testimony was concluded and Judge Murray announced a recess for lunch. The proceeding was rapidly winding down. Only Cowell remained to testify for the prosecution, and the defense did not plan to call any witnesses.

Shortly after two P.M. the trial was resumed and Cowell was called as a witness. Roger, whose testimony was completed, watched and listened from a seat near the front row of benches in the spectator section.

At the direction of the prosecutor, Cowell examined some of the driver's licenses and other documents previously placed in evidence, and identified the male shown in the photographs as Huberts. Ms. Sale asked how he knew Huberts.

Cowell explained that Huberts was targeted in a major credit card fraud investigation and arrested in Arlington County. Continuing to respond to the prosecutor's questions, Cowell said a warrant was later obtained for the defendant.

The prosecutor continued to move testimony along swiftly, and after ascertaining that Lisa hadn't been arrested on the warrant by the previous April 24, she concluded direct examination.

CitaraManis was also working quickly. After the witness testified that two arrest warrants were issued for Lisa on November 27, 1986, the defense attorney had begun questioning him about the case file prepared on Huberts, when the prosecutor objected. The line of questioning was not relevant, she claimed. The judge agreed, and CitaraManis announced that he had no further questions. Cowell had testified less than fifteen minutes when he walked from the witness stand. A few minutes later he left the courthouse, climbed into his police cruiser, and began the drive back to Arlington. He didn't plan to return to listen to summations.

Judge Murray invited the attorneys to approach the bench, and CitaraManis moved for a directed verdict of acquittal on grounds that the government hadn't shown what he described as "its apparent theory that Ms. Rohn was attempting to avoid arrest.

"That is a quote, unquote, unlawful intent, and I think unlawful is by its plain meaning something that's made illegal by virtue of some statute or law." There was no legal statute that made it illegal to claim to be someone else, he added.

The prosecutor responded by pointing out it is a violation of federal law to flee across state lines to avoid prosecution. "And the evidence viewed in the light most favorable to the government shows that Ms. Rohn was —her entire life was an attempt to avoid prosecution."

CitaraManis argued that the prosecution showed only that the defendant had used one other name, that of Johnnie E. Miller, besides her own during the time in question. He added again that no law made it illegal to be a fugitive, and that nothing during the trial had shown the documents were used or were intended for use specifically for crossing state lines to avoid prosecution.

Roger listened and watched intently, occasionally glancing toward Lisa as the court officers carried out the debate over CitaraManis's motion. Jurors remained quietly seated, idly watching the muted activity at the bench. Lisa also kept her eyes riveted on the judge and the lawyers, occasionally lightly tapping the end of a pencil on a yellow note pad as she waited for the conference to end.

At last Judge Murray advised the defense lawyer that the motion was denied. Following another jury break, and after Lisa formally advised the judge she chose not to testify, the panel was called back into the courtroom to hear summations.

The burden of proof in criminal trials is on the state. The defense does not have to prove their client innocent. The prosecution has to prove guilt. Consequently, the prosecution is given two trips to the plate during summations—before the defense, then again in rebuttal.

Sale led off for the prosecution, reviewing the evidence she claimed tied the defendant to the false identification documents. "Ladies and gentlemen, this woman was living a lie. Everything she did was a big lie." Lisa barely blinked her eyes as Ms. Sale half turned and swept an arm back in her direction. Being accused of living a lie wasn't the worst thing ever said about her.

Turning to the defendant's arrest, the prosecutor declared: "She ran like a rabbit and fought like a tiger— and said to the agents who were struggling to subdue her at that point, words to the effect of, 'How did you find me? How did you get me?' as she struggled to get free.

"She fought and she ran, and she had all of this identification because she knew she was wanted on the charge in Arlington. This man, Raymond Huberts, had been arrested in 1986, and in connection with his arrest a warrant was issued for Lisa Ann Rohn.

"Lisa Ann Rohn, Johnnie Elaine Miller, Dorene Davenport, all of these people have been running scared since 1986. Now, the question that you are going to be asked to address, and the issue I think that the defense will rely on is, was this unlawful? Was her possession of these unlawful? Did she intend to use them unlawfully?"

"Ladies and gentlemen, I submit that . . . every breath she took, every move she made since avoiding arrest in 1986 after she had fled across state lines, was all unlawful. She was unlawfully fleeing arrest."

The jurors listened intently as the words tumbled from the prosecutor's mouth forming an unbroken string of accusations.

"Filling out this W-4 was probably unlawful. Johnnie Elaine Miller! Who do they expect a tax return from at the end of the year?" she demanded.

"Every time she got in the car and turned the ignition on and drove off using who knows what driver's license, was that lawful?"

The prosecutor urged the jurors to use their common sense and to consider all the evidence during their deliberations. Even such seemingly innocent documents as library cards and club membership enhance the usability of other forms of ID, she pointed out. And although, as the judge would later instruct, only those issued under the authority of the state qualified as identity documents for the purpose of the indictment, they could all be taken into consideration during deliberations.

Sale asked the jury if there was any lawful reason for the defendant to have the identification, then answered her own question. "She was on the run from the charge in Alexandria." The prosecutor had made a small slip-of-the-tongue, citing the historic city just south of Arlington County, but no one seemed to notice and she rapidly concluded her presentation.

"That's why she had this briefcase full of phony IDs, all of them bearing her picture, some of them with wigs, some of them with glasses, and some without glasses," the prosecutor declared. "She was ready, willing, and able to be as many persons as she could be in order to avoid that charge."

Then, at last, it was the defense attorney's turn at bat.

CitaraManis began his summation by recalling that he had asked few questions of the witnesses during cross-examination. He explained that was because most of the facts weren't in dispute, and that, in turn, was because the government hadn't sufficiently proven its case. It simply wasn't shown that his client intended to unlaw-

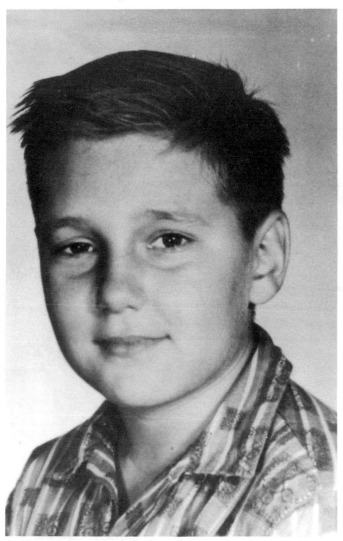

Roger Paulson, 10 years old, in a school picture.
(Author's Collection)

This photo was taken around 1963 in Hawaii, where Paul's father was stationed with the Navy. *(Author's Collection)*

Roger Paulson in 1980. *(Author's Collection)*

Raymond Arnold Huberts and Lisa Ann Rohn living it up and toasting their good fortune. Exact location and date unknown, but it was before November 1986, when Huberts was arrested in Arlington and Lisa went on the run.
(Courtesy William F. Cowell)

Bank photo of Lisa Ann Rohn and Raymond Arnold Huberts at ATM. *(Courtesy William F. Cowell)*

A few of the identification cards with aliases of Lisa Ann Rohn. They were found in her briefcase by Roger Paulson. *(Courtesy Laura Gwinn, Prince Georges County Assistant State's Attorney)*

Interior of Roger's apartment as police found it after he was shot to death. Lisa's full-length tweed coat is draped over the table, and the plastic garbage bag is on the floor. *(Courtesy Laura Gwinn)*

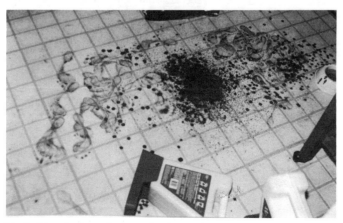

Lisa's bloody footprints on the floor of the kitchen where she placed the 911 call. *(Courtesy Laura Gwinn)*

Roger's Ruger Mark II .22-caliber target pistol with which he was shot. *(Courtesy Laura Gwinn)*

California arrest photo of Lisa Ann Rohn circulated by the Arlington County Police Department to other police departments and news media during the period she was a fugitive. *(Courtesy William F. Cowell)*

Laura Gwinn, Prince Georges County Assistant State's Attorney, in front of the historic county courthouse where she obtained a first-degree murder conviction in the trial of Lisa Ann Rohn for Roger's slaying. *(Photo by Lon Slepicka)*

Detective William F. Cowell, head of the White Collar Unit of the Major Crimes Division, Arlington County Police Department. *(Photo by Lon Slepicka)*

A photograph of Roger Paulson taken shortly before his death. *(Author's Collection)*

fully use the identification documents that were in her possession.

"It's not unlawful to be a fugitive. It's not unlawful to have a warrant out for your arrest. It's not unlawful to pose as someone else," he declared.

"I don't know if Ms. Sale might contend, in her closing remarks, that Ms. Rohn crossed state lines to avoid detection. But those charges were in Arlington," he said. "Where she was working! Arlington, Virginia! Certainly there was no—I don't think any rational person could find that she avoided flight by living in Virginia. She worked in Arlington!"

The defense attorney's reference to his client working in Arlington was a puzzling remark, which hadn't been supported by earlier testimony. At the prosecutor's table Sale scribbled a note to herself on a yellow legal pad.

CitaraManis turned to the question of the ID documents found in the briefcase that carried masculine names and photos. He said the jury could infer that Huberts hadn't used them in 1986 to avoid arrest. "I think what the government wanted to show you was that these were kept for safekeeping, essentially. . . . Well, if Ms. Rohn was keeping them merely for safekeeping, again, that's not unlawful.

"I think you can infer that perhaps a similar reason for her keeping the identifications that the government has admitted apparently, with her picture on it—that's not unlawful either—in her safekeeping."

The jury was learning that lawyers in real-life trials don't always talk in picture-perfect grammatical sentences or in dramatic sound bites, as they do in novels or on television shows. But the defense attorney was getting his message across. The question remained to be answered whether or not the jury would accept it.

CitaraManis forged ahead, advising the panel that no evidence had shown that his client had committed crimes or done anything unlawful during the four and a half years the warrants were outstanding for her.

"Indeed, the only evidence they had was that she was leading, I guess what you could characterize as a straight life," he declared.

"She met Mr. Roger Paulson. You saw him testify. He had fallen in love with her. In fact they had a very close, loving relationship, and he was intending to marry her." CitaraManis told the jurors he believed they would find his client not guilty.

In rebuttal, Sale told the panel that the defense lawyer had added an element to the offense. "And he has added it so that, of course, he can shoot it down," she said. That's a well-known tactic.

"The element that he added was that she must have actually used a document for an unlawful purpose. You are not going to hear that anywhere in Judge Murray's instructions," she declared.

Drawing on the defense argument that the prosecutor hadn't proven its case because Lisa used only one false name they knew about, which she had only two IDs for, Sale said it wasn't necessary to prove she used five documents. "We have to prove that she possessed five with the intent to use them unlawfully."

Then she turned to the defense attorney's remarks that Lisa couldn't have been on the run from charges in Arlington, because she was working in Virginia.

"Rosenbloom and Associates is in Bethesda. She was working in Bethesda, Maryland," the prosecutor declared. "That is not Arlington, Virginia. And she was working under a name certainly other than the name Lisa Ann Rohn."

Sale reminded the jury that at least six of the documents entered into evidence carried unexpired dates. She conceded that the government didn't know what Lisa did with them, but said that wasn't the jury's concern.

"The issue for you is what did she intend to do with them," she stated. "And the only conclusion you can draw, based on the evidence . . . is that she was running from the charge in Arlington and that she continued to be able to run.

"If the Johnnie Elaine Miller identification was burned, well look, she could turn into Johnalee Erma Smitter. She had it ready to go at any time. Did she intend to use it unlawfully? There is not another conclusion that can rationally be drawn from this evidence."

The prosecutor told the panel that Lisa was prepared to use as many IDs as were necessary to avoid apprehension. "You heard how she fought and how she kicked and screamed. What does that tell you?" she asked.

"Was this somebody who just wanted to live a quiet life and put the past behind her? Or is this somebody who is actively daily living a lie and living essentially an unlawful life with every breath she takes?

"Now, what is she? A collector of documents? You know, does she like to see her picture on plastic, or did she have an unlawful intent?" None of the jurors smiled at the sarcasm. The prosecutor was presenting a powerful argument.

A few minutes later she concluded the rebuttal, and another bench conference was called. CitaraManis renewed his motion for directed acquittal, and it was noted on the court record.

The judge began his charge to the jury, but after about twenty minutes adjourned the case until noon the next day in order to take care of other matters before the court.

The next day the judge completed his instructions and the jury retired to deliberate. The panel had barely begun deliberations, however, before sending a note to the judge asking if fleeing to avoid arrest was against the law. Judge Murray conferred with the prosecution and defense attorneys, then responded to the question. It was a violation of federal law to travel or to move in interstate commerce with intent to avoid prosecution for a felony, he advised.

Early that afternoon, less than an hour after Judge Murray responded to the query, the jury returned a verdict of guilty. The trial, including deliberations, had taken only a little more than one day.

The day after her conviction, Judge Murray sentenced Lisa to six months imprisonment. She was given credit on the sentence for the nearly two months already spent in custody. Roger blinked back tears that welled in his eyes as his girlfriend was led out of the courtroom to be returned to the jail. Lisa was stone-faced.

CitaraManis filed an appeal.

Chapter Seven

Shootings

"Beneath this face that appears so impassive,
Hell's tides continually run."
　　　　"You Felons On Trial In Courts"
　　　　Walt Whitman

About one month after Lisa's sentencing, she packed up her meager belongings at the Baltimore City Jail and federal marshals drove her to the Kent County Detention Center on Maryland's Eastern Shore to serve the remainder of her term.

Federal prisoners serving short sentences are frequently farmed out to area jails, which accept them on a space-available basis and are paid a daily rate for their upkeep. Located in a more rural area, isolated from the state's major urban centers, Kent County had more room available than the Baltimore Jail, which processed a steady stream of male and female inmates.

When Lisa was transferred from Baltimore, she left behind a thick stack of letters she had collected from Roger because corrections officers refused to allow her to take them with her. The move was so abrupt that she didn't have an opportunity to notify him of the date she was being transferred.

A couple of days after Lisa settled in at the Kent County lockup, she received an eight-page letter from Roger that he mailed twice. He wrote it on the day she was transferred. He first sent it to her at the jail in Baltimore, and when it was returned to him at the apartment because she had been moved, he remailed it to her at the Kent County Detention Center.

Roger began the letter in German. *Guten Abend, Mein Liebchen,* Good evening, my darling. Most of the letter was bright and cheery, filled with humor, and he closed by affectionately describing her as his friend, lover and future wife. But a few more sinister references were made between the romantic greeting and the tender farewell. At one point he fretted that he believed she blamed him because she was behind bars. But it was her own fault, he said. Her past had merely caught up with her. Another time he wrote, rather mysteriously, that there was an element of her character that frightened him.

He said he had pretty much forgiven her and hoped someday to forget, but judging by her intentional insult to him she thought of him with a lot of resentment, anger and hostility. He said he loved her, but she could tell him if she hated him. Roger was torn by love and anger, and his pride was wounded. In his mind, remarks by Lisa about not wanting to be under FBI surveillance during their possible future life together were apparently perceived to be a grossly offensive insult.

The day before Lisa's transfer, he had written another letter, asking at one point if he may have secretly wished for her to have an affair.

On August 14 he wrote and told Lisa he had checked

with Kent County jail authorities and was informed no CD players were permitted at the institution.

The couple's relationship was precarious enough as it was. But Lisa's transfer to the prison in Chestertown across Chesapeake Bay on the Eastern Shore also added at least another hour under normal driving conditions to the trip for Roger's visits.

Instead of driving north up U.S. Highway 1 or Interstate 95 into Baltimore, he had to pick up the Beltway, follow it southeast to Interstate 50 and 301 near Glenarden, and drive almost due east past Annapolis and, skirting the northern edge of the U.S. Naval Academy, cross Chesapeake Bay and Kent Island on the toll bridge. Then he was ready to begin driving the approximate hour-long leg of the journey along 301 to State Road 213, and swing north into Chestertown.

The drive past the profusion of scenic towns, islands, bays, and capes could be a pleasant experience for a tourist who never made the trip before. But it was an exhausting exercise in monotony for a motorist such as Roger, who had things other than relaxation and sightseeing on his mind.

Nevertheless, Roger drove to Chestertown several times for meetings with his girlfriend on visiting days. The hour-long visits were monitored by guards, but corrections officials at Kent County were more generous about personal contact than at the Baltimore lockup.

When Roger walked into the building through double doors, he was required to show identification, sign a logbook and give his relationship to the inmate. He wrote that he was Lisa's fiancé or boyfriend. After signing in, he moved on to a large lobby area to the left of the entrance, where three or four long tables with chairs were set up.

He was usually standing near the tables when Lisa

was shown into the room by a corrections officer. Like
others who were visiting elsewhere in the room, Roger
and Lisa were allowed to hug and kiss, and to hold
hands while they sat across from each other and talked.
At the conclusion of the visits they hugged and kissed
again.

Immediately after her arrival at Kent County, Lisa
was housed in the female work release area. But after a
few days she was made a trusty and assigned to kitchen
duties, helping the cooks prepare trays for other inmates, washing dishes and other cooking utensils, and
generally cleaning up. Assignment to kitchen duty
meant that she had to climb out of bed at five A.M.,
dress, and begin helping the cooks get ready to serve
breakfast. But the job had its advantages, and it was
better than the enforced idleness that many other inmates had to endure.

As a trusty she had access to collect call telephones in
her living area as well as in the booking area. She resumed the collect calls to Roger, and during their long
talks, frequently asked him to bring things to her.

On one of his first trips across the bay, he brought her
two yellow roses. A corrections officer confiscated the
gift because regulations at the jail didn't permit visitors
to give flowers to inmates.

But Roger was permitted to deposit small amounts of
money into an account for his girlfriend at the jail com-
missary and to bring her certain other gifts that didn't
violate regulations. He also made deposits into a private
bank savings account he set up for her, and brought her
the passbook. The deposits included money she had left
in a desk at the apartment, and the proceeds from the
sale of her eight-year-old Ford, which Roger was unable
to keep in running condition and got rid of.

Among his gifts to her while she was locked up were

cosmetics, clothing, and an audio disk player with batteries and tapes of some favorite musical selections he recorded for her and wanted her to hear. Roger still preferred old favorites from groups like the Beatles and Rolling Stones to the newer heavy metal and acid rock.

He also paid for a subscription for her to the *New York Times*, and provided postage stamps and envelopes for her letters. Lisa used lots of stamps. While she was locked up in Baltimore, and during the early weeks at the Kent County Detention Center, they exchanged letters almost every day. In keeping with regulations, each letter that she sent to someone or received was carefully recorded in a mail log that was kept by corrections officers.

While she was jailed in Kent County, just as when she was in Baltimore, the letters Lisa exchanged with Roger weren't always filled with protestations of undying love. During their brief relationship, the emotions of Roger and Lisa had been whipsawed and put through a meat grinder. The letters talked of love, but they also continued to be spotted with bitter accusations and talk of mistrust. Roger was loving one moment, bitter the next.

There were times he was afraid to love her, he wrote in one particularly poignant message. The remark would be publicly repeated later and recalled as eerily prophetic.

Roger continued writing every two or three days. He began one letter, "Yo, Sweetie," and helped her with some math problems. He began others with "Dear Lisa" or with "Dearest Lisa." He ended one letter, "I love you, Roger," another, "I still love you—Roger," and yet another, "I still love you, though it is too painful."

But the messages in his love letters were erratic, betraying his jealousies, suspicions, and spitefulness as often as they expressed his affection. The pathetic, love-

sick bachelor appeared to have been especially lonely
and depressed in a letter he wrote saying that he didn't
plan to seek revenge against her for his own failures. In
another, however, he bitterly blamed Lisa's problems on
someone named "Doug." In another he talked about a
ring. He said he didn't deserve to wear it because she
had slept with a couple of men he named as "Gene"
and "Habib." He ended the angry note, "Goodbye,
Roger."

He denied in yet another letter that he intentionally
snooped through her possessions looking for any sort of
evidence. He complained that her annoyance was de-
tracting from her affection for him. Another time he
wrote that he had tried to return the engagement ring,
adding that it was never worn.

Yet, almost always he ended his letters with, "I love
you," "I miss you," "I'll see you Saturday," or with other
affectionate assurances. And he told her in one letter
that he had written her into his will.

After the trauma of discovering the phony IDs, Lisa's
arrest and the revelations at her trial, it was difficult for
Roger to believe much of anything she told him. He was
quick to accuse her of lying to him, and it didn't take
much to arouse his suspicions. When she kept asking for
stamps, he counted up those he had already given her
and realized that she was writing to someone else at
least as often as she was writing to him. He complained
about buying her so many envelopes and stamps, and
worried that she was writing to her old boyfriend or to
another man. He closed one angry note by threatening
to dump the possessions she left at his apartment.

He was only partly right about his suspicions. After
her transfer to Kent County she began carrying out a
spirited lopsided correspondence that averaged two or
three letters a week to Dolores Swickert in Illinois. Lisa

wrote a total of fourteen letters to her Midwest correspondent, and received three from her in return. Lisa identified the north-suburban Chicago woman to corrections officers at the jail as her aunt. Lisa eventually told Roger who her other correspondent was. She had also written a letter to Christopher, telling him she was in love with his father.

Roger didn't drive to see Lisa at the Kent County jail as often as he visited when she was in Baltimore. Before her transfer, he had seen her almost every week, except for a brief summer vacation he took with Christopher to Hawaii. The father and son flew to Honolulu for a week, and Roger took Christopher to Pearl City and to view the USS *Arizona* National Memorial at Pearl Harbor. They also shared the magnificence of Diamond Head, and strolled Waikiki Beach together. Roger brought a souvenir ukelele home with him, strummed it a few times, then stored it in a hall closet.

He tried to fill every valuable minute he and Christopher had together with father-son activities. Among other interests Roger shared with his son was his burgeoning love for firearms. He continued to buy weapons, adding a Colt 5.56 caliber target rifle with a twenty-two-inch barrel, a Ruger 5.56 caliber carbine rifle, and a .22 caliber Remington rifle to his collection.

He was very safety conscious around Christopher, and cautioned the boy to always be careful when handling weapons, never to point a gun at anyone, to keep the barrel pointed down when not firing at a target, and not to shoot animals. He also showed Christopher how to work the safety on the pistol and how to clean the weapons.

A few times he took his son to a nearby shooting range and they practiced firing the guns. Roger always kept the firearms empty of cartridges until they got to the range and were ready to begin target shooting. Then he loaded them. A few times he allowed Christopher to load the guns, under his direction. Gun enthusiasts fired a variety of weapons at the target range, and Christopher sometimes collected a few of the spent casings and took them away with him as souvenirs.

Christopher knew where the weapons were stored in the apartment, but he was cautioned never to handle them without his father present. Roger kept the unloaded pistol in a black, plastic case in the master bedroom closet, where ammunition was stored. The long guns were sometimes stood up and stored against a corner in the closet, and at other times they were carefully stowed under the bed.

After Lisa's transfer, Roger quickly developed a lack of enthusiasm for weekly visits. He drove to Chestertown once in late August a few days after her transfer, and twice the following month, on September 14 and September 28. Between the two visits he wrote a letter talking about his fantasies of her walking out of jail a free woman while "Every Heartbreak" or "Unchained Melody" played on the CD.

Despite the warm letter that expressed almost childlike anticipation of her impending release, he skipped visiting days on the first two Saturdays of October. But he told Lisa he would drive to the jail for a visit on Saturday, October 19. Lisa was nearing her release date, and he promised to bring some of her clothes from the apartment.

On October 19, however, he telephoned the jail and talked with corrections officer Deborah A. Loller. Roger said he had been in a car accident and wouldn't be able to visit that day with Lisa. He asked the officer to inform his girlfriend he had been treated at a hospital, and to ask her to telephone him at four P.M. Loller told a colleague, who passed on the information to Lisa.

Lisa was disappointed and very upset. She insisted on talking with Officer Loller. The corrections officer confirmed the story when the distraught inmate confronted her: Lisa's boyfriend had telephoned and said he couldn't make the Saturday visit. Promptly at four P.M., Lisa placed a collect call to the apartment in Beltsville. Roger answered and assured her that he wasn't seriously hurt. He apologized for not being able to visit. Lisa said she would try to get permission for him to make a special visit later in the week.

But Roger didn't miss his Saturday visit to the jail because of a car crash. Important changes were occurring in his life. On August 15, two days after Lisa was moved to the jail in Kent County, Roger changed jobs. He went to work for the CSICED Corporation in Bethesda, a company that was more widely known as Contract Distributors. Roger joined the carpeting company as an estimator and salesman.

He had whipped up an imaginative résumé describing himself as a highly decorated U.S. Army veteran who served in Vietnam from July 1971 to July 1973 and earned a Silver Star and Purple Heart. He also earned a Bachelor of Science degree from the University of South Florida, according to the document.

Roger barely settled into the new routine at Contract Distributors before he developed a romantic interest in Cheryl New, the office manager. As part of her duties, the thirty-year-old woman kept track of the whereabouts of Roger and other estimators and salesmen so they could be reached by customers if they were needed. She stayed in touch with the salesmen by car phone and beepers.

Roger's desk and telephone were just around the corner through an open doorway from her working space. If she turned around from her desk and looked behind her, she could see directly into his office. Roger kept three or four photographs of Christopher on his desk, and had several pieces of the boy's grade-school artwork on the wall. A Purple Heart, and some other medals and ribbons that he explained were collected during his tour in Vietnam, were also framed and prominently displayed in the office.

Pleasant but efficient, like Roger, Ms. New was a single parent. She lived in the Montgomery County hamlet of Germantown, a few miles west of Beltsville, and was the mother of a five-year-old girl, Michelle.

Near the end of September, about a month after Lisa was transferred to the Kent County Detention Center, Roger and Ms. New began to date each other. In addition to dinner dates, they went to the movies and shared family outings with Christopher and Michelle in Baltimore and other area cities and towns.

As the new relationship developed, Roger began to realize that Cheryl had many appealing qualities that Lisa lacked. She was honest and hardworking, and appeared to show a sincere affection for him. He was already troubled about Lisa, and his enthusiasm for keeping their romance alive after her release from jail began to dwindle even more.

Juggling relationships with two women, even with one locked behind bars, was a challenging new experience and difficult enterprise for Roger to handle. He had always been a one-woman man, and he wasn't good at subterfuge.

As their affection for each other grew, Roger began occasionally staying overnight at Cheryl's apartment. He packed fresh clothes and a few grooming items, including shaving gear and after-shave lotion in a burgundy-colored fold-over luggage bag with a brown stripe for the overnight stays.

Roger didn't volunteer any information about his new girlfriend to Lisa in his letters during their telephone conversations, or when he was visiting at the jail. But he began to be evasive and tentative when he talked about the future and their lives together after Lisa had completed her jail term in Kent County and settled up with authorities on the charges still pending against her in Arlington County. Unknown to Lisa, he had begun to refer to her to acquaintances who knew of their relationship as "my little jailbird."

Nevertheless, after Lisa obtained permission for him to make a special visit on the following Wednesday, Roger made the long drive from his apartment to the Kent County jail to see her. He took several items of her clothing she had asked for along with him, for her to wear when she was released. It was his last jailhouse visit.

In October jail authorities notified Cowell that Lisa was scheduled to be released in a few days. The white-collar crime investigator told them he would be there to accept custody and return her to Arlington.

Early Monday morning, October 28, Cowell climbed in his police cruiser to prepare for the drive to Chestertown to pick up his prisoner. Before leaving, however, he arranged for a female officer to accompany him. It wasn't something that was required by regulations, simply a last minute decision that he settled on to protect himself from any possible accusations of sexually harassing or abusing his prisoner. Cowell later described the decision to take Sgt. Karen Schoembs with him to pick up the prisoner as one of the best moves of his career.

When Lisa was escorted from the cell-block area into

an anteroom to meet the Arlington County detective, she looked about as sexy as she could be. She was togged out in a tight, bright red miniskirt that hugged close around her hips, matching red high heels, hose, and a crisp white blouse. The prisoner looked like she was dressed for a party or a night out on the town.

"You could tell, she wasn't happy to see Sergeant Schoembs," Cowell recalled.

During the long ride to Arlington, the prisoner joined in occasionally as the two police officers chatted about the scenery or other mundane subjects. But Cowell and Schoembs were careful not to discuss the charges in Arlington that were pending against the woman in the backseat of the cruiser. Lisa appeared to have gotten over the surprise of being greeted by Cowell's companion, and behaved as if she was happy for the fresh air and change of scenery after the long months behind bars.

But her behavior changed the moment she was led into the third-floor interview room at the police building. "She was the sweetest thing you ever saw until we hit the interview room," Cowell recalled. "Then she turned as hard as nails, and wouldn't respond to anything. All she would say was, 'I want my attorney.'" Lisa knew the routine, and she knew that she couldn't be forced to talk to Cowell or any other police interrogator.

The demand to confer with an attorney left Cowell with no choice. He terminated efforts to interview the prisoner and led her downstairs to the first floor for booking. He remained with her while she was fingerprinted and her mug shot was snapped by a photographer. Then he accompanied her to a hearing before a magistrate on the third floor of the courthouse, where preliminary bond was set at $5000. At last, after the hearing, he turned over responsibility for the prisoner to a sheriff's officer and she was locked in a holding cell.

The $5000 bond wasn't enough to satisfy Cowell, however. He was convinced that she could easily raise the money and would go on the run again as soon as she was free. The next morning he appeared at a hearing in Arlington County Circuit Court with a deputy prosecutor to plead for higher bond. Lisa's bond was raised to $20,000, and she was moved upstairs from the booking area to a permanent cell in the detention center. At the hearing, Janelle Wolfe, a local Arlington lawyer, was appointed as Lisa's public defender.

Roger contacted court authorities about posting bond, but didn't follow through on efforts to get her out of jail.

With Lisa at last behind bars in Arlington, and the judicial processes for her prosecution on the local charges under way, Cowell turned his attention to other investigations. Lisa continued to place collect calls to Roger for regular talks. And she resumed her efforts to get out of jail.

Early Saturday afternoon, November 16, less than three weeks after she was transported to Arlington, Lisa dressed in her civilian clothes once more, packed up the remainder of her belongings in a large plastic trash bag provided by corrections officers, and walked out of the detention center.

Huberts's sister had posted $22,000 in cash to cover the $20,000 bail and an additional ten percent fee for the bondsman. No one notified Cowell that his suspect was released, and no one telephoned Roger.

According to terms of her bail agreement, Lisa was required to remain in Virginia, where the charges were filed against her, unless she filed a petition in the local courts and was permitted by a judge to leave the state.

But Roger and most of her belongings were in Maryland.

She headed back to Roger's apartment in Beltsville. With no one to depend on but herself for transportation, Lisa lugged her trash bag across the busy street to the entrance to the Metrorail Subway system and boarded a train. The Metrorail was cheap and fast. The basic fare, except for rush hour, was one dollar, and trains ran every ten minutes. It was perfect for Lisa, even encumbered as she was with her clumsy trash bag.

The throwaway bag was a poor substitute for luggage, but one that had become familiar to thousands of released prisoners around the country. They provide a convenient and cheap solution for prisoners who are released without luggage, and in the rude, often politically incorrect vernacular of police and prison guards in East Coast cities, they are commonly described as "Puerto Rican Samsonite."

A few commuters stared curiously at the pretty, well-dressed woman with the plastic bag at her feet while she rode across the Potomac, through Washington, and into Maryland. When Lisa traveled as far as she could on the Metrorail, she transferred to a taxi for the remainder of the trip into Beltsville.

It was approximately three-thirty P.M. when the cabbie dropped her off in front of the Powder Mill Apartments. But Roger's Honda was missing from its usual parking space next to the trash Dumpster, and no one answered when she knocked at the door. FBI agents had taken away her door key when she was arrested and turned it over to Roger, so she couldn't let herself in.

Lisa waited, huddling close to the building, hoping that he might drive up in a few minutes. It was a slate-gray late autumn day, the crisp temperatures had dipped into the mid-forties, and she was anxious to get inside.

After a while she decided to walk to a shopping center just across Powder Mill Road where there was a Giant Food supermarket, Ramada Inn, a couple of restaurants, a bar named Margarita Maggie's, and a string of other businesses, to wait until Roger returned home. She left the trash bag on the porch near the front door to his apartment while she walked to one of the restaurants and ordered a snack. When she crossed the road, she left Beltsville and entered the adjoining town of Calvert.

Lisa telephoned the apartment from the restaurant, but no one answered. Several more calls she periodically dialed to the apartment weren't answered either. At last, shortly before dusk, she decided she should pick up her belongings, and walked across the road to the apartment. The trash bag was gone, and Roger still wasn't home. Lisa walked back to the strip of businesses across the road to wait. Every half hour or so she tried the telephone again.

Roger picked his son up after school Friday afternoon and they spent a quiet evening together talking and watching television. About mid-morning the next day, Cheryl and Michelle arrived at the apartment, and they all drove together in Roger's car to Baltimore. There they strolled through the National Aquarium and ate a late lunch. The children especially enjoyed an aquatic show staged by dolphins. After spending two or three hours viewing the various fish and other forms of sea life, Roger drove the group south along I-95 back to Beltsville. They stopped at the apartment to freshen up and decide where to have dinner, and quickly settled on the Mongolian Barbecue Restaurant in Washington's

Chinatown. It was one of Roger's favorite places to eat out. While he and Christopher changed into fresh shirts, Cheryl telephoned the restaurant to find out what Metrorail stop was closest to their destination.

The sun had just set minutes before, and it was dusk when they pulled away from the apartment building on Evans Trail for Bethesda. Roger and Cheryl each drove their own cars. They parked near the carpeting company offices and caught the Metrorail for Chinatown in Washington.

After dinner they rode the train back to the Bethesda Metro Center and stopped into the office at Contract Distributors. They played a *Mad* magazine hide-and-go-seek game with Christopher, he tinkered with some video games on the computer, and the adults chatted.

At last they locked up the office and walked back to their cars. They had enjoyed a full day together, but planned to meet again early Sunday afternoon and watch football on television. Roger watched from the parking lot as Cheryl and Michelle drove away, headed for their home in Germantown. Then he and Christopher climbed into the Honda for the drive back to Beltsville.

When the father and son walked inside Apartment 102 and turned on the television, Christopher glanced at the clock on the VCR. It was almost exactly midnight.

Lisa shuttled impatiently back and forth across the road all afternoon while the sun dipped lower, until it at last faded below the tree line. The early evening shadows turned from dishwater-gray to the black of night, and still no one was home at Apartment 102. The apartment complex was quiet and the two-story buildings were silhouetted against the weak light of the moon when she walked impatiently across the road once more and at last saw Roger's metallic blue-gray Honda parked beside the Dumpster.

This time when she knocked at the door, Roger opened it up and was confronted by Lisa. Her face was crossed with spidery webs of fatigue and she was standing on his doorstep looking like a weary Cinderella. Christopher watched and listened from the front room for a few moments. Roger had been taken by surprise, and asked Lisa what she was doing back at the apartment.

Christopher moved back into his own bedroom as the adults continued to talk. Roger's voice was a little louder than normal, but the boy couldn't make out what Lisa was saying. He climbed into bed and quickly fell asleep. A few minutes later Roger flicked off the living room lights and he and Lisa walked into the master bedroom and also went to bed.

Sunday morning they got up late and Lisa prepared breakfast for herself, Roger, and Christopher. Roger finished dressing and leafed through the Sunday edition of the *Prince Georges County Journal* while waiting for her to finish up in the kitchen. After everyone had eaten, taken showers, and dressed, Lisa and Christopher walked across the street to a softball field and playground behind a community center. Roger complained that his back hurt and he was tired, so he stayed behind.

As soon as Lisa and his son were out the door, Roger reached for the telephone and dialed Cheryl's number. He told her something unexpected had come up and he and Christopher wouldn't be able to make it to Germantown to watch the Redskins game with her on television. He said he was calling from his car phone, and his voice was serious. He didn't explain what the problem was.

At the playground, Lisa lounged around, enjoying the

fresh air and freedom while Christopher played. They were there about a half hour before Roger joined them.

The trio spent the rest of the day together, puttering around the apartment, watching some of the Redskins game on TV and chatting. About the most memorable event of the idle day occurred when they ate a pizza Roger ordered delivered to the apartment. As she usually did, Lisa stayed behind when he left at about seven P.M. to drive Christopher back to his mother's home. On his way home, Roger used his car phone to call Cheryl again. He told her he was in Gaithersburg and had just dropped Christopher off with his mother. He told Cheryl he would see her in the morning.

Roger was back at the apartment a few minutes after eight P.M., and he and Lisa talked about her plans and the court proceedings she was still facing in Arlington. Lisa said she wanted to pack her clothes and other belongings and put them in storage. She also had to talk with her lawyers and appear for a court date in Arlington the following week.

She planned to travel to Baltimore on Monday to meet with CitaraManis and pick up $3300 he was holding for her. It was cash that was confiscated by FBI agents after her arrest in Bethesda. The Bureau had to return it because it had no bearing on the federal charges.

On Tuesday she had a morning meeting scheduled with her court appointed lawyer in Arlington. Roger gave a new key to the apartment to her so she could come and go as she pleased while he was at work.

Early Monday he roused himself from bed and was out of the apartment a few minutes after seven A.M. Lisa lingered in bed until about eight-thirty or nine before she got up, showered, dressed, and fixed breakfast for herself. Then she caught a cab for Baltimore and her meeting with CitaraManis.

She was back at the apartment by noon and was there a half hour later when Roger returned home for lunch. It was less than an hour's drive from the company offices in Bethesda to the apartment. He stayed about thirty minutes, and before leaving he told Lisa that he would take her to Margarita Maggie's for a drink, then to the Plata Grande Restaurant next door to the bar for dinner that evening.

Lisa spent the afternoon sorting through her clothes and other belongings. It was about six P.M. when Roger telephoned and told her he was working late at the office and didn't know what time he would be home. She hadn't prepared anything for dinner because they had planned to go out, and she was hungry. But she decided to wait for a while because there was still time for them to have a late dinner together.

At eight P.M. Roger telephoned again and updated his earlier message. He was busy working and didn't know when he would be home, he said. Lisa had just spent nearly seven months locked behind bars, and she was anxious to get out of the apartment. She told him she would go across the street and eat.

After hanging up, she slipped on a pair of blue jeans, a red blouse, red heels, and a red wool jacket and walked to Margarita Maggie's where she ordered a drink.

Brian Rohloff, an iron worker from Albany, New York, who was in the area to work on tower lines, was in the bar with several companions and noticed the attractive woman in red sitting by herself sipping at her drink. He was impressed, but when the group finished their drinks and walked next door to the Plata Grande for a Mexican meal, he went along with the others.

A few minutes later Lisa finished her drink as well, and also walked next door to order dinner. She barely sat down before Rohloff pushed his chair back from the table where he was sitting with his companions, walked over to Lisa and introduced himself. He invited her to join him and his friends.

Lisa agreed that it was a good idea, and she had dinner with the handsome dark-haired man and his friends —three other men and a woman. It was late and there were only a couple of other customers remaining in the restaurant when they finished dinner. The other woman and the other men left and returned to their rooms at the Ramada Inn, just across a parking lot, about a five-minute walk away. Lisa and Rohloff went back to Margarita Maggie's for a nightcap.

They were nearly finished with their drinks when a couple of Rohloff's friends showed up and told him they had all been asked to switch rooms from the second floor to the fifth floor at the Ramada. Members of a senior citizens' group had previously booked the entire second floor.

When Rohloff left the tap room for the motel, Lisa went along. She rode the elevator to his room on the second floor to help him gather up his clothes and other personal belongings for the move, then returned with him to the lobby so he could drop off the old room key and pick up the new one at the registration desk.

They were walking back to the elevators when Lisa glanced toward the front door and saw Roger. He was standing just outside the doorway glaring at her and the iron worker. He had tried calling her on his car phone, and when she didn't answer, he went looking for her at Margarita Maggie's. Then he checked out the motel.

Silhouetted in the artificial light of the entrance, the

bulky trench-coated figure with the small, neat mustache loomed from the pre-midnight darkness behind him like some kind of angry avenging angel. His face was flushed and he was glowering. Lisa told Rohloff she had to talk with someone, and hurried over to Roger. The iron worker glanced at the man and noticed that he was big, with a receding hairline. But he didn't study him closely, and turned away to talk with a couple of his friends who had walked out of the elevator moments before Lisa noticed her boyfriend.

Roger, who had moved just inside the door, was outraged and demanded to know who her companion was. Lisa tried to calm him down, but he looked like the air had been sucked out of his soul. While Roger raged, a night manager of the motel and the handful of people in the lobby stared at them, or peered curiously in their direction, then embarrassedly averted their eyes. Lisa insisted on continuing the conversation outside, and he lurched out the door with her.

But he still wanted the same questions answered. He demanded to know who the strange man was and what she was doing at the motel.

Lisa had an explanation ready on the tip of her tongue. She said the man waiting inside was just someone she had met at the restaurant, and she was helping him move his things. Roger knew Lisa too well to take much of what she told him at face value. And he didn't believe she was telling him the whole story about the strange man she had left at the elevators.

"What did you do, have sex with him?" he croaked. His anger-mottled face was almost purple with jealous fury and he was shaking with frustration.

Lisa denied having sex with the iron worker. But when Roger told her to come with him back to the apartment, she refused. "No, I'm not going back," she told him. Then she returned to Rohloff, who was still waiting at the elevators.

There was no angry click of heels as Lisa walked back across the lobby. While she rode up to the iron worker's new fifth-floor room with him, she appeared as composed and cool as if she had been doing nothing more emotional than ordering a cheese and pepperoni pizza.

Rohloff was curious about the man downstairs and about Lisa. He wanted to know what was going on. As they settled into the room and prepared for bed, she explained she had gotten into trouble for credit card fraud and had just been released from jail. The angry man she talked to in the doorway was her boyfriend, and he had turned her in to the police.

Lisa said she was an accountant and had to work a half day the next morning but would be free later. The couple agreed to meet again for dinner Tuesday evening, then spend the night together.

Rohloff left for work early the next morning, and it was just after seven-thirty when Lisa got out of bed, showered, and dressed. Before leaving the room, she wrote the iron worker a note, reminding him she would meet him at about six that night so they could have dinner together. She left the note on top of a dresser and let herself out of the room.

Wearing her heels, it was about a fifteen-minute walk for Lisa from the motel across the road to the apartment in Beltsville. A small plastic bag had been left on the porch next to a mat in front of Apartment 102 and a note was taped to the front door. Lisa picked up the bag but didn't look inside. She was more interested in the note. The message didn't mince words, and it was chillingly blunt.

Be here tomorrow at 2 p.m. to pick up your stuff
—Bring some help, since I'm not moving it for
you. Leave your key under the mat. If you try to
enter, I'll shoot you. If you aren't here by 2:30 it
goes in the Dumpster.

The word "shoot" was underlined.

She had no trouble recognizing the angry hand-
printed scrawl. It was Roger's.

Lisa is the only person who knows the exact details of
the occurrences immediately after she read the note.
But according to her later sworn courtroom testimony,
she took a key from her jacket pocket, turned it in the
lock and pushed at the door. It only opened a couple of
inches before it was stopped by a security chain.

Moments later the barrel of an assault rifle was poked
out the crack of the door pointed directly at her. She
lurched backward in alarm.

"Are you crazy?" she demanded.

"I want your key," Roger growled. Lisa couldn't see
him behind the door. But she could see the barrel of the
rifle in the crack between the door frame and the door.
And she could recognize his voice.

She said she needed to go inside and pick up some of
her belongings. "You know I have to see my lawyer this
morning," she reminded him.

Roger wasn't ready to give up on his hard-line stand.
"I'll just throw your stuff over the balcony," he threatened.

Lisa wasn't in the mood for protracted pleadings or a
long quarrel. If Roger wanted to toss her belongings
over the railing, there wasn't much she could do about
it.

"Roger, go ahead," she shot back at him.

Lisa turned and stalked out of the entranceway of the

building. As she reached the outside and began walking down the sidewalk, Roger was already right behind her. He had cooled down. His hands were empty and there was no trace of the gun. He still wasn't ready to capitulate completely, but he was willing to compromise.

"Go ahead and come get your stuff," he told her wearily.

The feuding couple walked back inside the apartment together. The rifle was lying on the couch, and Lisa's belongings were scattered all over. Bags and boxes were stacked on the living room floor near the front door; some were on the balcony, and a few were next to the couch.

Lisa sorted through the material until she found an envelope filled with legal papers she needed for her meeting with the lawyer in Arlington. She noticed a pet carrier on the floor and asked Roger if he was taking one of the cats somewhere.

He replied that he was going to take Jellybean to a nearby veterinary clinic at nine A.M. to be spayed before continuing on to work. Lisa asked if he would take her along and drop her off at the Metrorail station in Bethesda. Roger agreed to give her a ride, if he was able to drop the cat off at the veterinary clinic early.

After a telephone call to the Beltsville Veterinary Hospital confirmed that staff members had already arrived at work, Roger put Jellybean into the carrier and he and Lisa left with the cat. Lisa slipped on a brown tweed overcoat before stepping outside into the crisp late fall air. The animal clinic was only a few blocks from the apartment.

While Roger was inside the building with Jellybean, Lisa began applying her makeup. She was carrying it along with her in a brown paper sandwich bag. She continued working on her makeup during the remainder of the awkwardly silent drive to the Metro station after the cat was dropped off.

Still dressed in the blue-jean outfit she wore the night before, Lisa rode the Metro through the District of Columbia to Arlington and exited at the Clarendon station. The station was almost exactly across the street from her lawyer's office.

Lisa walked into Janelle Wolfe's office a few minutes ahead of the ten A.M. appointment. The lawyer greeted her and asked how she was doing.

"It could be better," Lisa replied. "My boyfriend just tried to kill me."

The attorney didn't immediately follow up with any questions about her client's dramatic opening to the meeting. Instead she opened Lisa's file and discussed the case with her. They concluded their business almost an hour later, and Lisa had gotten up and walked to the door when Ms. Wolfe asked her what the boyfriend trouble was about.

Returning to her chair, Lisa recounted her story of the trouble with Roger, her need to get her possessions out of the apartment, and showed Ms. Wolfe the note. Lisa told the attorney about Roger sticking the muzzle of the gun out the door and threatening her.

At about the time Lisa was meeting with her lawyer, a few blocks away at the police building, Cowell was being advised by an FBI agent that Roger had agreed to testify in Lisa's Arlington trial. Roger didn't share that information with Lisa.

After the meeting with her lawyer, she ate a snack at a nearby restaurant while she tried to figure out how she was going to move and store her clothes and other belongings. She didn't have a car or a driver's license. Although she had a fistful of licenses from various states and in different names only a few months earlier, they were gone. The FBI had taken them all and turned them over to the federal prosecutor.

Lisa walked to a pay telephone at the Metro station to make a few calls. She located a commercial storage company near King Street in Arlington that had space available for her luggage and boxes. Then she placed more calls, attempting to find someone with a car who would transport her belongings from Roger's apartment to the commercial storage spaces in Arlington. She couldn't find anyone to help.

Roger had ordered her to have her belongings out of his apartment by two-thirty P.M., and Lisa was rapidly running out of time. A couple of minutes before the early afternoon deadline, she telephoned Contract Distributors and asked to talk with him. She knew he would normally have a break in his work schedule about that time, and hoped to be able to coax him into helping her move her possessions.

A temporary employee working as a receptionist for the flooring company answered the telephone and explained that Roger wasn't in, but was expected back any minute. Lisa asked the receptionist to tell Roger she had called and said she couldn't make the two-thirty meeting and wanted to change the time to six P.M. It was already after one P.M.

After Lisa hung up, the receptionist paged Roger and passed on the message. About a half hour later Lisa telephoned the office again. This time Roger was there and took the call.

Lisa asked if he had gotten her message about not being able to meet his deadline to move out. He said it had been passed on to him. She told him she didn't have any means of moving her possessions from the apartment. She didn't even have a driver's license anymore, so she couldn't rent a car. There was no one she could depend on for help but him.

"Well, why don't you have Brian help you?" Roger responded. Lisa wasn't having much luck with her efforts to soften Roger up and get him to pitch in and help move her things.

"Roger, if you want me to move this stuff out, I need help. Can you help me move it?" she demanded.

Roger's temper was flaring, and initially, at least, he refused to budge. He was out of patience with Lisa, and he told her he carried her things out of the apartment and left them in the outside hallway to the building. According to her later account, Roger finally relented, however, and agreed to help her move. But he still had to work through the rest of the afternoon, and meanwhile just about everything she owned was piled outside the apartment. Anyone who was in the area or passing by and saw the clutter of boxes and luggage could help themselves to whatever they wanted and probably get away with it.

Hanging up the telephone, she hurried down the station steps and boarded a Metro for Maryland. Lisa didn't have many possessions left to show for her twenty-nine years, but she was determined to salvage what she could. It took her about an hour to reach the apartment, and her clothes and other personal possessions had apparently been untouched since Roger moved them outside. But suitcases, boxes, bags, clothing, and other items were stacked all over the hallway. Some were even outside on the sidewalk.

There was also another note with a message that seemed impossible to misinterpret. "It would be considered very unwise on your part to show your face around me again. Ever!" it warned. "Ever" was underlined. The handwriting was the same as that on the earlier note. It was Roger's unmistakable scrawl. Lisa crumpled the note up and stuck it into a pocket of her coat. Then she unlocked the door and began carrying the luggage and boxes back inside the apartment.

She stacked everything in the front room just inside the door. Then she began going through her things, re-packing some items for storage and making a casual mental inventory to make sure all of her belongings were there. Roger had passed over a few items when he dumped everything outside, and there were still some coats in the closet of the master bedroom, some toiletries in the bathroom, and a few other things here and there.

Lisa hadn't had an opportunity to check out or organize her clothing and other belongings since her arrest in April, and she wanted to make sure she took everything with her so she didn't have to return. She began making a careful room-to-room check, packing overlooked belongings while she went along. She prepared an overnight bag, which she kept separate from the items slated for storage.

Roger usually left Contract Distributors about four-thirty P.M., but he had to work late Tuesday night. Cheryl was concerned about his handling of a flooring job and wanted some changes made. Cheryl, Roger, and Bruce Dempsey, who was the company's branch manager, planned to hold a skull session after normal quitting time to work the matter out.

Roger wasn't at all bothered by the prospect of working late. He wasn't anxious to return home, and was hopeful that if he took his time and stayed away long enough, Lisa would be gone when he finally returned to the apartment.

He was beginning to resemble Sisyphus, the greedy

king from Greek mythology condemned in Hades through eternity to roll a boulder up a hill, only to have it roll immediately back down so he had to begin the job all over again. But Lisa was Roger's boulder. Everytime he thought she was out of his system and he had gotten rid of her, she turned up once more.

The problem with the job was quickly worked out, and Cheryl left for home. Roger and his boss walked a couple of blocks from the office to the Pizzeria Uno to have dinner together. They ordered pizza and a couple of beers. At about seven-fifteen P.M. they polished off the last of the pizza, finished their drinks, and walked out of the restaurant. Roger told his boss he would see him in the morning and headed for his car.

As soon as he climbed into his car to begin the short drive home, Roger called Cheryl from his car phone. He was worried she might be angry at him because of their disagreement over his handling of the job they had the meeting about earlier in the evening. She wasn't angry.

Roger told her he had shared a pizza with their boss, but he would rather have gone home with her. He ended the call by advising her he had just pulled into his parking space at Powder Mill and would ring her again when he got upstairs. Roger never talked with Cheryl again.

Erik Astheimer had a nasty cold. He was miserable and dropped off to sleep early on a mattress he and his wife had spread out on a bedroom floor in Apartment 202 at 11346 Evans Trail when a loud noise jarred him suddenly awake. It sounded like a shotgun was being fired. There was one blast after another.

Astheimer was a U.S. Army photographer who had just settled into the apartment less than two weeks earlier after being transferred from Germany to the huge

Walter Reed Army Medical Center nearby. His furniture hadn't even arrived yet from Europe. As a soldier who recently served in the Middle East during the Persian Gulf War, he had heard gunfire many times before. But he was sick, had been suddenly awakened by loud noises, and it was difficult to tell exactly where the ruckus was coming from.

The GI got to his feet and wobbled over to the window to see if he could spot anything that would help pinpoint the source of the gunfire. Just as he pulled the curtains back, he heard one more gunshot. Astheimer lurched backward and jerked the curtains shut. There was no more shooting, but he could hear children screaming in an apartment across from him. Adults, apparently their parents, were yelling back.

Astheimer cracked open the door and peered into the hallway. No one was there, so he eased the door shut. When he opened it again a few moments later, the outside hallway was alive with the movement of other tenants. But his attention was riveted on a young woman in her stocking feet who was screaming and moaning.

"Oh, God. Oh, God!" she screeched. "What did I do?"

The soldier briefly considered hurrying down the hallway and trying to help the distraught woman. She could be hurt. But his survival instincts clicked in and he eased the door shut again. Astheimer didn't really know what was going on, and was worried that he might hurry outside right into the middle of the trouble and wind up dead or injured with a gunshot wound himself. She could be carrying a gun.

He dialed 911 and reported that a "humongous" domestic ruckus of some sort was going on at the apartments, and someone was firing shotguns. It was exactly 7:58 P.M. when his call was logged in.

Lisa had placed her emergency call about a minute and a half earlier and reported the shooting. The 911 line she used was still open.

Lacey Tyler, a uniform officer with the Prince Georges County Police Department, was driving his patrol car in Calvert a few blocks from the apartments when he received a radio call about the disturbance. A three-and-a-half-year police veteran, Tyler was assigned to the Beltsville-Laurel area, which was designated by the department as "Charlie Sector." Tyler's call number was "Charlie 12."

He was about halfway through his shift and it had been a quiet night for "Charlie 12," but that changed in a hurry. Tyler turned on his siren and hurried toward 11346 Evans Trail a few blocks away in the adjoining town. The sprint to the apartment building took him approximately two minutes. At 7:59 P.M. he radioed that he had arrived at the scene. Fifty-seven seconds later, exactly at eight P.M., the first ambulance arrived from the Prince Georges County Fire Department substation in Calvert about a block away.

Moments after Tyler pulled his squad car to a stop in front of the garden-style apartments, a woman lurched from the hallway leading into the building. She was wearing a red jacket and blue jeans, but was without shoes.

"My God, I'm shot!" she wailed to a police officer she saw half hidden in the darkness behind a tree. "Can you help me?"

The woman was bent over slightly to the left, with her arm and hand pressed tightly against her side. But accounts differ over other aspects of her behavior at that point. According to Tyler's later recollections, there was no screaming, no sign of hysteria, and no cries of pain.

He didn't notice any blood. Lisa later recalled, however, that she was hysterical.

But moments after the policeman stepped from behind the tree, other figures began to emerge from the darkness. Paramedics and police were soon swarming all over the place.

"Is there anyone still inside the apartment?" Tyler asked.

A man was inside, she replied.

Tyler helped her sit down on a hip-high retaining wall in front of shrubbery landscaping the building, then radioed for an ambulance and backup from other officers. She was still perching hunched over on the retaining wall when patrolman Mark Riedl arrived. As he approached her on the wall, Riedl peered through the yellow light toward her hands as he had been trained to do after joining the department about a year earlier. They were partly obscured by her body and by the darkness and it was difficult to tell for certain if she was holding a weapon or anything else.

"Where's the gun?" he asked.

"Inside," she replied.

That was only part of the information Riedl wanted from the woman in the blue jeans. It was fairly obvious that she had been shot, and the patrolman wanted to know where the shooter was.

"Where's he?" Riedl asked.

The woman's reply was basically the same as it had been to the earlier question. "In there with it [the gun]," she said.

Another ambulance from the Prince Georges County Fire Department arrived moments later, and the policemen turned the injured woman over to the Emergency Medical Technicians, EMTs. One of the paramedics began snipping off the left sleeve of her jacket with scissors as the vehicle nosed away from its parking spot a few feet behind a police car and headed with siren blaring for the Greater Laurel-Beltsville Hospital.

Before the ambulance was out of sight and earshot, Tyler, Riedl, and a couple of other uniform officers had spread out and begun walking up the sidewalk and across the tiny lawn, cautiously approaching the front of Apartment 102.

Events were moving quickly, and the police officers didn't know exactly what they were faced with. At that point the only thing they knew for certain was that a woman was in the ambulance with a fresh gunshot wound. And she claimed a man was still inside the apartment with a gun. For all they knew, he could be barricaded with an arsenal of weapons and might suddenly begin blasting everyone within sight any moment.

The police officers called out for whoever was inside to leave the apartment. There was no response. The county lawmen whispered together for a moment, then Tyler broke away from his companions and moved around toward the back to cover the rear of the building. Riedl opened a foyer door leading into the building and moved a few steps inside the cinder-block hallway.

The other officers remained just outside the door, with their service revolvers at the ready while they radioed for a K-9. They could see into the darkened foyer through windows that flanked the outer doorway on both sides. Inside the building, the metal inside door to Apartment 102 was cracked open two or three inches.

Riedl realized that he was set up for a classic ambush, if someone wanted to quickly eliminate him from the tense drama that was being played out. He was alone in the stark hallway with no cover, nothing to hide behind if someone chose to begin shooting at him from inside the apartment door. He made a strategic retreat, back-

ing from the hallway and slowly easing himself through
the outer door. Then he crouched behind the low con-
crete wall next to the shrubbery that lined the front of
the building. He kept his eyes focused on the inner
doorway that showed faintly through the outside windows, while waiting for the dog and handler to arrive.

The flickering colored rooftop lights from the squad
cars and from the fire department emergency vehicles
silhouetted the darkened figures and professionally systematic movements of police and paramedics in the increasingly busy parking lot and lawn in front of the
apartment building. A few neighbors gathered in curious knots outside nearby buildings, hugging the en-
trances as they peered through the darkness watching
the activity and listening uncomprehendingly to the
raspy clatter of police radios.

More immediate neighbors who shared apartments in
Roger's building, peeked out windows from behind half-
closed curtains and drapes.

About ten minutes after Riedl eased out of the hallway and took up his position outside, a K-9 officer arrived with a German shepherd named Sam. The dog led
the way into the building, followed by his handler,
Riedl, and a police department corporal.

With the handler holding tightly onto Sam's leash and
flanked by his colleagues, the entry team eased open the
inside door and moved quietly into the apartment. Their
service weapons were drawn and at the ready in their
hands.

In a situation like the officers were facing, which appeared to be loaded with the possibility of danger and
more violence, they don't simply charge into a space
and spread out looking for anybody they can find. And
there is no room for *Dirty Harry* grandstanding in the
deadly serious real-life police work they were involved

in. They couldn't simply barge inside and begin blasting at anything that moved with a hail of hollow-point bullets and pick up the pieces later.

They entered the apartment exactly as they had been trained to do, clearing or securing one area or room at a time, with police academy perfection. The men and the dog worked as a unit, covering each other as they slowly moved through the interior of the apartment. There was a moment of startled distraction when a cat skittered across the floor and faded into shadows under the furniture. Sam noticed the traditional enemy, but was too well-trained to bark or lunge after it.

Continuing to assiduously follow police procedures, the team moved through the apartment and peered into the kitchen. The wall phone next to the microwave oven was off the hook, dangling from the cord. It was smeared red, and bloody prints of bare feet were traced across the tile floor in a crazy-quilt pattern of capricious gore. Many of the prints overlapped each other. The kitchen floor looked like a flight of vampires had danced their way through a macabre blood feast. A few pieces of cutlery, an empty coffee cup, and a half-filled bottle of water on the kitchen counter provided a curiously mundane contrast to all the blood.

As the entry team approached the end of the hallway, the policemen observed the feet of a man who appeared to be lying on the floor inside the master bedroom. Riedl was closest to the bedroom, and he slid his weapon back into its holster. Then, with the corporal covering them, Riedl, Sam and his handler moved into the bedroom.

The body of a middle-aged man was lying facedown on the floor of the doorway between the bedroom and the adjoining bathroom. It was Roger. Riedl scrambled over to him with a pair of handcuffs to snap on his

wrists. The left hand was cuffed easily, but the policeman had difficulty with the right hand. Two of Roger's
fingers were tightly gripping a maroon garment bag that
was wedged partially under the body. Riedl pulled the
limp hand up and around the shoulder before he was
able to cuff it with the other behind Roger's back.

The action may have seemed unnecessarily rude and
cruel to a casual observer unfamiliar with the dangers
and training tied to professional law enforcement. But it
was a necessary part of the established procedure for
protecting the officers while securing the apartment.
There was no movement from the body as the policemen and the dog approached, but that was no proof the
man was unconscious or dead.

With the German shepherd still in the lead, the police
officers moved into a smaller bedroom on the right side
of the hallway. Taking care not to disturb anything that
didn't have to be moved, they cautiously slid open the
closet door. There was nothing immediately obvious inside except a few articles of boys' clothing, some toys,
and a scatter of odds and ends. A more detailed search
of the closet and other rooms could be conducted later.
Riedl and his companions were looking for people;
someone who might conceivably pose a threat to their
safety.

At last the entry team was satisfied that no other civilians were in the apartment, except for the man who was
stretched out facedown on the floor between the master
bedroom and the bathroom. The body was straddling
the door frame. The policemen walked outside and announced that Apartment 102 was secure.

Additional police officers, paramedics, and personnel
from the fire department began moving into the apartment as Sam's handler made a path through the crowd
and put the dog back inside the cage car he had arrived

in. Riedl found himself an out-of-the-way spot near a desk in the area of the living room Roger had used for a study. Homicide detectives would be seeking him out for information.

Four paramedics trooped through the living room and down the hall into the bedroom as soon as they were allowed inside after the apartment was secured. When they bent over the prone body to check for vital signs, the strap of the garment bag was still around Roger's neck. When they turned him over, they saw his ruined forehead. He had been shot in the face and a ragged, bloody hole stared back at them from just above his right eye. Another bullet had apparently torn through his midsection. A quick, cursory examination produced no pulse and no other signs of life. A more intense examination of the body and the official cause of death would be determined by an autopsy.

Residents of nearby Washington, D.C., had earned an unenviable reputation for their city as the murder capital of the United States. Although larger cities such as New York and Los Angeles annually recorded more murders, they were several times larger than the capital city. Washington, with roughly 626,000 people, racked up the unenviable record of most killings per capita in 1988, repeated in 1989, and as the new decade began, it was getting worse instead of better. During 1990, 483 people were murdered in Washington, breaking the record and holding the per capita killing title for the third straight year. News reporters and many law enforcement officers had begun to refer to the District of Columbia as "Dodge City."

Beltsville and Prince Georges County weren't Washington, D.C. But much of the runaway violence that plagued Washington and Baltimore, the other big city in the area, had followed nervous residents into the sprawl

of suburban towns in the county. Areas of the county
that hugged the District of Columbia border were especially plagued with the constant danger and crime; the
drive-by shootings, the prostitutes, pimps, and dope ad-
dicts.

In one particularly nasty outbreak of savagery a little
more than three years earlier, five people were shot to
death and a woman from Jamaica was badly injured in a
Landover neighborhood known as part of a notorious
drug traffic corridor. Police investigators said the execu-
tion-style slayings marked the bloodiest day in the sixty-
year history of the department.

Beltsville and other suburbs in Prince Georges
County and in neighboring Montgomery County
seemed to offer a welcome measure of insulation from
that kind of behavior by professional criminals. Many of
the approximately 9000 people who lived in the unincor-
porated community along the Capital Beltway had
moved to the near suburbs of the capital city to escape
the carnage.

But the violence had followed them. Although the
exact numbers differed, according to which law enforcement agency's statistics were used, it was agreed that
Roger's slaying broke the one-year record in Prince
Georges County for homicides.

Prince Georges County police records indicated his
shooting marked the 128th homicide of the year, one
more than the number of people murdered in the
county during all of 1989, and six more than in all of
1990. Those statistics did not include homicides investigated by other police agencies operating within the
county, or justified shootings by police and accidental
killings.

Even using Maryland State Police statistics, which are
more specifically discriminating, Roger's death marked

the 123rd "unjustified homicide" in Prince Georges County. That was one more than the 122 their figures showed for the record year in 1989. It was a staggering murder rate for a single county that didn't overlap or include a major city of one million or more.

Most of the slayings in Prince Georges County were committed with guns, but unlike Roger's, most occurred inside the Capital Beltway, in neighborhoods similar to the brutal and explosive ghettos of Washington's northeast and southeast sides. The more remote suburbs north of the Beltway were generally expected to be quiet, safer, and more free of the killing savagery of the capital city's worst neighborhoods.

Consequently, a homicide at the Powder Mill Apartments was cause for an intense investigation. Patrol officers, corporals, a sergeant, and a lieutenant colonel were soon milling around with detectives as the crime scene was secured and evidence technicians began snapping photographs, dusting for fingerprints and collecting other material expected to eventually find its way to police laboratories and/or a courtroom. The only latent prints picked up were from the bloody telephone in the kitchen.

Evidence technicians Gary Taylor, a ten-year police veteran, and William Greene, who had logged more than nine years on the job, took the lead in processing the crime scene.

Someone, probably one of the detectives, removed the handcuffs from Roger's wrists shortly after it was determined he was dead. But his arms were left in the same position they were placed in by Riedl, behind his back.

Roger was fully dressed, including the light beige trench coat he had been wearing outside ever since the evening temperatures turned snappy and begun to dip into the low forties. His trouser legs were soaked with water, which had cascaded from the fish tank along with its occupants when a bullet shattered the glass. The dark green carpeting in the master bedroom quickly soaked through and picked up the dirt on shoes, turning it to a thin slick of ugly mud while medical technicians and police worked around the corpse.

When the body had at last been studied and photographed from almost every possible angle, it was loaded onto a gurney and covered with a white sheet. The evidence technicians collected some cartridge casings and a pair of eyeglasses from the pooled blood where the body had been lying and bagged them with other evidence. The casings under the body were among a total of six collected from throughout the room. One casing was picked up from behind the shattered fish tank at the foot of the bed. The bloody suit bag was also picked up and set aside on the bathroom floor for later attention.

One of the first and most significant pieces of potential evidence collected was a .22 caliber semiautomatic, Mark 2 Ruger, which investigators found a few inches from Roger's feet on the bedroom floor next to the dresser. The magazine was still inside the handgun. But there were no cartridges inside the magazine, or in the chamber of the weapon. The investigators carefully recorded the serial number: 21716851.

Several rifles, including some that were old and badly rusted, were found in closets. Investigators also inspected and recorded the presence of three boxes of ammunition and a three-foot saber with a sheath.

Taylor found four deformed metal slugs from bullets and bullet fragments; one on the floor next to the dresser, one behind the fish tank, one inside the tank, and one that he pried from a wall behind a dresser with a shattered mirror. The slug taken from the wall was in pieces.

Another investigator retrieved a lady's red jacket from the floor of the living room and turned it over to Taylor. It was wet and smeared with blood. The detective examined it briefly, then placed it in a yellow plastic evidence bag to be transported back to the evidence unit at the police department and checked out more carefully. Later, Taylor went through the pockets and retrieved three or four paper notes, which he read, then bagged and tagged along with other evidence.

A woman's full-length brown tweed coat found on the dining room table was also examined and yielded one more note. Like the others, the note was bagged and tagged and sent to the CID offices. A pair of red high-heel ladies shoes were on the dining room floor. One of the shoes was tipped over and lying on its side.

There was a large amount of blood in the apartment, much of it in the kitchen, where it trailed from the floor under the telephone almost out to the hallway. More blood speckled the floor of the master bedroom and the floor and lower portions of the walls in the bathroom, where a pan of kitty litter had been spilled and tipped over near the dead man. Samples of the coagulated blood were collected in evidence vials.

Careful notes were made of the exact location each piece of evidence was collected from, who collected it, the date and time. Detectives or technicians initialed or signed each envelope, bag, or tag. Similar information would be noted on the containers and tags by each individual who handled it as it moved from police officers to laboratories and to the courts, to ensure that the integrity of the chain of custody was maintained. It is a necessary precaution that must be followed to prevent later

legal challenges and possible disastrous repercussions in
court.

About an hour and a half after the first 911 call was
logged from Lisa, Prince Georges County Police Chief
David B. Mitchell arrived at the scene to confer with
senior officers and detectives. He was attending a community meeting with other high-ranking county officials
when he was notified of the shooting. Bright yellow
crime-scene tape was already strung in front of Apartment 102, and other residents of the building were being interviewed. Astheimer was relating his story to a
detective of being awakened by gunshots. It wasn't the
only time he would be asked to tell his story; merely the
first.

While investigators continued to scrutinize the area
for evidence, paramedics wheeled the gurney with
Roger's body outside and transferred it to a waiting fire
department ambulance. Then it was driven to Baltimore
for autopsy later that morning at the Maryland State
Medical Examiner's office.

Detective Larry Beverly was working in the county police department's Criminal Investigations Division headquarters when he was sent to Greater Laurel-Beltsville
Hospital in Laurel to interview the surviving victim of a
shooting. He arrived at the hospital emergency room a
few minutes before ten P.M., where a woman had been
taken for treatment of a gunshot wound to her left arm.

A single small-caliber slug had entered and exited her
bicep. The bullet passed cleanly through the fleshy part
of the limb without touching the humerus, the long
bone that extends from the shoulder to the elbow.

The twenty-nine-year-old woman had already identified herself to hospital staff as Lisa Ann Rohn before
the Prince Georges County Police investigator walked

inside. Moving purposefully past the collection of the injured and the ill, flat on their backs or hunched over and perching uncomfortably on the edge of gurneys with legs dangling listlessly and heads drooping in their hands, he made his way to one of the cubicles.

Lisa was lying faceup on a gurney, moaning occasionally and grimacing as if she was in a great deal of pain. She was wearing the engagement ring Roger had gotten for her. A costume jewelry bracelet was around the wrist.

Beverly introduced himself as a Prince Georges County police detective and advised her he was there to take a statement about the shooting. Before Beverly began the formal interview, photographs were taken of Lisa and of her injury. William H. Clelland, a civilian evidence technician with the county police department for seven years, was summoned to take the pictures. He arrived at the busy hospital emergency room a few minutes before ten P.M.

Doctors removed a temporary bandage from Lisa's arm so Clelland could photograph the wound. The technician made detailed entries in a notebook, stipulating the direction of travel the slug had taken, the presence of powder burns, and measurements around the entrance and exit points.

After Clelland completed his job, Beverly turned to the task of obtaining a formal statement from the lightly medicated woman. Before moving on to actual questions, however, he carried out the obligatory reading of the Miranda warning.

Reading from a typewritten sheet, he repeated his name, his job with the Prince Georges County Police Department, the date and time. It was 10:05 P.M. Then he moved on to Miranda:

"Number one, you have the right to remain silent. If

you choose to give up this right, anything that you say can be used against you in court.

"Number two, you have the right to talk to a lawyer before you are asked any questions and to have a lawyer with you while you are being questioned."

After each point, Beverly asked Lisa if she understood, and she replied that she did. It was a familiar litany, a dreary singsong recitation she had listened to many times before. As Beverly continued to move through Miranda, Lisa verbally responded that she understood the statement and inked in her initials, LAR, next to the appropriate paragraphs.

Despite her obvious pain and discomfort, her speech was even, her words were clear, and her handwriting was neat and legible. Although she broke into tears a few times, it appeared to the homicide detective that she was coherent and aware of what she was doing. When Beverly completed his reading, she signed her name at the bottom of the form. She agreed to make a statement without the presence of a lawyer.

Beverly had another printed form ready: a "Prince Georges County Police Department statement of victim-witness/suspect." They filled in the information at the top of the form with Lisa's full name, social security number, her vital statistics, and other information. She listed Roger's apartment as her address. Beverly's last name and badge number were also listed, along with the date and the time, which was jotted down in military and police style as 2217. In civilian terms it was 10:17 P.M. when the interview began.

Lisa began her statement by briefly tracing her version of the events, beginning from Roger's return home that evening, through the shooting and her call to 911. She wrote her initial account herself, before the detective moved to specific questions. It covered most of the first page of the "victim-witness/suspect" statement.

A few minutes into the statement, a doctor entered the cubicle to treat Lisa's arm and Beverly had to interrupt the interview. After the doctor left, Lisa and the detective resumed work on the statement.

According to the scenario initially recounted by Lisa, she was packing her things when Roger returned home from work about seven or eight P.M.. She continued to pack and make sure she had everything, and was in the bedroom when Roger suddenly pointed a gun in her face. Lisa said she thought he was trying to frighten her, and she didn't know the gun was loaded.

"I grabbed the barrel of the gun out of my face and he pulled the trigger. I got shot in the left arm. It scared the hell out of me," she continued. "I panicked and pulled the gun. Roger shoved me against the wall. I fought. He was yelling at me, but I don't know what he said. He came at me and I was trapped in the bathroom and I just pulled the trigger. I called 911."

Lisa had traced a dramatic and chilling account for the detective of an enraged boyfriend who had suddenly confronted her and shot her in the arm. In her desperate struggle to save her life, he was also shot. Based on the injured woman's statement, Roger's fatal shooting was clearly a case of self-defense. But the brief statement had left glaring unanswered questions, and it was Beverly's job to get answers.

He continued the interview, neatly recording everything in question-and-answer form. Writing quickly but legibly, the detective transformed Lisa's statement onto the paper forms as she talked, being careful not to miss a word. The detective wrote down his questions, and he recorded her replies. Lisa penned in her initials on the forms after every answer.

"Which room were you in when Roger shot you?" Beverly asked.

"The master bedroom."

"Where were you in the room when Roger shot you?"

"My back was to the mirror."

Beverly asked if it was a dresser with a mirror and how close she was to it. She said it had a mirror and she was standing about four feet away from it.

Continuing, he asked which room she was in when she shot Roger. The bathroom, she replied.

"Where were you standing in the bathroom when you shot Roger?"

"Inside the door frame in the bathroom," she said.

"Is that the wall against the door?" Beverly asked.

"Yes," she said. "He was coming in."

Lisa responded to the series of questions without suspiciously long hesitations that might indicate she was struggling to think up answers to fit in previous statements she had made about the tragic events earlier that evening. There was no backing up and correcting herself; no pleas that she was confused, or lame excuses about blacking out.

"Where was Roger standing when you shot him?" Beverly asked.

"In the bedroom outside the door of the bathroom."

"How many times did you fire the gun?"

"I don't know," she said. "I just kept pulling it. He wouldn't stop."

Beverly asked what Roger did after she fired the first shot.

"He just kept barrelling in," she said.

"What did Roger do after you shot him?"

"He fell on the floor!"

Asked if she touched Roger after shooting him, Lisa replied that she didn't. She just stepped over his body.

Beverly asked if Roger was carrying anything when she shot him, and Lisa replied that he had something but she didn't know what it was. It was a dark color.

Backtracking a few minutes to before the shooting, the detective asked Lisa where she was when Roger first arrived home that evening. She said she was in the kitchen, and heard him come inside.

"Did he say anything?"

"You didn't get your stuff out yet," Lisa quoted Roger. "I thought you were going to help me," she said she replied.

Lisa stated that after the verbal exchange with Roger in the kitchen, she walked back to the bedroom to finish her packing and to make sure she had everything that was hers. Roger told her then that he didn't feel like helping her, she said.

"How am I going to get my stuff out?" she asked him. "Why don't you have Brian help you?" she quoted him as replying. It was a question Roger had asked before, and one she apparently never answered.

Lisa said she told Roger to let her use his car and she would take care of the move herself. Then she went into the den, picked up a box of books and returned to the bedroom. "The next thing I knew, I turned around and he had the gun in my face," she said.

"Do you know where he got the gun from?" Beverly asked.

"He kept it in the closet," she replied.

"Did you see him get the gun?"

"No, I didn't know that he was in the bedroom."

"Did Roger say anything when you turned around?" the detective continued.

"He just called me a dirty tramp, and he said, 'I'll blow your head off!' " she responded.

"Did he say anything else?" Beverly asked.

"No," she said.

Beverly asked what Roger did with the gun.

"He held it to my face," she said.

"Did he touch you with it?"

"No!" she replied. "He pointed it right between my eyes."

Beverly asked what happened after that.

"I grabbed the gun in my right hand," she said, "and he shot me in the arm."

The injured woman on the gurney was sketching a chilling, brutal picture with her story of rage, fear, and violence. But Beverly wasn't shocked. He had been a cop long enough to witness firsthand some of the misery and savagery that seemingly normal people sometimes wreak on each other. He also shared the healthy skepticism that police officers inevitably develop, and he knew that people didn't always tell the truth.

"How did you get the gun?" he asked.

"I just grabbed the gun and pulled it away from him," Lisa replied. "I couldn't believe he shot me."

"Did Roger say anything after you grabbed the gun?"

"Kept swearing at me. Backed me into the bathroom and he called me a tramp, and said he hoped it was worth it," she replied.

"After Roger shot you, did he touch you?"

"He grabbed me and threw me against the wall. I hit the chair. I kind of stumbled."

Beverly asked if she had the gun when she was slammed against the wall. Lisa said she had the barrel in her hand. "I didn't let go. I still had it in my hand when he shot me."

Beverly asked what she was wearing at the time. A red jacket, jeans, and a laced top, she said.

"What did you do with the gun after Roger?"

"I just threw it on the floor," she said.

Once Lisa had described the shooting and the immediate events leading up it, Beverly steered the interview to matters of background. Responding to the detective's lead, Lisa recited Roger's full name, date of birth, and recounted how they met after he placed the ad in the personal columns of the *Washingtonian*. She explained she hadn't been going out much when she looked through the ads.

Asked who she was living with at the time, Lisa said she was looking after a child in Silver Spring. "I had a room in exchange for watching the lady who owned the house's son," she explained in slightly fractured grammar.

Lisa told about moving in with Roger and said they began having troubles with each other in April when she was arrested on a warrant for credit card fraud. She added that she had been in jail from that time until the previous week, when she was bailed out.

"Who got you out?" Beverly asked.

"My ex-sister-in-law in Illinois," she replied.

Beverly asked her why Roger didn't get her out.

"He didn't have the money," she said.

Continuing to respond to the same line of questioning, Lisa explained that the bond was $20,000, that she and Roger wrote to each other while she was locked up and visited her about once a week. He was happy when she was released on bond, she said.

In response to a question about why she decided to move out, Lisa said she planned to put her things in storage because she knew she was going back to jail. When she said her next scheduled court date was a preliminary hearing on November 26, he asked why she believed she would have to return to jail.

"Dolores wanted her money back by December first,

and she was going to revoke my bond," Lisa explained. She said the woman couldn't afford it.

When Beverly inquired why she couldn't continue to leave her possessions at Roger's apartment, she claimed she wasn't sure how long he would keep it for her.

Beverly turned his questions to the previous night and the confrontation at the motel. Beverly asked how Roger knew where to find her when she went to Margarita Maggie's. She explained they had planned to go there together before Roger's work interfered. So she went by herself. Then she told about joining Rohloff and some other men and a woman for dinner.

"When did Roger show up?" Beverly asked.

"After dinner," she said. "We went back to the hotel, then back to Margarita Maggie's. I had mineral water." Lisa said Roger and Brian didn't talk with each other.

"Why did you go to Brian's room?" the detective inquired.

"He just asked me to. If I wanted to walk over to his room. So I did!"

"Did you have sex with Brian?"

Not at that time, she said. "It was after I saw Roger."

"Why did you have sex with Brian?" Beverly asked.

"Because I didn't want to go home. Brian asked me if I wanted to stay there."

"Why didn't you go back with Roger?" the detective persisted.

"He was mad because he saw me talking to Brian," she replied. "And he was always jealous and I didn't want to hear it."

Lisa said she didn't know Brian's full name, but thought he was from Albany, New York. At Beverly's request, she related a physical description of the iron worker and provided his room number at the motel.

When Lisa was asked if Roger had any relatives in the

area, she replied that his ex-wife lived in Germantown. She didn't mention Christopher.

"Has Roger ever been violent with you before?" Beverly inquired.

She said he never hit her, but told of angry words after he telephoned her the night before she moved in with him and she wasn't home. Lisa didn't mention the mini-crisis that erupted at that time after Roger learned he and the landlady knew her by different names.

Responding to another question, Lisa said Roger kept the .22 pistol on a shelf in the bedroom closet. "He just showed it to me Sunday," she said. Beverly asked why Roger showed her the weapon, and she replied that he was an ex-Vietnam veteran who like to target shoot.

Beverly turned once again to a more personal question: why Roger called her a tramp.

She said Roger was always jealous and thought that if she talked to another man, it was because she was trying to pick him up.

"His first wife left him for another man," she volunteered. Beverly didn't inquire how she knew that: whether it was something Roger believed and told her, or if it was even true. It could be sorted out later if it was considered important enough and thought to have any bearing on the earlier violent events of the evening.

Beverly asked Lisa if she was tired of Roger.

"It wasn't easy, with me being in jail," she responded. "When I saw him again, all the good memories came back."

Beverly asked if she told Roger she had sexual relations with Rohloff. She said she admitted having sex with the iron worker after she left the motel and Roger confronted her about it. He was angry, but didn't do anything about it. And she told of returning to the apartment from the Ramada Monday morning and find-ing the plastic bag, and the note on the door.

"What did the note say?" Beverly asked.

"Something to the effect of 'get your stuff by two or two-thirty, or I'll throw your stuff out. If you try to come in I'll shoot you,' " she related.

Lisa told about trying to enter the apartment anyway, and being confronted with the muzzle of a gun. She said she could tell he was upset, but thought he was just trying to scare her and finally went inside.

"Did he threaten you after he let you in?" the detec-tive asked.

She said he didn't, and subsequently drove her to the Metro.

Once again Beverly shifted gears, and returned to the shooting. "Where did you go after you shot Roger?" he asked.

According to Lisa, she went down the hall to the kitchen and dialed 911. "I told them that I was shot and was bleeding over the floor," she added in response to a follow-up question.

Lisa said after making the call she heard an ambu-lance and went out to open the door, but didn't see the emergency vehicle and returned inside the apartment. Then she turned around and went outside again.

"Did you go back into the bedroom?" Beverly asked.

"No," she replied. "I don't think so."

Beverly was out of questions. The exhausting ques-tion-and-answer session had produced a ten-page hand-printed statement, and a rough sketch Lisa made of the master bedroom. The location of the window, closet, hallway, bathroom, furniture, and Roger's body were designated on the drawing.

The detective showed her the statement and told her to look it over and tell him if there was anything she wanted to change or add to it. He asked her to pay special attention to the questions and answers, and if she agreed with the statements as he had hand-printed them, to put her initial next to each reply.

Lisa didn't have anything she wished to add to the statement, and scribbled her initials next to each answer. She also signed her distinctive, cramped straight-up-and-down signature at the bottom of each page.

Shortly after Lisa completed her statement, Beverly drove her to the Criminal Investigations Division at the police department headquarters in Palmer Park, a few miles south of Beltsville. A doctor had indicated she was well enough to leave the hospital. There was no need for her to be admitted as a patient.

It was shortly after twelve-thirty A.M., Wednesday, November 20, when they arrived in Palmer Park. Later that morning Lisa was advised that she was under arrest as a suspect in Roger's murder. Investigators had already interviewed several other people with links to the tragic events of the previous evening, examined the shooting scene, and checked with local and FBI computers for police records on Lisa and Roger. If anyone with the CID believed Lisa's account of the shootings, they were keeping it to themselves.

The shooting made the front page of the Metro section of the *Washington Post*. The identities of Roger and Lisa, and information about her arrest, weren't released by authorities in time for the morning edition of most area newspapers, but the story made Wednesday's evening television news. That night Roger's shooting was a prime subject of discussion among men and women at Beltway singles bars.

A neighbor who lived in a town house near the Powder Mill Apartments was interviewed by a newspaper reporter, and appeared to be much less concerned with the different methods of police agency record keeping than she was by the spread of the danger and violence. She was quoted in the news story as saying she moved to the Beltsville neighborhood because she thought it was safer than other areas of the county. If she could afford to, she nervously added, she thought she would move to Alaska.

While Lisa was once more being walked through the familiar booking process at the police headquarters. about an hour's drive away in Baltimore an associate pathologist was beginning the autopsy on Roger's body. It wasn't the first autopsy conducted there that day. The Chief Medical Examiner's Office in the port city serves as a clearinghouse for the violently and suspiciously dead in Baltimore as well as those from many other communities throughout the Old Line State.

When Roger's body was wheeled into the morgue he took his place among a collection of corpses, men and women who were shot to death, knifed, bludgeoned with clubs or baseball bats, or mangled in traffic accidents. Like others that arrived before his, the body was immediately photographed, weighed, and measured. Roger had been five feet eleven inches tall. His fondness for pickup meals of sandwiches, fries, or pizza and a beer had ballooned his weight to a flabby 235 pounds. He was assigned a case number that was scrawled on a manila tag and tied around one of his big toes.

Because Roger's remains arrived at the morgue before noon, he was scheduled for autopsy that day instead of being held in a freezer overnight for attention Thursday. The swift and painstaking attention that is paid to autopsies in Baltimore provides one of the better examples of efficiency by medical examiners in American cities. Not every community is always so fortunate.

In West Texas a pathologist lost track of the head of a man police in Odessa were investigating as a suspected murder victim. The pathologist, who worked out of Lubbock County, said he detached it from the body and sent it to Austin so a reconstruction could be made by a forensic artist. Authorities in Austin said they never received it.

For a while in Los Angeles the year before Roger died, a horribly burgeoning homicide rate and severe staff shortages were cited for part of the blame because some cadavers had remained in the medical examiner's office for four or five days or longer before autopsies were conducted. At least once, employees complained they had to use military-style gas masks to enter a refrigerator where bodies were stored because of the terrible odor. It was a deplorable situation that often left homicide investigators at a critical disadvantage because the cause of death in many murders isn't always obvious before medical determinations can be made.

Forensic pathologists also pointed out that results of various tests on blood and tissue samples that are part of the normal procedure in a full autopsy can be altered by a long wait. And long delays add to the sad memories of family members and other survivors, who must wait for the medical examiner to release the remains before they can move on with the funeral and burial or cremation.

Dr. Junaid Shaikh was the forensic pathologist assigned to Roger's autopsy. Dr. Shaikh had traveled halfway around the world, before settling into the job of associate pathologist in the office of the Chief Medical Examiner in Baltimore. After graduating from the Dow Medical College in Karachi, Pakistan, and completing another year of training in surgery and medicine, and working briefly in private practice, Dr. Shaikh moved to the United States to continue his career. After supplementing his earlier training and work, at hospitals in Columbus and Cleveland, Ohio, and in Philadelphia, he found his way to the job in Baltimore.

There, amid the odors of the dead, body fluids and strong chemicals, stainless steel sinks, bowls and body trays, scales and sharp instruments, he worked to unravel the mysteries linked to people dead from criminal violence, suicide, accident, or merely because they expired suddenly when they were in apparent good health. If someone died in prison or police custody, from a disease considered a special threat to public health, while unattended by a physician, or under any suspicious circumstances, their bodies were likely to come under the keen scalpels and careful professional scrutiny of Dr. Shaikh or his colleagues.

Forensic pathologists are medical sleuths; Sherlock Holmeses in smocks. Dead bodies and death are their business.

When the sheet was pulled off Roger's remains in preparation for his autopsy, Dr. Shaikh and his assistants began their grim task with practiced precision. Their first step was to make a careful visual study of the corpse, from head to toes, front to back. Then additional color photographs were taken and the body was undressed. It was then cleaned up and more pictures were snapped.

In addition to the terrible injury to Roger's head, two other bullet wounds were observed. One of the slugs had entered the left side of his abdomen at the bottom edge of the rib cage. The other sliced into his body at the top of his right shoulder and coursed downward through the soft muscle of his back. Dr. Shaikh also observed some small cuts and abrasions around Roger's eyes, and others on the shin of his left leg.

In a classic full autopsy, the body is opened by making a Y-shaped incision; first cutting a line from the shoulders to the breastbone, then slicing straight down to the groin. Then the skin is peeled back and a small electric saw is used to remove a section of the breastbone.

Once Roger's body cavity was opened, Dr. Shaikh was able to trace the path of the low-caliber bullet that entered his abdomen. The projectile had moved downward a bit to the right, lacerated his stomach, cut through his pancreas and severed the large artery feeding the left kidney. The pathologist recovered the deformed slug from the back muscles where they had at last lodged.

While tracing the trajectory of the bullet, the doctor removed Roger's internal organs, which were later cut up into sections for closer study with microscopes.

A section of Roger's skull was also sawed through and removed so that Dr. Shaikh could examine the brain and the damage inflicted by the bullet that crashed through the victim's forehead. Probing among the neat ridges and crevices, the blood and the cool sleekness inside with his eyes and fingers, the pathologist tracked the path of the final gunshot wound. The bullet had smashed through the skull, tore through the right frontal lobe of the brain, crossed to the left side and lacerated the cerebellum there. The deformed slug from a small-caliber bullet was recovered from the back of the skull.

The spinal cord was snipped so the brain could be removed and set aside with other organs for further study. Additional samples of blood, urine, and tissue were also collected to be sent to a laboratory for later analysis. Scans would be run on the samples to detect the possible presence of alcohol, prescription, or over-the-counter drugs or illicit substances.

Dr. Shaikh determined that Roger died from multiple gunshot wounds.

At the Arlington County Police Department headquarters, Detective Cowell was sipping his second cup of black coffee and considering if he should slip outside to the front of the building for a few moments to take a smoke break when his telephone rang. It was his friend from the Secret Service, Jim Gaughran. The federal agent told him that as he was driving to work he heard on his car radio that Roger Paulson had been shot to death overnight by Lisa Rohn.

"No way! She's still in jail," Cowell spluttered. He growled to Gaughran that he had personally seen to it Lisa was safely locked up downstairs in the adult detention center. He had picked her up at the Kent County jail, returned her to Arlington, and watched as she was processed. But Gaughran insisted Roger's shooting by Lisa was a morning news story.

The burly detective forgot all about taking a smoke break. He barked a quick good-bye to his friend in his scratchy Marlboro voice, slammed down the receiver of the telephone and headed for the elevator. Moments later he was talking with the booking officer at the jail. The sheriff's deputy couldn't tell him if Lisa had shot anyone or not, but he confirmed that she had posted bail and was released from the lockup only five days earlier.

Cowell's suspect walked out of the jail while he was busy at work only two floors overhead, and no one had said a word to him. Now, less than a week later, Roger was dead and she was charged with his murder.

Curiously, with Roger's slaying, four of the most significant events in his life had occurred in November: He was born on November 26, married on November 10, divorced on November 27, and died on November 19. Only the August birth of his son, Christopher, occurred outside the seventeen-day window.

Chapter Eight

Preliminaries

Leonard and Joyce Paulson were looking forward to driving to Maryland in a few days to spend the Thanksgiving holiday with their youngest son and with their grandson, Christopher, when they learned the dreadful news.

They were roused from sleep at their home in Charleston into a nightmare of reality at five o'clock in the morning by a telephone call.

Police in Prince Georges County informed them their son was shot to death a few hours earlier at his apartment. Few other details were passed on to the shocked couple at that time. They were merely advised that an investigation was still under way. Roger was killed exactly one week before his thirty-eighth birthday.

The Paulsons left for Maryland as soon as they could pack a few clothes, close up the house, and notify relatives and friends of the tragedy and their destination. Then they began the bleak drive west to Interstate 95 and swung north, following the super highway through the Carolinas and Virginia, past Washington to Beltsville.

Instead of exchanging the easy chatter of loving parents on their way to share a holiday meal and a birthday celebration with the baby of the family, they were faced with the dreary task of coping with his sudden, violent death. It was a nightmare trip.

When they arrived in Beltsville, there would be no mundane chatter about such inconsequential matters as whether to have turkey or ham, or how to prepare the potatoes for their holiday dinner. Instead there would be funeral arrangements and other heartbreaking decisions to make.

And the pleasant young woman whom the Paulsons first met at their son's home less than a year earlier on another more cheerful holiday trip to Maryland was in jail, charged with his murder.

Before the heartbroken couple's arrival in Beltsville, Clelland was dispatched to meet Detective John Harhai at Roger's apartment to collect additional samples of blood or other body fluids. Harhai was a senior detective with primary responsibility for the investigation.

Clelland took blood scrapings from the kitchen floor, snipped a swatch of blood-spotted material from the armrest of a floral cover for a love seat in the front room, cut a piece from the bloodied carpet in the master bedroom, and clipped a chunk of a bloodstained pocket off Roger's burgundy garment bag. The piece of luggage was still lying on the floor of the bathroom where it was placed when Roger's body was moved.

By Friday night when Roger's parents entered the apartment after detectives and technicians finished their work there and the couple was permitted inside, the bag had been draped across the dining room table. They saw the blood on it and noticed that a large swatch was cut from the fabric.

Mrs. Paulson was curious about why the bag was on the table, and opened it. It was filled with a complete change of clean clothes that appeared as if they would fit a large man. There was a suit, white shirt, necktie, underwear, and socks. There was also some shaving gear.

The apartment was a disaster. The kitchen floor, telephone, the carpeting in the master bedroom, and the bathroom were still smeared with blood. The bedroom carpet was soaked through with the water from the fish tank, chunks of glass were scattered here and there, and bullet holes were still plainly visible in the wall and dresser.

It's not part of the duties of police officers to clean up crime scenes after they are through with it, although commercial cleaning and restoration services are available in some communities and can be hired to do the job. But no one attempted to contact a cleaning service to put Roger's apartment back in shape. Leonard and Joyce Paulson handled most of the grim task themselves.

They picked up the shattered glass in the bedroom, scrubbed the blood from floors and walls, and reorganized, packed up, and moved out the disarranged furniture and other belongings scattered through the apartment. They even picked Jellybean up from the veterinarian clinic, and eventually found a new home for her and Roger's other cats.

A couple of men who had worked installation jobs with Roger volunteered to pull up the ruined carpeting in the bedroom and toss it away. Early Saturday morning as they were ripping the carpeting out, they pulled one edge away from a wall and exposed two empty .22 caliber cartridge casings. Roger's father was watching as they worked, and all three men saw the casings at about the same time. They had been scrunched between the edge of the carpet and the wall.

Paulson telephoned Detective Harhai at the CID headquarters to tell him about the discovery, put his initials on a letter envelope and slipped the casings inside. Harhai sent Detective Green to the apartment to pick them up. Investigators sent the shell casings, blood samples, and other evidence collected during the searches of the apartment for clues to the FBI laboratories in Quantico for analysis and other tests.

The Paulsons arranged Saturday services for their son at the Collins Funeral Home in Silver Spring. He was interred at the Fort Lincoln Cemetery in Brentwood, a small suburb at the north edge of the District of Columbia border. The Paulsons wanted Roger buried in Maryland so he would be near his son.

Lisa was charged with first-degree murder and with use of a handgun in the commission of a crime of violence.

In many states, laws provide for a broad range of charges for homicide, all the way from first-degree premeditated murder, the most serious, down to involuntary manslaughter, the least serious. In Maryland the charge of first-murder is initially lodged against defendants in all homicides, but that can be reduced to lesser counts at the probable cause hearing, which is required to legally establish in court that a crime has been committed, by a grand jury, or in other proceedings.

Although Maryland is one of seven states with a gas chamber for condemned prisoners, Lisa didn't have to worry about being given the death penalty. (One of those states, Colorado, provides for execution by lethal injection of prisoners whose crimes occurred on or after July 1, 1988.) The circumstances of the shooting didn't meet the specifications of the statute, which calls for certain aggravating factors such as killing a police officer or prison guard, the murder of a child, or multiple murders.

But the death penalty is rarely sought by Maryland prosecutors anyway. At the time of Lisa's trial, only ten men were on death row at the old state prison directly across the road from where Lisa was locked up after her arrest in Bethesda. The last killer put to death in the gas chamber was Nathaniel Lipscomb in 1961. No one has been executed by Maryland penal authorities since a U.S. Supreme Court ruling in 1977 permitting states to reinstitute the death penalty.

As the case moved from on-the-scene investigation into the court system, Laura J. Gwinn was assigned as the senior prosecutor who would be charged with the task of obtaining a murder conviction. She quickly announced she would seek the maximum available penalty for Lisa according to state criminal statutes: life in prison without the possibility of parole.

The Prince Georges assistant county prosecutor took a circuitous route to her job, swapping an early career as a pharmacist to follow the legal profession. She grew up in the town of Sanford in North Florida, and after graduation from high school enrolled at Florida State University. After marriage, giving birth to a baby girl, and transferring to Florida A&M, she earned an advanced degree in pharmacy. She was serving a pharmacy internship in Orlando when she moved to Maryland to take a job with a Veteran's Administration hospital on a work study program for her master's degree. She was working at a local pharmacy when she started attending night school at the University of Baltimore. This time she had set her sights on a law degree.

Her first job after completing law school, earning her degree, and passing the Maryland bar examination, was with the Prince Georges County States Attorney's Office. She had decided it was a job, especially prosecuting homicide cases, that permitted her to repay society, which had given her so many opportunities. "You can't give parents a son or a daughter back," she explains. "But at least you can give them justice."

Approximately two years before Roger was shot to death in his apartment, State's Attorney Alexander Williams, Jr., formed a special unit that would prosecute only cases involving homicides. Gwinn was selected as one of four prosecutors on the staff.

By the time she was given the Paulson slaying to prosecute, the former pharmacist was an experienced professional who knew criminal law, how to assemble a case, and how to present it to a judge and jury in the courtroom.

She immediately began putting together a thick folder on the shooting and contacting police investigators, court officers, and others with knowledge of the case and of the suspect's background. Gwinn talked with Harhai and other Prince Georges County Police officers who investigated the shooting. And she exchanged information with her colleague with the federal prosecutor's office in Baltimore, Barbara Sale; with Zacur and other FBI and Secret Service agents; with Cowell; even a representative from the U.S. State Department.

Officers, agents, and prosecutors from so many law enforcement jurisdictions were interested in various aspects of the case that they began facetiously referring to themselves as members of the Lisa Rohn Task Force. The war room for the unofficial task force was the prosecutor's cramped office on the third floor of the Prince Georges County Courthouse in Upper Marlboro.

The office was awash in a litter of legal forms and papers, telephone call slips and memos that creeped over the prosecutor's desk and onto side tables. A bulletin board was equally busy, with thumbtacked newspaper clippings and notes overlapping each other, and a large wall calendar filled with hurriedly scrawled reminders in the squares. A huge plastic garbage bag, the same kind of utilitarian carrier Lisa used to move her possessions from the jail in Arlington to Roger's apartment, slumped in a corner of the office, abulge with thick legal files and more papers.

Despite the location in Upper Marlboro of the Prince Georges County Detention Center, and the grim business often conducted at the county government complex, a visit to the hamlet just east of the huge Andrews Air Force Base and the Capital Beltway can be like stepping back in time to America's colonial period.

Upper Marlboro lies on the fringe of Maryland's picturesque tobacco country. Sidewalks in and near the community's small shopping and business area are red brick and tree-shaded. But the showpiece of the quaint, hilly town is the stately old colonial courthouse.

The old, original section of the courthouse was the birthplace of John Carroll, who lived from 1735 to 1815. In 1776, at the request of the Continental Congress, he accompanied Benjamin Franklin and other early American patriots to Quebec, where they attempted unsuccessfully to convince Canada to join the thirteen colonies in the revolution. Carroll was also the first Roman Catholic archbishop in the United States, and a little more than a decade after the abortive trip to Quebec, he founded Georgetown College.

Today, the majestic two-story red-brick courthouse constructed with a cupaloed bell tower and two huge white columns at the entrance, fronts on Main Street at West Court Drive. The sleek, modern Prince Georges County Public Administration Building and U.S. Post

Office directly across Main Street provide a dramatic contrast between the old and the new.

Visitors don't have to venture far inside the front doors of the courthouse before they realize that the quaint functional beauty of the colonial period has given way to more modern times there as well. On the far side of the foyer, a security checkpoint has been set up with uniformed guards and metal detectors. Everyone passing beyond that point into a new larger section of the courthouse opened in 1990—spectators, county bureaucrats, police officers, and officers of the court—must move through the scanners. Often they are required to open briefcases and purses for hand-checking by the guards, and to empty coins, keys, and other metal objects from pants pockets.

Courthouse security is a serious business, and although there have been no major incidents of violence at John Carroll's birthplace in Upper Marlboro, knives, guns, and bombs have been sneaked into courthouses in other counties and states, sometimes with dire results.

In one of the most spectacular examples of a security failure, a criminal defendant in Kokomo, Indiana, set off an explosion in the Howard County Courthouse in 1987. The suspected drug dealer had stuffed four pipe bombs filled with shrapnel in a briefcase, and when he detonated it, he was killed, and his defense attorney and the county sheriff were badly injured.

But courtroom violence has occurred in many areas of the country. In the Bexar County Courthouse in San Antonio, Texas, a criminal defendant stabbed a woman in one of the courtrooms, then stabbed an Assistant District Attorney in the heart while fleeing through the halls. The Assistant D.A. survived and later became a judge. And early in 1993 an outraged single mother stalked up to a man in a Sonora, California, courtroom who was accused of sexually abusing her son, pulled a gun and fired a fatal shot into his head.

The new addition of the Prince Georges County Courthouse was constructed with a high, almost cathedral-like ceiling, with offices strung in clusters around the borders of a central gallery. A smooth, sloping ramp and elevators provide access for the wheelchair bound, as well as others with business there.

But Lisa had more immediate and important problems to concern herself with than the aesthetics of the courthouse where she would be put on trial for Roger's murder. In the county detention center where she was locked in the women's unit about a mile north of the courthouse, there was none of the charm or beauty of the historic old building. The lockup was noisy, grim, and filled with the same vitality-eroding institutional smells and regulated subsistence shared by almost every other jail or prison in the country.

She put her fate in the hands of Harry J. Trainor, Jr., an experienced criminal defense lawyer with the Landover law firm Greenan, Walker, Steuart, Trainor & Billman. The final partner in the law firm is Trainor's wife, Leslie Billman. At the detention center the murder defendant and the lawyer set up a fee arrangement that called for her to pay him over a period of time. The exact details of the pact, including where the money was coming from, were not shared with the area press.

Trainor was recommended to Lisa by some of her fellow female inmates whom he was representing. She made a good choice. The defense attorney was respected by his colleagues, by judges, and by prosecutors he found himself matched against in the deadly serious winner-take-all legal contests played out in the courtrooms.

"He's a nice guy," Gwinn said of him months later.

"It's a real pleasure to try a case against him." They were generous remarks, and an attitude that wasn't obvious when the two squared off against each other in the courtroom.

But even though good prosecutors and defense attorneys are expected to fight like furies in the court, it works best for everyone involved when they are able to forget their professional differences once they are outside.

Trainor was the kind of successful and confident professional who made it easy to do that. A nonsmoker, he worked hard on his physical fitness and kept in shape with regular jogging near his home in Annapolis. With his lean, near six-foot frame, straight brown hair, and wire-rimmed glasses, he had the look of someone who might have been picked by Hollywood casting to play the role of a lawyer. But he wasn't a make-believe lawyer, and that was obvious in the courtroom, where he was respected as a scrappy and tenacious opponent.

A native of Montgomery County, Trainor grew up a couple of blocks from the house in the Sligo Park neighborhood of Silver Spring where Lisa was living when she first met Roger. After graduating from Montgomery Blair High School in 1963, he earned his undergraduate degree at the University of Maryland in College Park a few minutes' drive from his childhood home, was accepted for an MBA program, and earned his law degree at the Catholic University of America in Washington, D.C.

Although he was initially attracted to labor law, he decided to change his specialty after clerking for lawyers who were involved in criminal defense work.

Years later, when he accepted Lisa as a client, Trainor appeared to be locked into a defense strategy. Lisa's statement to Detective Beverly had made her position clear: Roger attacked her, and she shot him in self-defense.

The Assistant State's Attorney was developing a courtroom strategy built around a far more sinister motive as she assembled and organized her case. She was determined to prove to a jury that Lisa shot Roger in revenge for turning her in to the FBI then testifying against her.

Gwinn was convinced that Lisa lurked inside Roger's apartment until he came home, and shot him to death in cold blood. Then, as he was lying on the floor with his life seeping out of him, she deliberately shot herself in the arm to set up an alibi.

The prosecutor's preparation for the trial was a grueling task. There was physical evidence to arrange; witnesses to interview and subpoena; and significantly, strategy to plan. There were also the pretrial motions, both hers and those of the defense, to deal with.

Defending or prosecuting a homicide case is a demanding ordeal that requires the understanding and cooperation of family members. Gwinn's family had grown to include a son as well as the firstborn daughter, but as she worked on the Rohn case and others, she found herself increasingly tied to the job on weekends and nights.

Her land surveyor husband was cooperative, and so were the children—after they made a deal with their mother. She gave them a choice: would they rather she worked late two or three nights a week, or on weekends? The children made an easy decision. They preferred for her to take weekends off work to spend with them. Except for a couple of hours or so early in the evenings, they were asleep nights anyway.

Gwinn kept the schedule and her word as best she could, although as other cases intruded, she eventually had to fudge a few hours on weekends now and then to keep up. Other professionals in the criminal justice system were busy with preparations for the trial as well.

Associate Judge James P. Salmon, one of the most experienced jurists on the local bench, was selected to preside over the case in the Prince Georges County Circuit Court.

At the FBI laboratories in Quantico, firearms analyists with the Firearms and Tool Mark Unit used high-resolution microscopes and other state-of-the-art equipment to examine the .22 caliber target pistol, the bullets and fragments found in the bedroom near Roger's body. The experts were seeking to determine if the grooves in the barrel matched the almost infinitesimally fine markings on the bullets.

Only two could be identified as .22 caliber long rifle bullets. It was definitely determined through the tests that one of them was fired by the target pistol. The other was so mutilated that experts were unable to make a positive determination, although they concluded that markings indicated it could have been fired by the same pistol or another with similar barrel characteristics.

The fingerprint lifted from the wall phone in the kitchen was confirmed to be Lisa's. But no usable prints were obtained from the pistol or from the empty cartridge casings dusted by investigators.

In other laboratories, toxicologists and serologists were completing tests and preparing reports on the blood collected at the crime scene and on the body fluids and tissue samples taken from Lisa and from Roger during his autopsy. Two vials of blood were drawn from Lisa's arm early in January and used to match bloodstains in the apartment. A few weeks later she provided samples of her handwriting for examination at the FBI laboratories.

There was no evidence in Roger's body fluids or tissue of any illegal narcotics, or of over-the-counter painkillers and drugs. Curiously, despite the beer he drank with his boss at the pizza parlor, there wasn't even a trace of alcohol.

In the courtroom, Trainor won an important preliminary contest when Judge Salmon ruled that information about the charges pending against Lisa in Arlington would not be admissible. Testimony and evidence linked to the criminal charges in the adjoining state were not to be presented to the jury during the murder trial.

But the call favored the prosecution in regard to the admissibility of testimony relating to Lisa's arrest in Bethesda and her conviction in U.S. District Court in Baltimore. Judge Salmon's ruling was made over stiff objections from the defense, and later permitted to stand through the period of the trial, even though Lisa's conviction in Baltimore had already been reversed by the United States Court of Appeals for the Fourth Circuit in Richmond, Virginia.

On May 5 the three-member panel unanimously ruled the prosecution did not prove Lisa had used the IDs for illegal purposes. The published opinion noted that Congress adopted the False Identification Crime Control Act of 1982 creating federal offenses relating to possession of, counterfeiting, and trafficking in false identification documents.

"Congress could have criminalized mere possession of false identifications. It did not, however, write the statute in this way," it was observed. "Rather, an essential element of the offense Congress created is an 'intent to use unlawfully' the false identification possessed."

Consequently, the court decided that the mere possession of the documents constituted a crime only when their intended use would violate a federal, state, or local law. And the government failed to show that intent.

The judges specifically singled out the prosecutor's cautioning the juror's not to check their common sense at the door of the jury room as suggesting Lisa intended to use the ID unlawfully, because there were no "possible lawful uses for phony identifications."

The court wrote: "This, we think, is an insufficient basis for the jury to conclude that the appellant's intended uses were unlawful. In effect, the government's argument represented an impermissible effort to shift the burden of proof. . . ."

Even though Lisa had already served her jail sentence, the higher court decision was a bitter disappointment for the government. Essentially, it wiped her record clean of that particular alleged offense. It was as if she had never been arrested, convicted, or jailed on the charges of possessing the multiple ID. Almost as if it had never happened. Almost—but not quite.

Despite the reversal, it was a fact that she was arrested, she was convicted, and she was jailed. And the information was critical to the state's case, which could have been shattered if the prosecutor was not permitted to demonstrate to the jury the key role Roger played in putting his girlfriend in jail. It was central to Gwinn's contention that Lisa was motivated by revenge to kill him.

The decision led to one of several stipulations, agreements to certain information that was accepted as fact by both sides in the contest. The opposing lawyers agreed to allow into evidence certain information from Barbara Sale related to the case in Baltimore. Sale would not be called to the witness stand during the trial.

But Gwinn was permitted to present information the federal prosecutor would have testified to.

Trainor's agreement to the stipulation about the statements from the federal prosecutor was reluctant. He pointed out to the court he would not have agreed if it hadn't been for Judge Salmon's earlier ruling permitting introduction of evidence relating to the case in Baltimore.

As the Landover lawyer shaped the defense, he began drawing a picture of the victim that was far different from that of the prosecution. It was a picture of a disturbed man who was living unsteadily on the edge of violence and schizophrenia before the final dreadful confrontation that led to his death.

Trainor obtained records of the guns, including the .22 caliber Ruger used in the fatal shooting, that were purchased by Roger while Lisa was in jail. The notes left on the door to the apartment during the last three days of Roger's life were also studied and analyzed by FBI experts, who confirmed the handwriting was his.

In addition to the overt threats contained in the messages, there were additional aspects of Roger's notes and other writings to Lisa that appeared to shed additional light on the troubled state of the author's mind. One of the threatening notes was hand-printed. Another was penned in script. His writing habits were disturbingly scrambled and inconsistent.

The defense lawyer also expected to make use of color photographs of Lisa taken at the hospital, which showed ugly bruises on her neck. They appeared to be classic strangulation marks, the kind of bruises that would be left if someone grabbed her around the neck with powerful hands. If he was allowed to submit them as evidence, they could provide a powerful argument to the jury that Lisa was in a desperate life-and-death struggle with her jealous lover when he was shot to death.

Trainor, furthermore, simply didn't believe that Lisa lurked inside the apartment, waiting to waylay and murder Roger the night of the shooting. She was too streetwise and savvy, even if she had wanted Roger dead. It would have made more sense for her to ambush him outside the apartment as he parked his car or left it next to the corner Dumpster, which he had formed the habit of doing.

One more robbery murder by an unknown gunman, amid all the other violence in Prince Georges County, wouldn't have appeared so strange. And Lisa wouldn't have been such an obvious suspect, and wouldn't have had to deliberately shoot herself in the arm to establish an alibi, as police and prosecutors were contending she did.

Early in 1992, several weeks before the trial was scheduled to begin, the prosecutor got some help. One of her younger associates, Judy L. Woodall, was assigned to assist her with the prosecution. It was the newcomer's first homicide case. Rebecca Dieter, a young attorney with Trainor's law firm, had already joined him and would serve as the second chair for the defense.

But Detective Harhai, who headed the police investigation, had dropped out of the picture. He retired from the police department shortly after the new year began. Although the prosecutor could still call on him if she wished, various colleagues of the retired detective were available to testify about the investigation in his place. It was a case that called for more routine police work than imaginative sleuthing of the kind that would challenge a Sherlock Holmes. Harhai and his colleagues in homicide had touched the necessary bases and neatly wrapped up the investigation before he was pensioned off.

At last, early Monday morning, August 3, almost nine months after Roger was shot to death, attorneys assembled in the county circuit courtroom in Upper Marlboro to select a jury and begin Lisa's trial on charges she carried out his cold-blooded murder. The trial was being held in the same courthouse where Roger's divorce was granted and the papers were filed.

Judges and other officers of the court in Prince Georges County don't fool around for six weeks or six months selecting a jury. In many other jurisdictions around the country, long-drawn-out battles over jury selection has almost become the rule rather than the exception for major criminal trials. Jury selection can become a financially taxing and time-consuming battle of wits between opposing lawyers and professional jury experts ranging from high-paid psychologists to astrologers.

Even if prosecutors and defense attorneys in Prince Georges County decided to call on the help of astrologers, behavioral scientists, and social psychologists, it isn't likely it would do them much good. The judge in the case handles the voir dire—he reads the prepared questions to the jury panel. And the queries usually don't vary much from general efforts to flush out prospects who are related to or know figures in the case, have too much prior knowledge of the events, have been recent victims of crime, and are in law enforcement or careers with the courts—or are closely related to other people who are.

An attorney may produce a question asking prospective jurors if they are members of the National Rifle Association, or some other query may occasionally intrude. One of the questions asked of members of the circuit court jury pool drawn on for Lisa's trial was whether they would be troubled by viewing photographs showing a dead body or blood. But there were no long, drawn-out debates over sun signs or pop psychological claptrap and efforts to probe individual quirks in an attempt to predict if the prospects would be more symathetic to the defense or prosecution. The object of the voir dire is clearly and simply aimed at weeding out anyone with obvious biases that might affect their judgment of the defendant or of the case. Jury selection for a murder case in the Prince Georges County circuit court is typically completed in two or three hours.

Lisa's trial was typical. A twelve-member jury of eight women and four men with a male and a female alternate was selected in less than three hours. Judge Salmon and the attorneys settled on the panel before noon of the opening day. Juror Linda Thompson was designated the forelady.

Then the judge advised the jury not to discuss the case among themselves or with anyone else, and dismissed them for the lunch break. The jury and court officers were advised to return at one-thirty P.M. for presentation of opening statements.

When the prosecutor left the courtroom for lunch, she believed in her case but she wasn't overconfident. She knew she was up against a formidable opponent, and almost nothing in a murder trial can be taken for granted. She realized any victory that was won by either side would have to be earned after a hard fight.

Gwinn was uneasy about the jury's reaction to Lisa's injury, even though she was firmly convinced the gunshot wound was self-inflicted. But she worried about her chances of convincing a jury that the petite young woman on trial for murder could coldly and deliberately send a bullet smashing into her own arm.

The jurors were average men and women who weren't daily witnesses to the casual violence of the streets and were unlikely to accept such a painful and grisly act as matter-of-factly as veteran professionals within the criminal justice system, who had seen and heard it all.

Gwinn quietly confided to some of her colleagues that she would be pleased to get a conviction for manslaughter. A conviction for second-degree murder would make her ecstatic, and a first-degree murder verdict would be a crowning achievement—a tour de force.

Chapter Nine

The Trial

It was a hot and muggy early afternoon outside, good tobacco-growing weather, when the Assistant State's Attorney began her opening presentation to the jury.

Reporters from the *Journal* in Hyattsville, the *Washington Times,* the *Washington Post,* and the *London Daily Mail* were seated among a sprinkling of observers in the spectator's section of the courtroom, but there was no massive stampede by the press to cover the trial. Much of the world's media attention was on Spain, where the summer Olympics were under way in Barcelona.

Some area television stations would deal with the proceedings in the Upper Marlboro courtroom by devoting a minute or two of their evening newscasts to remarks gleaned from wire services; others would ignore it altogether.

But no one inside the courtroom ignored the lead prosecutor as she faced the jury and began her story of a star-crossed romance, of deception, betrayal, and a murder motivated by revenge.

"That's what this case is about: revenge! Lisa Rohn killed Roger Paulson three days after she got out of jail because Roger Paulson was instrumental in putting her there," Gwinn declared.

Describing the defendant as a woman whose life was a sham, she traced Lisa and Roger's meeting through the personals ad in the *Washingtonian;* their developing romance and cohabitation; the discovery of the false identification documents; and Lisa's arrest, conviction, and jailing.

The prosecutor told the rapt panel about Roger's continued devotion to Lisa; of his letters, the long telephone conversations, and the regular visits with her in jail, even though it was he who had turned her over to police.

"He was ready to forgive and forget, but there came a point in time when Roger had to get on with his own life. He took up with a new woman by the name of Cheryl New, and Cheryl and Roger maintained, or eventually got into, an intimate relationship," she continued.

Gwinn's style in the courtroom depends on the situation. She can be methodical and logical, or she can be emotional when the circumstances call for it. But she doesn't try to fool the jury, and if there are problems with a case, she gets it out up front and levels with the panel. But she didn't believe there were any weaknesses in her case against Lisa that had to be brought out up front. And there were no *Perry Mason* histrionics. The prosecutor's delivery was matter-of-fact, a bluntly grim recitation of murder and revenge. Roger turned Lisa in to the police, and she shot him to get even. It was as simple as that.

Gwinn told about how Lisa was released from jail and showed up ringing the apartment doorbell at midnight. Although Roger didn't want to let her inside, ultimately he gave in and sent his ten-year-old son back to the bedroom.

"What the hell are you doing here," or words to that effect, was the only thing Christopher remembered his father saying to the surprise visitor, the prosecutor said. "Christopher will tell you when he woke up the next day, Lisa was still there, and his father was not happy about it. He was uncomfortable about it."

The jury and the sprinkle of news reporters and other observers now knew that one of the witnesses they would listen to would be the schoolboy son of the victim. But the big question about whether the defendant would testify was still to be answered.

One of the women jurors peered past the lanky form of the prosecutor to look at Lisa. Wearing glasses, and with her hair just below her shoulders, Lisa was modestly dressed and sitting quietly and without obvious emotion between her attorneys. One elbow was propped on the top of the defense table and her chin rested pensively between the crooked thumb and forefinger of her hand. Only she and her lawyers knew if she would take the witness stand in her own defense.

Gwinn, meanwhile, was continuing her narration of the events leading up to the shooting. She told about the telephone calls to Roger at his office, which he didn't want to take; of the bags and suitcases dumped outside of the apartment; of the rescheduled appointment to meet, which he missed; and of Roger's call to Cheryl as he was driving home following the pizza dinner with his boss.

"Roger is expecting he's going to go home. Everything, all the bags will be gone. Lisa will be out of his life," she recounted. "And he goes home and gets murdered!"

The prosecutor allowed the flat, blunt declaration to

hang for a moment in the courtroom and sink into the consciousness of the jury. Jurors subconsciously swung their gaze from Gwinn to Lisa, as if to confirm for themselves the prosecutor was really talking about the attractive, composed young woman seated a few feet away. Lisa didn't look like a killer was expected to look. She looked like someone's daughter, sister, wife—or mother.

Gwinn moved on to the gunshot wound in Lisa's arm. It was "a flesh wound, a contact wound, and went from this part of the arm right out the other part of the arm," she said, capturing the fleshy portion of her own arm near the bicep between a finger and thumb to demonstrate.

"And I'm going to ask you during the course of this trial to keep your mind open as to whether or not that was a self-inflicted gunshot wound." It was obvious to everyone who the Assistant State's Attorney thought fired the shot.

Then Gwinn moved to the series of gunshots heard by neighbors the night Roger died. She expected testimony from a prosecution witness about the sequence of shots to provide some of the most compelling evidence of her case. According to the story Lisa told Beverly, she was shot first, and Roger was struck when the gun discharged several times during the ensuing struggle. The testimony of Gwinn's witness would trace a glaringly different succession of gunshots.

"There were several shots, there was a pause, there were several more shots. There was a long pause, and there was one final shot," Gwinn declared. Roger was struck three times, she pointed out.

The prosecutor's inference would be obvious to the jury, especially after it was backed up by detailed testimony from the witness. If the shooting began with a rapid series of gunshots spaced closely together, those must have been the bullets fired at or into Roger's body. The single shot fired after a pause would have accounted for the bullet that tore through Lisa's arm. She shot him before shooting herself!

But Gwinn wasn't yet through talking about the shooting. "She gave a statement to the police where she says Roger Paulson, who was a man of approximately five-eleven, two-hundred-thirty pounds, she says came home and got the gun and pointed it at her," the prosecutor declared. "And she, the petite little thing here you see before us today," Gwinn continued with a sweep of her arm in the defendant's direction, "was able to wrestle the gun away from him, she says. But not before he shot her!

"She was—she says in her statement—she was able to wrestle it away from him; that he came toward her and she shot him three times."

Lisa didn't change expression, but appeared to hunch her shoulders slightly, making her look even smaller as the Assistant State's Attorney drew the jury's attention to the startling contrast in size between the two people who were together in the apartment the night Roger died. He had weighed almost twice as much as Lisa.

The prosecutor had drawn a graphic image for the jury of a desperate David and Goliath struggle that hardly seemed credible. But she didn't mean for it to be, because it was the defendant's story. It would have taken an amazingly scrappy and lucky woman to turn the tables on such a huge man who was armed with a gun, especially after she was already shot in the arm. Gwinn wanted the jury to think about that.

She asked the jurors to keep open minds about the sequence of shots and whether the defendant's wound was self-inflicted. She said she would ask them to consider whether, "in the back of her mind, or in the front of her mind, she had not planned there to get revenge on the person who sent her to jail; to get the ultimate revenge of death for Roger Paulson."

Gwinn had delivered a strong presentation that set the tone for her case in clear and concise terms. But Trainor was primed and ready with his own opening statement to counter any early points she may have scored.

A skilled craftsman in the courtroom, the defense attorney was methodical and systematic as he began his presentation. He cautioned the jury to carefully weigh all the evidence before reaching conclusions. Then he swiftly moved to his client's background.

Lisa's past, if judged against almost any normal community standards, was unsavory and shockingly wanton. Her life story was a sad litany of exploitation and lawlessness that ranged from the childhood abuse of growing up in an unstable, violent home, to the reputed criminal acts and deceit that marked many of her adult activities.

Rules of law and judicial decisions by Judge Salmon would severely restrict testimony about her past, including her missteps in California. But enough information would be allowed into evidence to smother any possible illusions that the defendant was an angel.

Trainor, as almost any other good defense attorney would do, had decided to expose some of his client's troubles with the law. It was better to confront the panel of homemakers, salesmen, government workers, and retirees immediately with some of her blemishes than to let it come out later, and when it would look as if he'd been trying to cover it up.

"We're going to tell you some things about Lisa Rohn's past that jurors rarely hear," he promised.

"You're going to hear, and you already have heard, she went to jail."

The lawyer recalled the dates of her arrest and of her trial in Baltimore. He said Roger was subpoenaed and testified for the government, and that she was convicted and served a jail sentence.

"We don't usually tell jurors about what happened in someone's past like this because of the fear that they won't use it fairly, that the defendant won't get a fair trial because of that information," he said. "But you're being trusted with that information in this case, and I know Judge Salmon will give you some instruction on that."

Trainor didn't mention his pretrial efforts to block admission of the information about the federal trial and conviction as evidence. Instead he reminded the jurors that the case wasn't about events that occurred in April 1991, or five years before that time.

"It's what happened November 19, 1991, between the hours of approximately 7:48 P.M. and about 7:56 P.M., a period of roughly eight minutes. It happened at 11346 Evans Trail, Apartment 102, in Beltsville, Maryland.

"So I ask that you really focus in on that critical time period at that location," he declared. "The seven or eight minutes in November 1991 are what this case is all about."

Trainor briefly traced the meeting of Lisa and Roger beginning with the placing of the ad in the personal columns of the *Washingtonian,* and her response while using a false name.

"You will see that they developed a relationship that was apparently happy, apparently in love," he said. "In fact, they made marriage plans. But those plans were derailed in April of 1991. April 24, 1991, Lisa Rohn was arrested." Once more the lawyer moved through the arrest and jailing, of her transfer to the Kent County Detention Center, and of Roger's continued romantic devotion. Then he turned to Roger's suspicions and jealousy.

"He was accusatory that she was seeing other people at times during their relationship. He told her about that. He had some reservations, as anyone naturally would, about why she had used the false names that you're going to hear about," Trainor said.

"But he was jealous. He forgave her for what he saw as infidelity, but he let her know that he just couldn't tolerate it anymore."

Jurors were listening intently, their eyes on the defense attorney as he moved on to Lisa's release from jail in Arlington. "There's nothing that would tell her: Lisa, you're no longer welcome at your home. You can't come here!

"So she's released from jail. Where does she go?" Trainor asked. Then he answered his own question: "She goes home! She got there and Roger's not there. . . . Roger's not there because he's out on a date with Cheryl New." Trainor moved through Lisa's surprise midnight appearance at the front door, and the next day when Roger begged off an early trip to the park so he could telephone Cheryl and break their date to watch the Redskins play.

"Now, Lisa didn't know any of this. She didn't know who Cheryl New was, never heard of her until after this case was already under way. Roger never told her."

A woman juror narrowed her eyes and frowned as the lawyer talked of Roger's deceit. Now it was Roger who was living the lie, and pulling the wool over Lisa's eyes. Trainor continued to trace the carpet estimator's perfidy through the next day, and moved to Lisa's growing anxiety over the broken dinner date. After six or seven months in jail, she was anxious for a night out. Trainor said Roger didn't come home because he stayed at work with Cheryl to make up for the broken date to watch the football game.

Trainor carried his story on through Lisa's meeting with the iron worker in the restaurant, to Roger's sudden appearance at the front door of the Ramada Inn; the private talk between the couple outside; and Roger's storming away.

"You'll see that Lisa didn't go home that night. She spent the night at the Ramada Inn," the lawyer said. In his encapsulated version it wasn't stressed that she spent the night with her new companion, she merely spent the night at the motel. Earlier in his presentation, however, Trainor was careful to point out that after Lisa's surprise midnight appearance at the apartment, "She spent Saturday night in Roger's bed."

The defense attorney turned to the note Lisa found stuck to the door the next morning, and promised the jury they would get to examine it for themselves. Meanwhile, however, he paraphrased the message for them.

"It says, 'If you try to come in here, I will shoot you.' And 'shoot' is underlined!"

Trainor told about Roger greeting Lisa with the barrel of a gun, but finally letting her inside to get her things. He told about her errands later that day, and of Lisa returning to the apartment where she saw her bags and belongings on the walkway. "It appears . . . he may have moved things out, back and forth a couple times during the day," the lawyer said.

Then he moved on to Lisa's going inside the apartment to organize her belongings once more, of Roger's belated return home and of the final face-off with Lisa. At that point the lawyer's account heated up. The words tumbled rapidly from his mouth.

"So he gets there. There is an argument. There is a fast-moving, hot-blooded confrontation between the two of them. During this time both of them sustained gunshot wounds. You'll see her gunshot wound and photographs of it. Roger sustained three gunshot wounds."

Trainor told the jury that evidence would show Roger pulled one of his guns, as he had threatened. "The gun went off, injured Lisa. You'll see she got control of it, that she fired it, that she fired it in self-defense and that the gunshots she fired actually killed Roger Paulson in self-defense."

Although Trainor continued, providing additional details to fill in more of the chronology, his graphic description of the violent quarrel and the shooting had made his strategy clear. Roger was driven into a homicidal fury by jealousy, attacked Lisa with a gun, and was shot to death during her desperate struggle to survive.

The lawyer talked on about the statement Lisa gave to Detective Beverly, then concluded his opening presentation after cautioning the jury to do their best to fairly and honestly evaluate the evidence.

The prosecution called Officer Tyler as its first witness, then followed with Officer Riedl. Gwinn's colleague conducted the direct examination of the two policemen, using their testimony to establish the scene of the crime and the events that occurred immediately after the arrival of paramedics and police.

The young Assistant State's Attorney was cool and confident while she led the two county policemen through their testimony. There was no hint of nervousness or other glitches in her behavior that might indicate to the jury or court officers that she was prosecuting her first homicide case.

Riedl provided an intriguing glimpse into training and

behavior of police rank and file when Woodall asked if he had received training related to the securing of and preservation of crime scenes. He said he had. She asked what exactly he learned.

"Largely, as a beat officer and not a detective or technician, to leave things alone," he replied.

"Did this occur in this case?" she asked.

"Yes, ma'am."

During cross-examination, Trainor grilled the witness about the technique used to enter and secure the apartment, and the position of Roger's body on the floor. He paid particular attention to the position of Roger's arms and the handcuffs. But Riedl was unable to say for certain who removed the cuffs. When Trainor asked if he took them off, the policeman replied, "I don't think so. I think a homicide detective did."

"It would be routine?" The lawyer posed the remark as a question.

"My thinking, if I were to make that judgment now, that's what I'd do," Riedl responded.

"You're not real sure about who removed the handcuffs?"

"No, I'm not," the witness replied. The question of who removed the handcuffs was never resolved during the trial.

During redirect examination, Woodall quickly moved on to another mystery closely tied to the position of Roger's hands when the body was first observed by police. She asked where Roger's right hand was in relation to the garment bag.

Riedl said Roger was facedown with the fingers of his right hand hooked around the neck of the clothes hanger extending from the garment bag.

"So they were actually touching the garment bag?" she asked.

"Yes, ma'am," the policeman replied. "I had to separate them from the bag to handcuff them."

Trainor had one more chance at Riedl on re-cross-examination. He asked if it was true that the garment bag was under Roger. The witness confirmed that was correct.

"Under the upper part of the body?" Trainor asked.

"Yes, as though he had rolled on it and fallen." Riedl had made an assumption, and volunteered more information than he was asked for. Trainor pounced on the misstep.

"That's your conjecture, is it not?" he asked. Riedl conceded that the statement indicating Roger may have rolled onto the bag was speculation. Moments later Trainor advised the court he was through with the witness. The police officer was excused, and Judge Salmon called a brief recess.

There was good justification for the persistence of attorneys for both sides to pin Riedl down over the exact position of Roger's arms and the garment bag. Viewed in the light of Lisa's claim that he pulled the gun on her, the debate promised to raise interesting mental images about his ability to juggle the cumbersome garment bag and the weapon at the same time.

The attorneys weren't through probing the conundrum. They would return to the matter repeatedly during the proceeding.

Leonard Paulson was called as the first witness after the trial was resumed. Roger's father was courteous and direct as a witness, but the disciplined military bearing acquired after thirty years in the Navy didn't mask the emotional impact the devastating loss of his youngest son had inflicted on him.

Questioning by Gwinn quickly turned to the period when the overlooked shell casings were found as

Roger's friends were tearing out the ruined carpeting. At Gwinn's direction, Paulson stepped down from the witness stand, walked up to an easel and designated on a large drawing of the interior of the apartment exactly where the two empty .22 caliber shell casings were found. He also pointed out the location of the stand near the entrance where the car keys were left.

When Paulson returned to his seat on the witness stand, Gwinn asked if his son was right- or left-handed. Right-handed, the witness replied. The prosecutor didn't further pursue the matter of Roger's dominant hand at that time, but the significance was obvious.

Matters had turned back to the position of Roger's hands when his body was found, and just exactly what he was doing with them when he and Lisa confronted each other in the bedroom. Even if he held the gun in his left hand, the question was raised about why he hadn't set the garment bag aside and grasped the weapon with his dominant hand.

Gwinn asked the witness if he was ever introduced to a new woman who appeared in Roger's life about October 1990. When he replied he had been and that she was in the courtroom, the prosecutor asked him to point her out.

The witness pointed to the defense table and said she was sitting there. "Which woman?" Gwinn asked.

"The one with the glasses and the right—the one in the middle, I guess," he replied. Lisa's expression didn't change as Roger's father pointed her out, and the jurors turned their eyes to peer at her. Her quiet appearance didn't fit the typical image of a dangerous *femme fatale* who had taken her lover's life. She looked about as bland as vanilla pudding.

"By what name were you introduced to her?" Gwinn asked.

"She was introduced to us as Johnnie Elaine Miller."

During cross-examination, Trainor asked the witness if he was present in the apartment Saturday morning when the previously overlooked shell casings were found. Paulson said he was there.

"So you actually saw—"

The witness cut the attorney off before he finished the question. "Yes!" Paulson replied.

"It was clear—they weren't hidden under anything, were they?" Trainor asked.

"They, ironically, were under the edge of the carpet along the wall, where they weren't out in the open. When they pulled the carpet up is when they were exposed," Paulson said. He confirmed that he could see them clearly.

The witness said that although he and his wife hadn't originally gone to the apartment to clean it, they wound up doing the job because it was in such a mess.

Trainor asked if they found several firearms, ammunition, and clips while they were gathering up Roger's belongings. Paulson said they did. But he demurred when the lawyer asked if he found silencers. There were no silencers, he said.

"Noise suppressors?" Trainor continued.

"Ear muffs for shooting, yes!"

"So there were assault rifles?" Trainor asked.

"One of them!"

"SAR-48 assault rifle?"

The witness agreed there was an SAR-48. In response to another question, he also agreed there were a couple of other rifles.

"With clips that—for rapid fire?" Trainor inquired.

"I don't know how the rapid fire is," Paulson replied. "But there were clips."

The witness also confirmed that his son was never in

the military or in Vietnam. Judge Salmon interjected a statement of his own at that point. The jurist posed it in question form.

"Too young for Vietnam, wasn't he?"

"Probably. I'm not sure when the last went in, so I don't know," Paulson replied.

"Nineteen seventy-three was the last," the judge advised.

"No!" the witness said.

The peace treaty between the United States and North Vietnam was signed and the end of the military draft was announced on the same day, January 27, 1973. That was almost exactly two months after Roger's nineteenth birthday, after he had dropped out of community college, and nearly a year before he was married. Roger had been the same age as many other young men who were drafted or enlisted in the military service.

A little harmless lying about a military career may not have been such a terrible thing to do, but the information was enough to show that Roger wasn't without blemishes. The jury had learned that Lisa wasn't the only member of the ill-fated relationship who misrepresented herself. Roger told some tall tales of his own.

With that accomplishment under his belt, Trainor began questioning the witness about the garment bag. Paulson said he believed it was lying across the dining room table when he first saw it inside the apartment.

"Did you notice whether there was ever bloodstains on it?" the lawyer asked.

"I didn't pay particular attention to it. There was a piece cut out of it, I noticed," Paulson said. He estimated that a swatch about a foot or a bit less was missing from the bag.

"Did you notice whether there was a bullet hole in it?"

"I didn't pay any attention," Paulson replied.

Gwinn asked only two questions on redirect examination: Was Roger a gun collector? And did he sometimes practice on a target range? Roger had several guns, including a couple of very old ones, the witness said. And he frequently fired some of his guns on a practice range.

Mrs. Paulson followed her husband to the witness stand and repeated much of the same information he had provided. She said she previously met the defendant, and was told at that time her name was Elaine Miller. Trainor had no cross-examination, and Roger's mother was excused as a witness less than fifteen minutes after she was sworn in.

Woodall resumed the questioning when the prosecution turned again to testimony dealing with the murder probe. William T. Whigham, an investigator with the State's Attorney's Office for Prince Georges County testified he took handwriting samples from the defendant and that she was right-handed.

Gwinn took over the questioning when Taylor was called as the next witness. He described the crime scene as it appeared when he first entered Apartment 102 a few hours after the shootings. He also told about recovering a note from the pocket of a woman's brown tweed overcoat that was lying on the dining room table, and others from the pockets of Lisa's red jacket.

Asked to read aloud from one of the notes the prosecutor handed to him, he replied: "The writing is, it says, 'Number one, call Dolores Wednesday, with a phone number . . .'" He repeated a telephone number in the 708 area of suburban Chicago which hugs the edges of the city on the shores of Lake Michigan in a lazy crescent. Huberts's sister, Dolores, lived in the Chicago suburbs.

Taylor continued trying to make out the faded words.

"Then the next line has a number two circled, and call . . ." The words trailed off. The evidence technician appeared to be straining to read the barely legible message on the crinkled note paper.

The Assistant State's Attorney waited patiently while the witness squinted at the paper, then started over again. "I'm not sure what this is. 'Janelle,' I guess, or something of that effect. 'Wolfe, Thursday,' and it says 'lawyer Arlington, Virginia.' " Taylor added that the numerals 14 were written in parenthesis under the word "Thursday."

Gwinn showed him another note and asked him to read it. The writing on the second note was also difficult for the witness to make out. The notes were nearly a year old, and they had been crumpled up and stuck inside coat pockets.

Taylor managed, nevertheless, to identify the words, "Number ten," and "Vault Storage," and a telephone number with the area code 703 in parenthesis. He was unsure about the rest of the message, which appeared to be a partial address. But he said he thought it read, "Duke Street near King."

The prosecutor handed him another note. It was short and easy to make out. This time the evidence had only four words and a number to decipher.

"Ramada Inn. Brian. Rm. 517."

Gwinn skipped the next note, marked as State's Exhibit 12, and handed the witness State's Exhibit 13. All four of those notes were taken from pockets in the red jacket; the other note was inside the tweed overcoat.

"And so, State's Exhibit Thirteen says what?" she asked.

The writing was neat, still easily legible, and Taylor didn't have any trouble making out the message.

"State's Exhibit Thirteen says, 'Be here tomorrow at

two P.M. to pick up your stuff. Bring some help, since I'm not moving it for you. Leave your key under the mat. If you try to enter I'll shoot you. If you aren't here by two-thirty it goes in the Dumpster."

The note found in the overcoat was the last to be read, and the witness once more had difficulties making out some of the words. Taylor stumbled slowly from one barely legible word or phrase to another. A couple of times he was helped with prompting from the prosecutor, who provided a word and asked if that could be correct.

Pieced together, it was the message Lisa had found on the door of Roger's apartment advising that it would be "unwise" to show her face around him again.

Taylor said the notes were in substantially the same condition they were in when they were first discovered in the coat pockets. The court admitted them as evidence.

Then Gwinn turned her attention to the seven .22 caliber shell casings collected from Roger's bedroom, and to the .22 caliber target pistol. The witness pinpointed the location where each of the casings and the pistol were recovered.

One of the bullets found in the bedroom, and another, which was recovered from Roger's body during the autopsy, were entered into evidence. Most of the bullets were so badly fragmented they were not brought into court.

As Taylor continued his testimony, he identified blood scrapings from the kitchen, and described the condition of the apartment and the position of Roger's body and the garment bag on the floor of the bedroom. Gwinn used photographs at times as she led him through the testimony, and at one point asked him about something that could be seen around Roger's neck in one of the pictures. Taylor said it was a strap from the garment bag.

The evidence technician testified about blood trails, blood spatters on the walls, bullets, photographs, boxes and luggage piled near Roger's bed, the location of injuries that were directly noticeable, and the direction and angles taken by bullets that struck the body and other objects in the room.

When it was Trainor's turn to cross-examine the witness, he turned quickly to the search of the apartment for blood. He asked the witness if he cut the swatch of cloth from the garment bag. Taylor said someone else took the sample. He agreed, however, that there was blood on it.

"And there was perhaps a bullet hole in it?" Trainor continued.

"No, sir, I wasn't aware of that," the policeman replied.

Trainor asked if the piece of the garment was sent to the FBI for analysis, and Taylor said he thought it had been. "Do you know that?" the lawyer persisted.

The witness wasn't sure. After reviewing his records, he testified that it wasn't sent to the FBI laboratories after all. Trainor asked if a piece of bloodstained carpeting cut out from the bedroom carpet and bloodstains on the bathroom wall were sent to the FBI laboratories for analysis. Taylor said they were not

The cross-examination continued, touching on the bloodstained kitchen floor, the dangling telephone, bullets and bullet fragments. Taylor conceded in response to questions, that some of the bullets found in the master bedroom were so badly fragmented he couldn't tell exactly how many there were.

During the testimony, Trainor managed to read into the record once more the words to the note Roger wrote threatening to shoot Lisa if she tried to get into the apartment. It could only help the defense case to reinforce the depiction of Roger as an unstable, dangerous man.

The attorneys clashed during redirect examination when Gwinn attempted to have a photograph of Roger after police had moved his body accepted into evidence and Trainor objected. The judge summoned the attorneys to the bench for a conference. Lisa joined her lawyer and stood silently by while Trainor argued that the picture showed blood all over Roger's face and complained that the prejudicial impact to the jury would outweigh any value as evidence. He said he wouldn't object if some of the blood was cropped out before the picture was shown to the jury. It appeared the prosecutor wished to use the photograph to demonstrate the relationship of the blood in the room to the victim.

"Right, plus that's after he's been moved," Gwinn agreed. Trainor insisted it wasn't necessary to show the body in the picture.

Gwinn pointed out the jurors were questioned during the selection process about viewing photographs showing a body or blood, and they indicated they wouldn't have a problem with that.

"I have a problem with it," Trainor shot back.

Before Gwinn could reply, Judge Salmon added an observation that seemed to favor the prosecutor. "In this day of all the violence on TV and everything, I would think it's not really prejudicial to your client or anybody else," he said. "It's a sad picture, but nothing that turns your stomach."

Trainor responded by suggesting again that the portion of the photograph showing the body be removed before submitting the remainder to the jury as evidence. "If the relevant portion is the bloodstain, the irrelevant portion is the body after it has been moved," he argued. Gwinn stubbornly insisted the entire picture was relevant.

Judge Salmon ended the conference by ruling in favor of the prosecutor. He admitted the picture as evidence, over defense objections. A few minutes later, after a couple more questions from the prosecutor, Detective Taylor was at last excused as a witness. It was exactly five P.M. when Judge Salmon recessed the trial for the day after advising the jury to avoid listening to or watching news stories or talking to anyone about the case.

Roger's son, Christopher, was the first witness when the trial was resumed the next day. Lisa wore a neat, black suit for the second day of the proceeding. Outside, dark clouds were gathering as a late summer storm rumbled into the area.

But the boy didn't begin his testimony until after the lawyers tangled in another bench conference, this time over whether his mother would be allowed inside the courtroom while he was on the witness stand. Gwinn wanted his mother in the courtroom while Christopher testified. But the woman, who had remarried, to John L. Pickell, had been subpoened by Trainor as a possible defense witness, and under normal circumstances would have been barred from the courtroom prior to her own testimony.

Gwinn asked for the court to make an exception and waive the rule on witnesses, to allow Mrs. Pickell into the courtroom with her son because of the boy's age. "I have a problem with that, with a child witness," the prosecutor declared. "It's important for the parent to be able to be in the courtroom." It was three days before Christopher's eleventh birthday.

Trainor responded that the rule is mandatory. It couldn't be waived. But he offered to try to work out an agreement with the prosecution stipulating certain testimony from Mrs. Pickell. Presumably, if the agreement was reached, she would not have to testify on the witness stand and could remain in the courtroom during Christopher's testimony. Judge Salmon asked the lawyer what she was expected to testify to.

Trainor said he talked with her on the Friday before the trial started, after she contacted Gwinn and was referred to him. They talked about Ruth Ann's marriage to Roger, their separation and divorce, he said.

The lawyer said she told him Roger kept some old guns in the house during the marriage, but didn't begin shooting as a hobby until after their separation. Trainor quoted her as saying she learned Christopher was target shooting with his father after she found a photograph of the boy wearing noise mufflers on his ears. She also told him that Roger was never in the Army, didn't graduate from college, and had checked himself into a psychiatric hospital shortly before their divorce. Judge Salmon asked if hearing her son's testimony could be expected to help her shape her own testimony in any way.

"Sure! I mean, you know, I don't know what her son is going to testify to first of all," Trainor responded.

"Of course you do! You interviewed him," Gwinn shot back.

"I interviewed him," Trainor agreed. "But I don't know what he's going to testify to."

The debate flared on as the lawyers quarreled over what Christopher and his mother might testify about, and what potential testimony would be permitted. At last, Judge Salmon decided to call Christopher and his mother into his chambers for a private discussion of the matter with them.

The jurist was caught between his concern for protecting the boy's emotional well-being and following rules of law and evidence. The question of allowing Christopher's mother into the courtroom during his testimony, or barring her, was just the type of conundrum that could lead to troubles with an appeal if he made a legal miscue.

Exactly five minutes after the mini-conference began in Judge Salmon's chambers, he advised the lawyers that Mrs. Pickell had suggested being called out of turn. If she testified before Christopher, she could be in the courtroom when he was summoned to the witness stand.

Judge Salmon explained that he told the woman she could sit in a small anteroom just outside the courtroom while her son testified. He also told Christopher that if he was testifying and he "wanted emotional comfort or anything like that," all he had to do was to let the judge know. Christopher had said he didn't think he was too nervous.

Trainor asked if the boy felt he could testify without his mother present. Judge Salmon said he did, but that she preferred he wouldn't even have to be a witness. Christopher's mother had pointed out that the boy had "a normal adverse response" mentally to his father's death, the judge said. He asked the defense attorney if he was against calling her as a witness out of turn.

Gwinn was agreeable to calling Mrs. Pickell first, but Trainor didn't like the proposal. It was a matter of strategy.

Judge Salmon appeared to have little choice. He advised that they would go ahead with Christopher's testimony, but if the boy got upset, he could take a break anytime he needed or asked for it.

After all the fuss and concern, Christopher performed like a trooper on the stand. Gwinn conducted the direct examination and rapidly moved the boy through the details of his background. He said he was a

sixth grade student at Fields Road Elementary School in
Gaithersburg, and lived with his mother and stepfather.
He confirmed that his parents were divorced and that
he had visited his father every other weekend after the
split-up.

When the prosecutor asked if he knew "the lady" sitting a few feet away in a black suit, Christopher said he
did. What name did he know the woman by? Gwinn
asked.

"Johnnie Elaine Miller," Christopher replied.

Continuing to respond with no major discernible discomfort to the prosecutor's questions, Christopher said
he first met the defendant sometime before the winter
of 1990. He couldn't remember the month.

"What was the relationship between your father and
her?" Gwinn asked.

"They loved each other!"

Gwinn moved the testimony through the time the defendant moved in with Roger, then to Lisa's sudden absence from the apartment. Christopher testified that
was in 1991, but when he was asked what month it was,
he became confused. March, he said at first. Then he
quickly corrected himself and said it was October.

He was closer to being correct with the first answer,
but the prosecutor passed it by. Other witnesses could
be used to establish the time Lisa was arrested and went
to jail, after Roger discovered the false IDs. Gwinn led
the boy through the vacation in Hawaii, Roger's change
of jobs, his meeting and dates with Cheryl New.

At last the prosecutor began questioning the boy
about the weekend before his father was killed, the Saturday outing with Mrs. New and her daughter, and
Lisa's late night appearance at the apartment. Responding to a question about his father's attitude Sunday
morning, Christopher said he wasn't very happy.

Continuing to move the testimony forward, the prosecutor asked Christopher if his father owned guns. Christopher said he had a semiautomatic pistol and a couple of rifles.

After giving the Ruger to a sheriff's deputy to inspect, to make sure it was unloaded, she handed it to Christopher and asked if he recognized it. "It's my dad's pistol," he replied.

Gwinn asked a few more questions about Roger's instructions to his son about gun safety and where the pistol was kept in the house, then turned the young witness over to the defense lawyer.

Trainor retraced much of the same territory covered by the prosecutor, and added a few questions about weekend telephone conversations Roger had with Lisa after she vanished from the apartment. Christopher answered "Uh-huh" when the lawyer asked if the conversations were long and friendly and conducted in pleasant tones.

When Trainor asked Christopher if his father told him Lisa was in jail, the boy shook his head no. When Trainor repeated the question, Christopher replied "Uh-uh," prompting a gentle instruction from the judge to respond with yes or no.

Trainor asked the boy if the gun he had just inspected was the only one he was taught to shoot. "No," Christopher replied.

"Did he have a machine gun or an assault rifle?" the lawyer inquired.

"Yes!" Christopher said.

"With a big clip in it that would hold a lot of shells?" the lawyer continued.

Christopher forgot the judge's instructions of a few moments before. He nodded his head up and down. But he quickly moved back on track, uttering a soft "Yes" to

Trainor's follow-up question asking if Roger had other rifles as well. Christopher said his father allowed him to shoot one of them.

Responding to continued questions about where the weapons the lawyer referred to as "assault rifles and machine guns were stored," Christopher indicated some were kept in a corner of the bedroom closet or under the bed.

Trainor's questions returned to the pistol. Christopher indicated it was stored unloaded, but that his father had taught him how to load it. The handgun held twelve bullets, he testified.

Christopher also testified that sometimes when he and his father were at the shooting range, he picked up shell casings and took them back to the apartment. He indicated he also sometimes took the shells to his mother's home and showed them to her.

The lawyer concluded cross-examination after asking a few questions about the final weekend of Roger's life and Lisa's reappearance at the apartment.

Gwinn's redirect examination of the young witness was brief. She revisited the boy's earlier testimony about collecting empty shell casings at the shooting range from the .22 pistol and from other guns. She asked Christopher where in his father's house he left the casings, and the boy replied that he probably left them in his father's bedroom closet. "He kept some of the shells in his ammunition case," Christopher said.

Trainor's re-cross-examination of the boy lasted about one minute. He asked Christopher if he could remember exactly where he left the casings after bringing them back to the apartment from the shooting range.

The boy said he usually gave them to his father, who put them someplace.

Christopher was excused as a witness and left the

courthouse with his mother a few minutes later. Mrs. Pickell was never called to testify.

Roger's former boss, Dempsey, followed the boy to the witness stand and during brief testimony recounted what he knew of his late employee's last night.

Corey A. Williams, an eighteen-year-old student at High Point High School and a resident of a basement apartment at 11346 Evans trail, was the next to testify. Williams told of leaving his apartment at about seven-thirty Tuesday morning, November 19, and noticing a pile of luggage stacked against the wall. He said he stepped over a little yellow bag and went on to school. He didn't know if the luggage was still there when he returned in the middle of the afternoon because he used a different entrance.

Cheryl was the first witness of the afternoon. A pleasant-appearing woman who was soft-spoken on the stand, she began by briefly tracing her professional background and her meeting and friendship with Roger. She said after they began to date, he sometimes stayed overnight at her apartment, and carried the garment bag with shaving equipment and a change of clothes with him.

She also retraced their Saturday outing with the children, and told of Roger's telephone call Sunday morning breaking their date to watch the football game on television. She betrayed her apparent nervousness once when Gwinn asked how long she had stayed at Contract Distributors. The witness said she left the company in December 1991.

"No, I mean that night," the prosecutor said, referring to the stopover at the company offices following dinner in Chinatown. "Probably after midnight," Cheryl amended.

The witness also told of taking a break to pick up her

daughter Monday evening, then working late in the office with Roger. She said she and Michelle left about ten-thirty P.M., and Roger also apparently went somewhere else at that time. He was already back in the office when she arrived on the job at about ten A.M. Tuesday.

Then she told about overhearing the temporary receptionist page Roger and inform him Lisa had called and said she couldn't make the early afternoon appointment and wanted to change it to six P.M. She recounted the meeting to sort out the differences over the carpeting job, before the questioning finally turned to her last conversation with Roger over his car phone.

Cheryl's testimony was interrupted at times with objections from Trainor, primarily concerning claims of violations of the hearsay rule which prohibits repeating the reputed statements of other people.

After several minutes of intense argument in a bench conference, the judge decided to allow the prosecutor to continue with questions about the telephone talk. When questioning resumed, Cheryl told about Roger's remarking that he would rather have spent the evening with her instead of working late and sharing a pizza with their boss.

Gwinn followed up by asking if Roger had a specific spot at the apartment complex where he usually parked. Cheryl said he always parked near the Dumpster. When the prosecutor asked how long it would take to park a car, get out, and walk to the apartment, Trainor again objected.

He said she shouldn't speculate for the jury how long it would take her to get out of the car and walk to the apartment.

"I would allow her to say how far is it from the Dumpster to the door," the judge suggested.

Gwinn responded that she could ask the witness how long it had taken her to make the walk from the car to the apartment on previous occasions. But Trainor still wasn't satisfied.

"She has little legs!" he said of Cheryl. "Why don't you ask her, has she ever seen Roger, ever timed him how long it took?" Picking up steam, he continued the verbal punch-out, asking: "Do you know that the car was parked there that night? You're having her speculate he parked in the certain parking space."

"Habit!" the prosecutor responded.

Judge Salmon stepped into the squabble and suggested the prosecutor simply ask the witness to estimate how far it is from the parking space to the doorway. Returning to the witness, Gwinn asked her about how far it was from the Dumpster to the doorway of the apartment.

"I'm terrible at that," Cheryl began. "Probably—"

Trainor cut her off with an objection. It appeared they were back to square one. But the judge interceded again.

"All right! Just give your best estimate. If you want to point out anything, etcetera. If you want to use car lengths or courtroom distances or anything like that you can do it," he advised.

"Maybe two and a half of these rooms, maybe," Cheryl suggested. The judge helped pin the estimate down a bit more exactly with a couple of questions that established she was referring to a span about equal to the distance from the witness stand to the back wall.

The verbal dustup was an example of one of those mini-exchanges in a courtroom that consumes time and sometimes taxes the patience of judge and jurors, but which can also often take on tremendous importance and set or alter the course of a trial. The way the contests were played out in Judge Salmon's Prince Georges County Circuit Court would have much to do with determining how and where Lisa was going to spend the next decade or two of her life.

Gwinn had one more question for Cheryl before concluding direct examination. She asked if Roger had called her again Tuesday night. Cheryl said he didn't.

Trainor continued to focus on Roger's telephone calls during the early stages of cross-examination, and got the witness to concede that she wasn't sure he was using the car phone when he broke his Sunday date with her to watch the Redskins. Cheryl said she heard interference on the line and thought it was a car phone.

Questioning moved on to the time she and Roger began dating. Cheryl estimated it was probably late September, a month or a bit more after Roger was hired at Contract Distributors.

A few moments later, Trainor turned again to the question of where Roger parked the night of his death. Cheryl said she didn't know where he parked, or if he had an assigned space set aside by apartment management. But she said he once told her he always tried to park next to the Dumpster. If someone already had that space, he parked directly across the driveway from it.

Cheryl said Roger never showed her his gun collection or talked about his weapons. When Trainor asked if he ever showed her the medals he won in Vietnam, the prosecutor objected. Trainor adjusted course and took another route to get the testimony in about Roger's deception. He asked the witness to describe Roger's office.

"His desk, many pictures of Christopher, artwork done by Christopher. The frame that contained some medals and ribbons that were I guess from his military career," Cheryl responded.

"So, a Silver Star and Purple Heart, that sort of thing?" Trainor asked.

"Uh-huh."

"From Roger's military career?"

"As far as I know," she said. "I assumed that. Yes."

With his last question to the witness, Trainor changed direction once more. "Now, did Roger ever tell you that Lisa was staying with him this weekend?" he asked.

Cheryl's reply was short and to the point. "No, he did not tell me she was," she said. The courtroom ordeal of Roger's former girlfriend was over at last. Cheryl looked straight ahead as she walked out of the courtroom, without turning to peer at the woman who was accused of his murder.

The prosecutor was counting on the next witness to provide testimony that could be among the most important and crucial of the entire trial. She planned to use Erik Astheimer, the GI stationed at Walter Reed Army Hospital, to repudiate Lisa's version of the sequence of gunshots.

During questioning by Gwinn, Astheimer told about being awakened at about eight P.M. by what he at first thought was a shotgun being fired but later confirmed was a pistol. He said he heard six or seven shots in rapid fire. Gwinn asked him to describe the sequence.

"It was like, 'pop-pop-pop—pop-pop,' " he testified. "Then there was silence for about, I don't know, thirty seconds or so, and then another 'pop.' "

"The final one by itself?" the prosecutor asked.

"Yeah!" the witness replied.

The Operation Desert Storm soldier's description of the gunshots was startling testimony, which had the potential of being extremely damaging to the defense. According to the story Lisa told police, Roger shot her, then during the ensuing struggle, the gun discharged several more times.

If Astheimer's version of the sequence of shots was correct, it could appear to the jury that Roger was shot first in a hail of gunfire. Then, after a wait of several seconds, Lisa fired the final shot through her own arm.

The prosecutor wanted to be sure the testimony was shown in the court record to back up that version. "Your Honor, I guess the record should reflect that he did three—"

Judge Salmon cut her off before she could finish the sentence, and suggested another bench conference to determine exactly what the record would reflect. "The jury heard it," he pointed out.

Trainor was on his feet and in fighting fettle. "It reflects what it reflects," he said.

"The problem is the record doesn't necessarily reflect the time period," Gwinn shot back.

But the judge had decided that the matter should be sorted out outside the hearing of the jury, and he called the two attorneys to the bench.

"The way I heard it was he went 'pop-pop-pop' in close succession. Then he said 'pop-pop.' There was a pause in those two in close succession, then he said it was thirty seconds and the final 'pop,' " the judge advised the lawyers. "But I don't want to be saying that in front of the jury, because they heard it."

Both attorneys appeared to be satisfied, and there was no further argument at that time. It had been one of the shortest bench conferences of the trial. Trainor returned to his seat at the defense table next to Lisa, and Gwinn returned to the witness to resume questioning.

Astheimer told about looking from the window, then opening his door and peering out into the hallway, where a woman was screaming, and of calling 911. Gwinn passed the witness to the defense counsel.

Trainor began cross-examination by reestablishing through the witness's testimony that he was sick and asleep when he was awakened by gunfire.

"Now, isn't it true that when you heard this shot, you heard an initial shot and you heard somebody, the sound of somebody being thrown against the wall?" the lawyer asked.

"Oh, yes!" Astheimer agreed. "That came, see, when I heard the first initial shot, my wife grabbed my arm like in a death grip. That's when I realized something was really wrong, and that this was shots being fired. And before the next repetition of shots, I did hear a thunk up against the wall."

"So you heard a shot and then the sound of, like somebody being thrown up against the wall?" Trainor persisted.

"Or just a thunk," the witness hedged.

"That's what you heard?"

"Yes," Astheimer agreed.

"And then you heard a succession of shots?"

"Uh-huh," the soldier agreed again.

"By that time you're out of bed, aren't you?" Trainor continued.

Astheimer said that wasn't correct. "I got out of bed after the, I guess the first six shots, whatever it was."

Undeterred, Trainor turned to the soldier's call to 911. "And you told them that you had just heard a humongous domestic dispute and that people were firing shotguns, didn't you? At first?" he asked.

Astheimer conceded he said at first he thought he heard shotgun fire.

"But that's what you told the police?"

"Right!"

Trainor bored in, poking for any inconsistencies he could find or open up in the witness's 911 call, later statements to police, and his current testimony.

"On the 911! So this idea that what you heard was a handgun is something that you've—"

"I've established that," Astheimer interrupted.

"Established since then?" Trainor asked.

"Right!"

"That was not your impression at the time you heard it?"

"It was my impression because it was so loud," the witness explained.

"But you told the police it was a shotgun?" Trainor asked again.

"Right!" the witness replied once more.

Trainor asked Astheimer if it was true that when he told police he heard a shot and the sound of someone being thrown against a wall, he wasn't sure if it was the apartment below him or the apartment next to him. Astheimer agreed that was true.

The lawyer asked if he was clear about peering into the hall and hearing a woman yelling, "Oh God, Oh God." Astheimer said he was.

"She was hysterical, wasn't she?" Trainor asked.

"Well, crying. Yeah, if you want to call it that. Yeah!" the witness replied. He said he didn't know the woman.

"Would you describe it as a terrifying cry?"

" 'Oh God. Oh God, what have I done,' cry," Astheimer said.

He agreed in response to another question that he gave a statement to police the night of the shooting. Then Trainor produced the statement. After having it marked as an exhibit for the defense, he passed it to Astheimer and asked him to read his own description to police of the cry he heard.

"It says, 'Oh, God, oh, oh.' "

"The next three words," Trainor directed.

"A terrifying cry," the soldier read.

"So it was, 'Oh God, oh, oh, a terrifying cry.' Correct?"

"Correct!"

Trainor moved to the earlier noises Astheimer told of hearing just after being awakened by gunshots. "When you heard the sound of someone being thrown against the wall after the first shot, you heard yelling, didn't you?" he asked.

"I heard kids. I didn't necessarily hear yelling," Astheimer replied. "It sounded like kids yelling and the parents yelling back at the kids." He said he didn't know what was being said. Trainor responded by once more producing the witness's statement to police, and directing him to read a question and answer on the second page.

" 'Did you hear any yelling prior to the shots? No. During the shots I heard yelling, but I don't know what was being said,' " Astheimer read back.

Trainor asked if that was what he told police, and if he had tried to be as accurate as he could be. Astheimer replied "Correct" to both questions.

"The only thing the woman said in the hallway that you heard was, 'Oh God,' Correct?" Trainor asked.

"Yes," the witness said. "She repeated that over and over."

"Those were the only words?"

"Yes."

At last, Trainor had finished with his grueling crossexamination of the Persian Gulf War veteran. But Astheimer wasn't yet permitted to leave the witness stand. The prosecutor had one more question for him on redirect examination. She asked how many shots he heard before hearing the thunk he had described.

"Two, three," Astheimer replied.

Gwinn advised the court she was through with the witness, and Trainor also passed. But Judge Salmon had a question of his own that he wanted cleared up. He asked Astheimer where his apartment was in relation to Roger's.

"It was right above the incident," the witness replied.

"He was right below you?"

"I was in the bedroom exactly above where it transpired, I guess," Astheimer replied.

Given another chance at re-cross-examination after the judge concluded, Trainor asked a few more questions. In response, Astheimer described his apartment as having two bedrooms and a den, agreed that he was in the back bedroom and that he and his wife were sleeping on the floor because their furniture hadn't arrived from Europe. He said he had a cold, but hadn't taken any medication for it.

In the front row of the jury box, one of the jurors drew in a big breath and exhaled what appeared to be an audible sigh of relief when the young soldier finally walked from the witness stand. He had undergone one of the sharpest, most exhausting interrogations of the trial. No one during the entire grueling examination had asked if he saw the woman from the hallway outside his apartment in the courtroom.

Lisa sat quietly at the defense table showing little animation or emotion throughout most of the testimony until a tape recording of her 911 call was played for the jury. Then tears ran down her cheeks and she wiped silently at her eyes. By midway of the second day of testimony, the prosecution's case was rapidly winding down.

Kenneth H. Whittler, an FBI agent and firearms examiner, was called to testify next, and he traced his training, experience, and other credentials before being accepted by the court as an expert witness in the field of firearms identification. His status as an expert witness in the case meant that he could offer opinions within his field of knowledge. Other witnesses could not.

The federal agent was handed the bullets and fragments found at the shooting scene and in Roger's body, to examine. Then he testified about the ballistics tests he conducted on them. At Gwinn's request, he included a mini-lecture on the nomenclature of cartridges to help the jury better understand the technical testimony. He explained that the cartridge is composed of the container or jacket, the brass portion that holds the powder or priming material. The cartridge also holds the bullet, the lead or copper projectile that is stuck at the front end of the casing.

Whittler was only a few minutes into his testimony when Judge Salmon interrupted to ask the bailiff for more lighting. Fat rain clouds had been forming outside since early morning, and a late summer thunderstorm was rapidly rolling into the area, casting a gray pall over the courtroom.

Moments later the lights were turned up and the federal agent continued his lesson with the Ruger, describing its operation and working components. Before handling the pistol to demonstrate its parts and operation, Whittler examined it to make sure it was unloaded, just as every other law enforcement officer who touched it in the courtroom did.

The federal agent explained to the jury how cartridges were moved into the chamber by the mechanism of the pistol, fired when the trigger was pulled, ejected the old casing and loaded a new round. He said that the trigger had to be depressed each time a bullet was fired. The Ruger was a semiautomatic, not an automatic, which can continue to fire bullets until the pressure is taken off the trigger. He said the Ruger held ten bullets in the magazine and another in the chamber.

Whittler, who had been an FBI-certified firearms examiner for eight months at the time of the trial, also testified about his examination of Lisa's red jacket. The jury was treated to another mini-lesson from the witness to help them understand technical testimony about such exotic matters as speckling of a target with lead fragments or vaporized lead, sophisticated chemical tests to show the presence of gunpowder, and muzzle-to-target distance.

Muzzle-to-target distance was the key to that portion of the firearm expert's testimony. The witness said he determined through visual observation and laboratory tests on the bullet hole in Lisa's jacket that the gun was touching the fabric or was less than an inch away when the shot was fired. The pistol, bullets, and fragments were all accepted as evidence.

Trainor's cross-examination was brief. He established that the witness didn't know if all the casings had been in the magazine at the same time, or what order the rounds were fired in.

"So you're not able to say from your examination whether all of these cartridges were in the magazine that you examined at the same time?" Trainor asked.

"No sir, I can't say they were in the magazine," the FBI man replied. "I can only say they were at one time in the pistol when they were fired and ejected." A few minutes later Whittler was excused as a witness.

Clelland, the evidence technician who took photographs of Lisa at the Greater Laurel-Beltsville Hospital, was the next to testify. Most of the drama occurred during cross-examination when Trainor began grilling the witness about the marks on Lisa's neck, which could be seen in some of the color photographs.

Trainor showed him one of the pictures and asked him to describe what he saw. Clelland said it was a photograph of someone's neck, with visible red areas or markings around it. Trainor showed him another photograph, and Clelland again identified red areas on someone's neck. Two more photographs were produced, also showing what appeared to be bruises or marks on Lisa's neck.

The defense lawyer seemed to have scored a strong point. The ugly red bruises in the photographs that were so plainly visible on his client seemed to indicate her neck was gripped and squeezed with powerful hands. They were the kind of marks that police and pathologists find on the bodies of strangulation victims.

A few minutes later Clelland was followed on the witness stand by Corporal Beverly, who recounted his meeting with the defendant at the hospital and the taking of her statement. Six months before the trial began, Beverly was transferred from the homicide division to the department's Community Oriented Police program.

Responding to questions from Gwinn, he said at one point in his testimony that most but not all of Lisa's statement was taken at the hospital. "We left the hospital at nine minutes after midnight and we arrived at CID at 12:37, and she was placed in interview room Number Two and we began the statement, continued the statement, after that," he said.

After Lisa's statement was admitted as evidence and Gwinn passed the witness to the defense attorney a couple of minutes later, Trainor pounced on what appeared to be an inconsistency in the policeman's testimony.

The lawyer asked Beverly if he was saying the statement was begun in the hospital emergency room and completed at CID. Beverly agreed that was correct.

"But you had asked all your questions before you left for CID? There wasn't any further statement made at CID, was there?" Trainor asserted. He asked the police officer to check his notes for confirmation.

Beverly quickly scanned the statement, then replied: "The question and answer part ended at the hospital."

"So there were no questions asked at Criminal Investigations Division?"

"No sir," Beverly replied.

Trainor moved back once more to Beverly's meeting with Lisa at the hospital, and asked if it was true that when they talked, she was in a great deal of pain but coherent. Beverly said that was true.

"She was also very upset?" Trainor asked.

"She was emotionally upset," the witness said. He also agreed that she cried from time to time.

Trainor asked the witness what his response was when Lisa asked if she should make a statement. Beverly said he told her it was her decision, but that she was the only person who could tell him what had occurred.

As the lawyer neared the end of his cross-examination, he asked the police officer if he had seen the bruises on Lisa's neck. Beverly replied that he remembered seeing neck injuries.

During Gwinn's redirect examination, Beverly said he took Lisa back to the Criminal Investigation Division because it was customary to do that in order to obtain follow-up information. But he conceded that he didn't get any additional information there.

Trainor posed only one question for the police corporal on re-cross-examination. He asked if it was correct that the reason no additional information was obtained from Lisa at the CID was because she wasn't asked any more questions. Beverly said that was true.

If jurors were under the impression Lisa had balked at further interrogation, Trainor's final question to the witness seemed to have put those suspicions to rest. His client was apparently cooperative and helpful. A few minutes after four P.M., Judge Salmon dismissed the jury for the day. Gwinn planned to call two more witnesses.

Early Wednesday morning, William Greene, another of the evidence technicians called to the crime scene, appeared as the first witness of the day. During Gwinn's brief direct examination, he testified about finding the .22 caliber semiautomatic pistol and other items of evidence under Roger's body when it was moved. He said the magazine was still in the pistol when it was found. But there were no rounds remaining in the magazine or in the chamber.

The defense attorney began cross-examination by moving once more to the position of Roger's hands and asked the witness if they were pulled back. Greene said that as he recalled they were to his side.

Trainor asked the evidence technician to explain the meaning of bagging the hands of someone who was dead. Greene replied that paper bags are sometimes put over the hands to protect evidence, such as hair, fibers, or body fluids.

"How about if you were trying to detect whether someone had fired a gun?" the lawyer inquired.

Greene replied that could also be done. But Roger's hands were not bagged.

During redirect examination, Gwinn quickly followed up on the defense lawyer's line of questioning. "In this particular case, given the type of gun apparently used, would it have been of any use to swab the hands?" she asked. Trainor objected before the evidence technician could answer, but was overruled by the judge and the witness was permitted to reply.

Greene indicated it wouldn't have helped the investigation. He explained that .22 caliber ammunition does not produce antimony or barium, which investigators look for traces of to determine if someone has fired a weapon. Gwinn surrendered the witness once more to the defense for re-cross-examination.

Trainor asked the witness if he was saying there was no means of determining by checking someone's hands if they had recently fired a .22 caliber weapon.

The witness responded that an FBI memo advised .22 caliber ammunition does not produce antimony and barium. "Therefore, we cannot swab hands for gunpowder residue," he said. Trainor asked if the FBI memo was the reason Roger's hands weren't bagged. Greene said that was correct.

Moments later the prosecutor entered Roger's autopsy report into evidence and called Dr. Shaikh as her final witness.

The forensic pathologist's testimony began with the witness tracing his education and professional background. He said that during his career he was involved in about 1000 autopsies, including about 200 at the Medical Examiner's Office. All but about fifty of the 200 were homicide cases. Judge Salmon accepted the doctor as an expert witness.

Responding to the prosecutor's questions, Dr. Shaikh explained the autopsy process and pinpointed Roger's injuries and the damage inflicted by the bullets. The testimony was grim and gruesome, but jurors listened intently, drinking in the details as the pathologist continued the depressingly clinical dirge.

Gwinn asked if there was evidence that the wound to Roger's head was inflicted by close range or contact firing. The pathologist said there was no evidence of that on the skin of the entrance wound. He explained that gunshot injuries inflicted from contact or other very close-range firing leave stipples, or small punctate abrasions, on the skin near the entrance wound. Soot carried by gas from the muzzle is also deposited in and around the entrance wound. The witness said he didn't find either of those conditions on Roger's forehead.

After Dr. Shaikh testified it was his opinion Roger died of multiple gunshot wounds, the prosecutor allowed the statement to hang in the silent courtroom for a moment. Then she asked the results of toxicology studies on the fluids and tissue samples collected during the autopsy. The witness replied that the tests revealed no evidence either of alcohol or illicit drugs. There wasn't even any trace of antihistamines, which are included in most over-the-counter medications for colds and sniffles. Gwinn passed her witness to the defense.

Trainor began cross-examination by reviewing Roger's size, and the location and trajectory of the gunshot wounds in the dead man's body. Then he elicited a finer definition of Dr. Shaikh's earlier references to "contact" and "close-range" wounds. "By contact, you mean touching or nearly touching?" he asked.

"That's correct," the pathologist replied.

"And by close-range, is that eighteen inches or less?"

"Yes," Dr. Shaikh agreed.

Trainor asked if it was correct that it could be determined from examination of the wounds that the distance of the injuries from the pistol was more than eighteen inches. Dr. Shaikh again agreed.

"But we can't say whether it's three feet or five feet, can we?" the lawyer asked. The pathologist concurred once again.

Trainor turned to the apparent inconsistency between

the serology tests and Dempsey's earlier testimony that Roger drank a beer during the pizza dinner they shared. Roger was shot about an hour after the men parted at the pizza restaurant.

"Now, is it possible that, is it medically possible that someone could have consumed, say, one beer within an hour or two of his death and it would not appear on the heart blood or the urine?" the lawyer asked.

It wasn't possible, the pathologist replied. He explained that various bodily fluids and tissues are examined for alcohol as part of the autopsy process and it would have shown up.

"So, if this gentleman had consumed any beer within two hours, let's say, before his death, you would have been able to detect it?" Trainor asked.

"Absolutely," the pathologist replied.

The question of the beer Roger reputedly drank shortly before his death was one of the curiosities of the complex trial. The puzzle was never cleared up, and it was left to jurors to determine what they believed and to weigh the possible significance.

It was still mid-morning when Gwinn announced that the state rested its case. Judge Salmon dismissed the jury for a fifteen-minute recess, in order to hear a motion from Trainor before the scheduled opening of the defense.

As soon as the jury left the courtroom, Trainor asked for a judgment of acquittal on both charges. The move was not unexpected, and is almost de rigueur at the conclusion of the prosecution's case in murder trials. Trainor contended that, especially in the murder count, the evidence was insufficient to show willfulness, premeditation, or that the act was deliberate. Judge Salmon disagreed. He denied the motion.

A few minutes later he also excused the jury for an

early lunch after Trainor reported problems locating a witness. The jurors left the courtroom, still unaware if Lisa would testify in her own defense.

When they returned to the courtroom, the first defense witness was Daniel Weston Stewart, a young waiter from Beltsville who was working at the Plata Grande Restaurant in Calverton on the night Lisa met the Albany iron worker.

Stewart said he was talking with a couple of men in a group of five about deer hunting when one of the men at the table went into the dining room where Lisa was sitting. The witness said he went into the kitchen, and when he came back out, she had moved to the table with the group from New York. Trainor asked how he happened to remember her moving from her own table and joining the others.

"Well, that's the first time I've seen someone pick up a person . . ." he stumbled briefly over the words, adding, "what it looked like to me," before awkwardly finishing the convoluted sentence ". . . and brought her back to the table since I had worked there off and on. As long as I've been there I never seen nothing like that happen.

"And also that the tip they gave me I remember," he added. "They tipped me, I think it was thirty dollars. You don't get too many tips like that in that kind of restaurant."

During cross-examination the witness said he first learned of the shooting when his mother told him after hearing a news account on television. But he said he didn't know that the woman he saw in the restaurant was involved, only that the shooting occurred in an apartment near his home.

Gwinn asked if the investigator who talked with him about the incident at the restaurant had to refresh his memory about who was present that night and what he saw.

"That's right," he said.

"You didn't exactly," she began, before hesitating and slightly shifting gears. "Other than a thirty-dollar tip?" she concluded. It was an awkwardly phrased question, but the witness's reply was firm and absolute.

"I remember what happened that night with everything. I remember that real clear," he said.

Gwinn didn't let the matter rest, however. "But initially you did require some refreshment of your memory by the investigator?" she asked.

"That's correct," the witness replied.

Dennis Brian Hawkins, manager of the Ramada Inn, was the next defense witness, and told of observing the confrontation between Lisa and Roger at the hotel. Hawkins testified that when Roger showed up, he overheard Rohloff exclaim, "That's her boyfriend!"

When CitaraManis followed Hawkins to the witness stand, his testimony was interrupted by an early objection after Trainor queried the Assistant Federal Public Defender if he had asked Roger at the trial in Baltimore to describe his relationship with Lisa. Judge Salmon summoned the opposing lawyers to the bench for a conference. Lisa joined her attorney in front of the judge.

Trainor explained that he expected the witness's testimony to show that Roger stated in Lisa's presence they had a beautiful relationship and planned to marry.

"I just merely want to show the effect on the hearer in that she had no reason to believe that she was not welcome to go home again after her jail sentence was completed," he said.

The prosecutor argued that the statement was made in July, four months before Roger's death in November, and consequently it wasn't relevant because so much time elapsed in the interim. His feelings for Lisa could have changed during the four months she was in jail, Gwinn contended.

Trainor responded that he intended to show a chain of evidence extending from April 25, 1991, to the time of her release that would demonstrate Roger had given no signals that she wasn't welcome to return to the apartment. Judge Salmon ruled in favor of the defense.

CitaraManis said Roger testified he loved Lisa and they planned to be married.

The testimony of Christine Ann Barker, Custodian of Records for the Prince Georges County Fire Department, was used to move into evidence records of the 911 call and ambulance runs to the apartment building on Evans Trail.

Then Trainor's co-counsel Rebecca Dieter summoned Deborah Loller, the corrections officer at the Kent County Detention Center, as the next witness. Dieter ran into objections from the prosecutor early in the guard's testimony when she attempted to question Loller about possible discipline problems or dissatisfaction with Lisa's performance of her kitchen chores.

After the judge sustained the objections, the defense attorney moved on to other matters, establishing that Roger was a regular visitor. The testimony moved through Roger's story that he was in a car accident and the canceled visit. Responding to Dieter's questions, the guard indicated she never saw the couple argue or raise their voices to each other. She described the tone of the visits as, "Very pleasant. Happy!"

Gwinn used her opportunity during cross-examination to establish that during Lisa's last month at the jail, she was held in a holding cell, which normally means loss of some of the privileges shared by inmates in the general population, such as performing prison jobs. Despite that, Lisa was permitted to continue working in the kitchen; which under the circumstances seemed to be a special privilege.

Dieter responded during redirect examination by asking the witness if Lisa was still a trusty while she was in the holding cell. The guard confirmed she was, and the defense lawyer responded by asking why Lisa was assigned to the holding cell even though she was a trusty.

"The reason was, she was in the female work release section with, of course, other females, and she had to report for kitchen duty at 0500 hours every morning," Loller explained. "So as not to disturb the other inmates, she was placed in the holding cell because it was space available."

"The fact she was in a holding cell was not reflective of her status as a trusty?" Dieter asked.

"Nothing to do," the witness said in a rather oddly worded reply.

Gwinn was determined not to let the matter rest with that response, and asked for permission to approach the bench. Moments later, with Lisa standing beside her attorneys and listening in, the lawyers huddled with the judge to sort things out.

The prosecutor said the jail warden had advised her Lisa was put in the holding cell because of the detainer from authorities in Arlington. Trainor protested that the detainer had nothing to do with it. But Gwinn insisted she wanted to cross-examine the witness about the matter. Judge Salmon decided to send the jury out of the courtroom for a few minutes while the witness was briefly questioned outside their presence, so he could get an idea of what her testimony would be before making a decision.

Loller indicated in response to Gwinn's queries that although inmates are sometimes placed in holding cells because detainers have been filed, that wasn't the reason in Lisa's case.

"You're aware she had a detainer from Arlington?" Gwinn asked.

"We were aware of the fact on the twenty-third of October," the witness replied.

The lawyers huddled again with the judge. Trainor cited the pretrial ruling that the Arlington case was not relevant and wouldn't be admissible.

Gwinn claimed in response that the line of questioning was relevant. "I think it's a bias on this witness's part toward Miss Rohn to give some other neutral reason as to why she's in the holding cell other than the real reason," the prosecutor contended.

Trainor again argued that the line of questioning about the holding cell wasn't relevant. It was an attempt to go beyond the pretrial order about the Arlington case, he insisted.

"I don't think you need to get into that," Judge Salmon agreed. "Nothing's going to swing on whether she was in the holding cell or not."

Gwinn said she would abide by the court's ruling. But moments after resuming her cross-examination, she was back on the subject of the holding cell. She established from the witness that Lisa got out of bed at five A.M. every morning from the time she began working in the kitchen until she was moved from the jail. She asked if it was correct that Lisa was transferred to the holding cell so she wouldn't disturb other inmates with her five A.M. wake-up time. "Yes," Loller replied.

When Gwinn asked if it was correct that it was more than a month before Lisa was transferred to the holding cell, the witness said she didn't know. After peering at her records, Loller stated that September 23 was the first day Lisa was assigned to the holding cell.

"So she was disturbing the other inmates for over a month—is that correct?" the prosecutor persisted.

"Yes."

The prosecutor continued pressing the matter, and established that other holding cells were available for at least a week before Lisa was moved from general population. And except for a few days, one or both of the holding cells were available for her for five weeks or more before the move.

Redirect examination was brief. Dieter asked the witness if she knew who requested that Lisa be moved to the holding cell. "You're not aware whether it was Lisa or the other females?" she asked.

"I'm not aware of whether it was Lisa or the other female inmates," the guard replied.

A few minutes later she was excused as a witness and Judge Salmon dismissed the jury for the day. The trial was rapidly nearing its conclusion and there had still been no indication to the jury or spectators whether Lisa would be called to testify.

Trainor led off the final day of testimony at ten o'clock Thursday morning by calling Rohloff to the witness stand. The jury had heard from the other woman who played a role in Roger's life as the last days of the tragedy were being played out; now they would hear from the man Lisa spent the night with after the confrontation at the motel.

The Albany iron worker retraced the early events of the fateful Monday night he met the defendant. He said they spent the night together, but she never showed up the following evening for the dinner date they made. He said he waited awhile, but there was no message from her and he eventually went to dinner with his friends. Rohloff hadn't heard from Lisa since she left the note for him at the motel Tuesday morning.

When Rohloff left the witness stand after a brief cross-examination by Gwinn, he looked confident and relaxed. He had delivered his testimony as smoothly and cocksure as a lonely bachelor, or a married rakehell, might while pitching a successful pickup line.

Janelle Wolfe, Lisa's Arlington attorney, testified about their meeting the morning before Roger died. Then Trainor called the defendant as his final witness.

The decision determining whether a defendant will testify isn't always an easy call for defense attorneys to make. Despite the hours that may have been spent with a client, lawyers can't look into the future and somehow divine exactly how the defendant will behave on the stand or how he or she will come across to a jury or judge.

Furthermore, when defendants take the witness stand, they open up areas of inquiry that rules of law have previously closed to the prosecution. Trainor was aware that allowing Lisa to testify was a calculated risk, but he decided it was a gamble he had to take in order to increase chances of saving her from a first-degree murder conviction. Although the decision to put her on the witness stand seemed to increase the likelihood of a manslaughter conviction, it appeared to be a fair trade. If she didn't testify, first-degree murder might be the only option the jury would seriously consider.

The forty-seven-year-old defense attorney was determined, of course, to pull out all the legal stops and do his best to win a full acquittal.

Gwinn wasn't surprised at the decision. Trainor had revealed during one of the bench conferences that Lisa would testify. But the prosecutor was convinced even before then that she would most likely have an opportunity to cross-examine the defendant. Even though Lisa gave a statement to police that pinpointed self-defense for Roger's shooting, the explanation still had to be sold to the jury. And that's usually easier for a defendant to carry off in person than with a piece of paper.

The prosecutor had worked hard preparing for cross-examination, and she was looking forward to crossing verbal swords with the petite defendant.

Lisa looked anything but formidable as she scooted her chair back from the defense table, got to her feet and walked the few feet to the witness stand. The woman who was about to become the star witness at her own trial didn't have the appearance of a dangerous siren—or of any popular conception of a murderess. She looked more like a lonely woman who might reply to a personals ad.

As she was sworn in as a witness, she appeared even smaller than her five feet four inches. Her pale features were barely brightened by a smudge of cosmetics, and her light brown hair appeared lusterless and more frizzy than curly. Her eyes peered from behind red-rimmed glasses.

She was dressed neatly in a black paisley skirt with a trim black jacket and white blouse. Smart defendants with smart lawyers don't show up to testify in murder trials wearing hip-hugging miniskirts or low-cut scoop-neck blouses. Lisa's outfit was unobtrusively stylish and properly modest. As she settled into her seat, she appeared quietly composed; prepared, but not looking forward to the ordeal ahead.

Trainor opened direct examination by quickly leading the witness through a minimum of biographical information, to her reply to the personals ad in the *Washingtonian*. After some debate between the attorneys, she drew a circle around the magazine ad, and the single page it appeared on was accepted as evidence. Lisa testified that she used the name Johnnie Elaine Miller when she wrote to Roger.

Lisa had barely begun to testify when Gwinn leaned over to her associate at the prosecution table. "That voice doesn't go with that person," she said. Lisa's voice was deeper than might have been expected, and she replied to questions with an odd accent that was difficult to define. But her voice was audible and controlled.

"Why is is that you used a name other than your own?" Trainor asked.

"Well, back in 'eighty-six, I found out that I was accused of a charge in Virginia, and at that time I didn't want to face up with it," she responded. "So I decided to use a different name." She confirmed she also used other names while she was a fugitive.

The line of questioning moved back to her dates with Roger, which she said occurred about twice a week until she moved in with him. Trainor asked what their relationship was like when they began living together. "It was wonderful," she said. "It had escalated quickly, but we had—we didn't have any problems. It was a beautiful relationship."

Trainor moved the testimony through Lisa's arrest after Roger found the multiple IDs, through her imprisonment in Baltimore then in Chestertown. Several of the letters he wrote to her were admitted as evidence. The lawyer asked if all the correspondence between the two was always loving and polite, and she replied that it wasn't. They had problems over her arrest, being in jail, and with mistrust and jealousy.

But she didn't feel there was any reason she shouldn't return to the apartment after she was released. Roger always signed his letters affectionately, she said. The testimony moved through her release from jail in Arlington, the confrontation with Roger at the Ramada

Inn, her morning errands, and her return to the apartment.

Lisa said that after going through her things once more while waiting for Roger to return from work and help her move, she fell asleep on the living room couch. After about an hour and a half or two hours, she woke up, used the bathroom, and walked into the kitchen. She was hungry and thirsty, but there wasn't anything in the refrigerator that was appetizing to her. She hadn't grocery shopped. So she settled for a cup of water. She was still in the kitchen when she heard the key turn in the front door, and Roger walked inside.

The witness said Roger demanded to know why her things were still there, and she replied that she thought he was going to help her move them. Roger said he didn't feel like it and stomped into the back bedroom. She followed him and asked to use the car, then returned to the den, picked up a box of books and moved it to the bedroom. She set the box on the edge of the bed.

"After you put the box down, what happened?" Trainor asked.

"I turned around and I was going to go back down the hallway for . . ." Lisa hesitated for an instant, seemingly carried away by the drama of the moment, then resumed: "Roger was standing there and he had a gun in my face!"

Except for the woman in the witness chair and the man standing in front of her, everyone in the courtroom was silent. A couple of the jurors leaned slightly forward in their seats, intent on not missing a word of the vividly compelling testimony.

"What kind of gun was it? Do you know?" Trainor asked.

"It was a pistol."

"When you say it was in your face, how close was it to your face?" the lawyer persisted.

Lisa placed a finger on her forehead just over the bridge of her nose. "It was right between my eyes," she replied.

Trainor asked if Roger said anything.

"He said, 'I'll blow your head off,' and he called me a tramp," she said. The graphic testimony sketched a powerful and frightening mental image of an enraged lover whose emotions had flared dangerously out of control.

Lisa said she pushed the gun out of her face with her right hand. She thought he was merely angry and trying to scare her. She had no idea the gun was loaded.

"What happened?" Trainor asked.

Her reply was simple, but forcefully impressive. "He shot me!"

Trainor asked how close she was to Roger when the gun discharged.

"He was right on top of me," she replied. "It had been maybe two feet or less. He was right on me, because when he put the gun between my eyes, it was almost touching me."

"After you were shot, what happened?"

The petite defendant's reply was convincingly blunt and impossible to misunderstand. "It scared the hell out of me. And it was like a big punch, and I just grabbed for the gun." Lisa said she thought she got hold of the barrel, and pulled the weapon out of Roger's hand.

Roger grabbed her around the throat and slammed her up against the wall, and as they struggled, they crashed into a chair and stumbled, she said. "When we stumbled down, I kicked at him and he went back and I fell down and—" She hesitated, then finished, "—in the door frame of the bathroom."

In reply to a question about how close the gun was when she was shot, Lisa said Roger was so close that when she turned around to walk back down the hall she almost collided with him.

"When you grabbed the gun, how close were you to Roger?" the lawyer continued.

"Right there. I mean I hadn't moved after he shot me," she responded. "I just grabbed. I didn't move back or anything." She said she grabbed the barrel in her right hand.

Trainor again asked her what happened after that, and she repeated her story of being slammed against the wall and kicking at him. ". . . and he fell back and I fell down in the door frame and I had lost sight of him," she said. "And when I stood back up, he was coming at me. He was swearing and everything else and I just froze. I couldn't—"

Her voice caught before she finished the reply. "I couldn't move. He scared me and he just kept coming in with—he was cussing at me and calling me a tramp and everything."

She said she pulled the trigger of the pistol.

"How many times?" Trainor asked.

"I don't know," she replied.

The one-time criminology student said her only thought was that Roger was going to kill her. "He had shot me. If he gets the gun—I can't let him get the gun."

The cadence of her words picked up and tumbled from her mouth in a torrent as she relived her version of the dreadful events the night Roger was killed. "I had known he was in the war and had fired guns before, and had been in a mental hospital the year before. He had tried to commit suicide with a gun, and all I know was if he got that gun back from me, I was dead," she continued.

Lisa's staccato account marked the first time in the trial that mention was made of a reputed suicide attempt by Roger. Trainor didn't pursue the point, however, but continued pressing his witness for more details of the desperate struggle in Apartment 102.

He asked what room Lisa was backing into as she fired the gun. The bathroom, she said. He asked how far she moved into the bathroom.

"Well, when Roger kept barreling in at me, I . . . I was backing up a little bit when he kept coming in, and then when he fell on the floor, he fell at my feet. And then after that I jumped back and to the back of the wall, and I had stepped in the kitty-litter box or whatever it was." She explained she knew she stepped in the litter box because she was in her stocking feet.

Roger was in a crouch and had something in front of him as he barreled in on her, she continued. Again she said he was swearing and calling her a tramp. "I hope it was worth it," she quoted him as saying at one point.

"And you fired?" the lawyer asked once more.

"Yes," she replied. Lisa said after shooting Roger she stepped over his body, tossed the gun away, and ran to the kitchen, where she telephoned 911. She didn't use the bedroom phone because it was on the nightstand and she would have had to climb over the suitcases and boxes stacked at the side of the bed to get to it. She estimated less than one minute elapsed between the time the shooting stopped and she dialed the emergency number.

Judge Salmon interrupted the testimony at that time to order the lunch break. Despite the riveting testimony of the past hour or more, the jury had to discuss other subjects during their meal. The judge ordered them not to talk among themselves or with other people about the case.

When Lisa resumed her testimony at two P.M., Trainor backtracked to the subject of the letters Roger wrote to her while she was in jail. Copies of five of the letters were admitted into evidence.

Then he returned to the death struggle in the bedroom, and she added a few more specific details to her earlier account in response to the lawyer's probing. As she grabbed the receiver of the telephone, blood ran down her right hand and dripped onto the kitchen floor, Lisa recalled. She was hysterical, and when she heard the siren on the ambulance, she took the security chain off the door and ran outside. All she could think of was that the help she needed was there, she testified. She said she didn't know if Roger was dead or alive.

Continuing her account, Lisa said she ran into the hallway outside the apartment, then opened an outer door and peered into the darkness, looking for the ambulance. She couldn't see it. "The only thing I could think was, 'Oh, my God, they got the wrong address,'" she said. So she dashed back into the apartment to call for help again, but there was a big pool of blood under the telephone, so she turned and dashed outside once more. This time she ran through the outer door and onto the sidewalk in front of the building.

She slipped her shoes off after returning to the apartment earlier that afternoon and left them by the dining room table, she explained. Her feet were covered only by panty hose.

When questioning turned to her conversation with Beverly at the hospital, Lisa said she asked the detective two or three times how Roger was. The first couple of times Beverly replied that he didn't know yet, she said. At last, however, he told her: "He's dead!" She also confirmed she completed the written statement at the hospital. But Beverly and another detective continued questioning her throughout the morning after she was taken to the Criminal Investigation Division headquarters, she testified.

Trainor passed his witness to the prosecutor.

Gwinn opened cross-examination by asking Lisa if she was familiar with how a semiautomatic weapon operates. "Vaguely," she replied.

"Well, isn't it correct that you had in your possession at one time a .45 caliber semi-automatic pistol?" the prosecutor demanded.

Trainor was on his feet with an objection, and moments later the lawyers were huddled before Judge Salmon at another bench conference. Evidence about the .45 was suppressed at his client's federal trial and it was suppressed for the current trial, he declared. "That's the contents of the briefcase that was suppressed in the federal case."

Gwinn cited case law. The judge began to answer when Trainor interrupted, remarking again that the evidence had been suppressed.

"Was it suppressed in this case?" Salmon asked.

"Yes, you ruled on it," the defense attorney replied.

Gwinn argued that the evidence wasn't suppressed for all purposes, and she could bring the matter up in cross-examination. Judge Salmon complained he was having difficulty understanding the argument because both lawyers were talking at the same time. Trainor contended that the prosecutor was plowing new ground with her questions and delving into an area of suppressed evidence.

It was eventually decided that the prosecutor could ask the witness how familiar she was with semiautomatic weapons. Gwinn resumed cross-examination. "Have you ever fired a semiautomatic pistol prior to this occasion?" she asked. Lisa said she hadn't. "Have you ever

had one in your possession prior to that occasion?" the
prosecutor continued.

That brought another objection from Trainor, but it
was overruled by the judge. Lisa said she previously had
a .45 automatic.

"That .45 semiautomatic held eight rounds?" Gwinn
asked.

Lisa said she didn't recall.

The prosecutor either missed or ignored the distinc-
tion between Lisa's reference to an automatic and the
question, which was framed to refer to a semiautomatic.
Gwinn turned the testimony to the defendant's use of
the name Johnnie Elaine Miller and the backup ID.

Moments later Trainor asked to approach the bench,
where he observed that the prosecutor had a pile of ID's
and credit cards on her desk. If she tried to introduce
the material, he was going to "hotly contest" the effort,
he cautioned. Gwinn said she didn't plan to try to introduce it.

"But she's waving it in front of the jury," the defense
lawyer complained. He also insisted that he was strongly
against any references to the credit card charges still
pending against his client in Virginia. The prosecutor
responded that she expected the witness to claim she
couldn't remember if she had certain identification.
Gwinn argued that if that occurred, she had a right to
show the document to the witness to refresh her memory.

Judge Salmon eventually decided to have the ID
placed in a box and to permit the prosecutor to pull out
individual documents as they were needed. The device
would be less prejudicial than sorting through a clutter
of bulging envelopes and stacks of driver's licenses,
credit cards, and other forms of identification. The jury

was led out of the courtroom for a few minutes while the documents were arranged in the box.

As Gwinn had predicted, testimony barely resumed before the witness replied that she couldn't remember to a query asking if she had used a certain social security number. The prosecutor dug into the box, pulled out a driver's license, and asked Lisa to look at it to refresh her memory. Lisa peered at the license and said the number was correct.

Gwinn repeated the process with other ID whenever the witness said she couldn't recall something. One time after another, Gwinn got the witness to admit she had used a false name, a false birthday, a false social security number, or other bogus information and documents.

After a few minutes of the merciless cross-examination, it was beginning to look like there was hardly anything about Lisa's past life that could be counted on as having been truthful. Then Gwinn turned to a birth record from Louisiana, which Lisa previously had in her possession, listing the name Johnnie E. Miller. Lisa conceded that wasn't her name and the date of birth wasn't hers.

But when the prosecutor asked if the maiden name of the child's mother, listed on the records, was "G. L. Hart," the witness responded that the information was correct. At last something had turned up on the documents that was truthful. A few moments later, however, Gwinn quizzed the witness about a birth record from California in the name of Dorene R. Davenport, which indicated the birth mother's name was Thompson. The prosecutor asked if Thompson was really the name of her birth mother. Lisa conceded that it wasn't.

Gwinn continued her blistering cross-examination, repeatedly pulling documents from the box. She grilled the witness about vital statistics and other information

on prescription medicine insurance cards, telephone
calling cards, driver's licenses, state-issued nondriver
identification cards, social security cards, even a guest
membership card from the Smithsonian Institute in the
name of Dorene Davenport.

Trainor objected, citing the court ruling against using
information about the pending case in Arlington and his
client's Fifth Amendment rights against self-incrimina-
tion. Judge Salmon barred the prosecutor from a line of
questioning she planned to use showing Lisa lied when
she told her Silver Spring landlady she needed a job
because her husband was killed in an accident. But she
was permitted to continue her withering cross-examination about other ID. Later, however, Gwinn also had to
back off on questioning the witness about the marriage
to Martinez while using the name Stacy Linda Miller.

Despite the fitful starts and stops, the objections,
bench conferences, and pleas of Fifth Amendment protection, when Gwinn at last moved on to other areas of
questioning, Lisa's credibility had been ripped to shreds.
She was exposed before the jury as a woman whose life
was littered with so many lies, it seemed almost impossible to believe she could come even close to keeping
track of all her names, birthdays, birthplaces, social security numbers, and other information.

Gwinn asked who Dolores Swickert was. The defendant said it was her ex-sister-in-law. "Your ex-sister-in-
law. You were married to Raymond Huberts?" the prosecutor asked in obvious disbelief. Lisa admitted she was
never married to Huberts. As Trainor objected, Gwinn
hurried off another question: She's Raymond Huberts's
sister, isn't she?"

There was another bench conference. Trainor objected to any reference to Huberts, arguing that the
prosecutor was preparing to bring in the Arlington case

—and violate his client's Fifth Amendment rights. Judge Salmon ruled Gwinn could cross-examine the witness about whether Swickert was or was not her sister-in-law.

One more lie in a long line of lies had already been exposed, but Gwinn continued lifting up rocks and peering underneath them. She asked once again if Swickert was Huberts's sister, and Lisa said that was true. "You were not married to Raymond Huberts, were you?" the prosecutor continued.

"Not legally, no," Lisa replied. Judging from the testimony, it seemed that just about everything the defendant had anything to do with was tainted and warped by deceit.

When Gwinn asked Lisa if when she was at the Kent County Detention Center she had identified Swickert as her aunt and next of kin, Lisa said she couldn't recall, and the prosecutor handed her a document from the jail so she could refresh her memory. The witness glanced at the paper.

"Yes," she replied. "It says next of kin, Dolores Swickert. And next to it is a [sic] aunt. I don't know if I told them that or not, and it's not my writing."

Gwinn asked if the listed address in Aurora, Illinois, was correct. Lisa said it was.

Questioning continued, touching on Roger's telephone calls, letters, visits, and presents of stamps and other items while Lisa was imprisoned. Lisa agreed he was the only person who visited her while she was locked up, but said she received letters from other people. She claimed Swickert sent stamps to her.

Gwinn accused Lisa of being worried before moving in with Roger that he would find out her life as Johnnie Elaine Miller was a lie. The prosecutor asked Lisa if it was correct that some of the notes she wrote included such words and phrases as "danger," "stop," "think what danger will he cause if J.M. leaves." J.M. were the initials of Johnnie Miller.

The witness said she didn't exactly recall. Her reply was the same when Gwinn asked if she had also written R.P. for Roger Paulson, and described him as "suspicious," "clever," and "resourceful." When the prosecutor asked Lisa if it was true she wrote an introspective note on the same slip of paper, wondering if she should invest more time in Roger or cut her losses and begin over again, she got the same response once more.

Gwinn asked the witness if it would refresh her recollection to look at the slip of paper. Lisa looked and agreed the words were written there.

"In fact, you thought it out very carefully before you moved in with Roger Paulson, didn't you?" Gwinn demanded.

"Yes, I'd say I did," Lisa replied.

Despite occasional miscues and the prosecutor's harsh and demanding cross-examination, most of the time Lisa appeared to be reasonably calm on the stand. Except for the earlier brief display of emotion when the 911 tape was played, she didn't cry. She didn't get flustered and she didn't lose her temper. Her tone was flat and emotionless.

Continuing to respond to Gwinn's barrage of questions, she agreed that while she was in jail, Roger was worried about her harboring resentment against him for turning her in to police. He was afraid she wouldn't forgive him and marry him, she said.

Gwinn accused the witness of being worried while she was jailed that Roger was going to take the money she had left at the apartment.

"I was a little concerned," the witness conceded. "Because, through Roger's letters and talking to him on the phone, he would one day say, 'I love you very much. I want to marry you, still.' And then the next day he would say, 'I don't know if I can go through with this. I don't know if I want to be there for you. I don't know if I can continue.' "

Gwinn asked if it was true that she wished to hold on to Roger's affection because of the savings account he established for her and because her possessions were at his apartment.

"I didn't look at it that way," Lisa replied.

Gwinn asked what she would do if the money and her possessions were gone. "You didn't have anybody else, did you?" she demanded.

"I had my Dolores Swickert!" Lisa said.

A few minutes later, when Gwinn asked the witness if she was aware she was in Roger's will, Trainor objected. Lisa answered the question anyway. "No," she said.

At a bench conference Trainor told the judge that Roger's will was on file in another office at the courthouse, and Lisa was not listed as a beneficiary. Gwinn responded that she had one of Roger's letters, in which he had written that Lisa and Chris were each fifty-percent beneficiaries in his will.

Roger was apparently fudging the truth again. In the will, signed on March 28, 1991, he stipulated that if he were married, the bulk of his estate would go to his wife. If he were not legally married at the time of his death, the estate was to go to his son, unless Christopher's surname had been changed or he was legally adopted by someone else. Roger designated his parents as the next in line to inherit his estate if he weren't married and Christopher didn't qualify under the terms he established. He also directed that he be cremated and that his remains be given to his son.

Although the matter of the estate's value wasn't

deeply delved into at the trial, after paying off Roger's debts and funeral expenses, there wasn't much left to be contested by anyone. Except for the furnishings in the apartment, clothing and other personal items, Roger hadn't accumulated many valuable possessions. The Honda was valued at nearly $14,000, he had nearly $2000 worth of firearms and ammunition, another approximate $2000 in camera equipment, and less than $500 worth of jewelry, which included two watches and a ring.

Judge Salmon directed the prosecutor to rephrase her question to focus on what Lisa thought, rather than what was factual about the will.

"Do you recall receiving a letter from Roger in which he indicated also you're still a fifty-percent beneficiary in my will along with Chris. I see no reason to change this?" the prosecutor asked.

Lisa said she believed that was written on a card.

Gwinn announced that she was through with her questions. There was a mild stir in the courtroom as a few people leaned over to whisper to each other. In spite of the drawn-out, exhausting, toe-curling cross-examination the witness was subjected to, the prosecutor hadn't asked a single question about the shooting itself.

Trainor wrapped up redirect examination within a few minutes. He asked Lisa if she believed she was a fifty-percent beneficiary in the will, and she replied that she did not. The defense lawyer also asked her to explain the reference to an "intentional insult" Roger wrote of in his letter of August 13.

Lisa replied that he had warned he was going to be suspicious and mistrustful of her after she was released and they were together again. She said she told him she didn't want to be "under the eye of the FBI" after she was freed. But he also talked of his love for her in the letter, she said.

When Lisa left the witness stand to take her seat at the defense table, she looked as composed as if she had just finished placing a telephone order for Chinese food or a pizza.

After a brief recess, Judge Salmon reconvened the trial and informed the jury that the attorneys had agreed Lisa was not a beneficiary in Roger's will. In fact, the judge disclosed, the assets of the estate were exceeded by the liabilities. Roger obviously wasn't killed for his money, and if that had figured as a motive in his death, it would have been a dreadful miscalculation.

The prosecutor recalled Greene to testify as a rebuttal witness. The Prince Georges County evidence technician said he hadn't noticed any bullet holes in the garment bag, and that most .45 caliber semiautomatic pistols can hold seven rounds of ammunition in the magazine and another in the chamber.

It was late afternoon on the fourth day of the trial when Judge Salmon began his instructions to the jury. A few minutes earlier he had denied another defense motion for acquittal. He explained to the jurors that under the murder charge, they could find the defendant guilty of first-degree murder, second-degree murder, of manslaughter—or reach a finding of not guilty. The jury was also to return a verdict on the second charge, use of a handgun in the commission of a felony. It was 4:35 P.M. when the jury was dismissed for the evening and advised to return at nine o'clock Friday morning to hear closing arguments.

As Gwinn gathered up her folders and walked out of the courtroom, a couple of her friends asked her if she had made a mistake during cross-examination by not quizzing the defendant about the shooting and the events immediately leading up to it.

The prosecutor was surprised by the concern. She never intended to grill Lisa about the shooting. "No, I didn't make a mistake. I intentionally didn't ask her about the crime," she told her worried colleagues.

"Why would I ask her to reiterate everything all over again when I had all this wonderful impeachment evidence to show she's not a credible person?"

The prosecutor wasted no time during her closing statement Friday morning in taking up the issue of the defendant's credibility. She branded the defendant as a witness who was totally incredible and said her entire life had apparently been a sham. Lisa was probably the type of person who would wake up in the morning wondering who she was supposed to be that day, she declared.

Gwinn described the defendant as: "A person who scammed Roger Paulson, who scammed Rosenbloom Associates, who scammed the Armed Forces Benefits Association, who scammed Mrs. Olender, and who is hoping today to pull the ultimate scam."

The prosecutor claimed that when Lisa was released from jail and realized she couldn't use Roger anymore, she took "the ultimate revenge."

Sketching her version of the shooting for the jury, Gwinn said Roger was shot in the left side as he walked into the back bedroom carrying the garment bag. As he turned and was falling, she said, the defendant shot him twice more, in the shoulder, then in the right side of the head. "And 235 pounds of man go 'thud,' and that's what Erik Astheimer heard. Erik Astheimer said he heard a thud, thought it was somebody getting thrown against a wall, but 235 pounds of Roger Paulson falling on the floor will give you a big 'thud.' And then there was a long pause. Mr. Astheimer said about a thirty-second pause, and then Lisa shot herself."

The prosecutor continued hacking away at the defendant's credibility, pointing to the bogus names and bogus ID, and accusing her of plotting scams and revenge. It was time to tell Lisa that she had reached the end of the line for scams, Gwinn asserted. "You murdered Roger Paulson," she declared. She turned to glare at the defendant and deliver a final, stern condemnation: "The facts prove that you murdered Roger Paulson, and you will not walk out of this courtroom."

Trainor urged the jury to judge his client on what occurred at the Evans Trail apartment during the eight minutes between 7:48 P.M. and 7:56 P.M., November 19, 1991, not on her background. And he cautioned them not to be sidetracked by any suggestions that Lisa may have shot Roger for his money. She wasn't in his will, and there wasn't any money anyway.

He disputed Officer Tyler's testimony that Lisa was calm when he encountered her outside the apartment, and criticized some witnesses for reputedly trying too hard. And he said the piece of luggage found under Roger's body wasn't a garment bag, but was a suitcase-type bag with a handle and a shoulder strap.

It wasn't the kind of bag Officer Riedl referred to during testimony, the lawyer declared. "He said two fingers over the shoulder like he's carrying his bag over the shoulder as in a coat-hanger type bag. He would have no way to know there were no coat hangers on top of it because the body was on top."

The defense lawyer talked about the shell casings found in the bedroom, and suggested that some of them may have been casings Christopher brought home from the firing range to play with.

He picked at the professionalism of the investigation, pointing out that some evidence collected at the scene, such as the piece of the maroon bag, were never sent to the FBI laboratories for analysis. Scrapings weren't even taken from the blood splashes on the bathroom wall, he pointed out. "You have to question whether the investigation was really completed," he declared.

Trainor reviewed the threatening notes Roger left at the front door, and asserted that Roger's actions and writings proved he was a jealous man. Roger claimed in his letters he had discovered past infidelities, the lawyer told the jury. "He mentions Doug; he mentions Gene; he mentions Habeeb. Not to say that any of that was proven by Mr. Paulson, but it shows that he was jealous and suspicious."

Continuing to press his contention that Lisa acted in self-defense, Trainor said Roger had armed himself to the teeth, stocking up on assault rifles and ammunition. Finally, the defense attorney asked the jury once more not to judge his client on her past or her character.

Gwinn had one more opportunity to address the jury before deliberations began, and she reminded the members of the panel that only two people really knew what happened in Roger's apartment the night of November 19, 1991. They had only heard from one of them, and that was a person who hadn't lived a truthful day in her life for years, she said.

The prosecutor accused Lisa of ambushing Roger, and putting her things in the back bedroom so he wouldn't know she was there when he returned to the apartment. As he walked past the bedroom carrying the garment bag, Lisa called his name, then shot him as he began to turn, Gwinn declared. "If she had been shot before the struggle and before this occurred, you would have seen blood on the wall, on the carpet, in the bathroom. But it's not there."

Gwinn claimed Lisa arranged things to back up her murder scenario for investigators during the thirty seconds after the next to last shot was fired. She took her coat and shoes back into the living room, then returned to the bedroom and fired the final shot through her own arm, the prosecutor said. She described the defendant as a calculating woman who planned everything before Roger returned home, then waited in the bedroom for him with a gun.

It was a few minutes before eleven A.M., when Gwinn concluded her summation and Judge Salmon dismissed the two alternate jurors. The jury deliberated more than eight hours before sending a note to the judge asking for permission to go home for the weekend. Judge Salmon honored the request, and after warning them to avoid news stories or discussions of the trial with anyone, instructed them to return at nine o'clock Monday morning.

After conferring with the judge and checking with her boss, Gwinn gathered up a handful of paperback novels and headed for the inviting solitude of the beach. Lisa's trial was the second of three grueling back-to-back homicide cases she was responsible for prosecuting, and she had promised herself a three or four day break relaxing by herself, with no case files, no husband, and no kids. But she provided her boss with her telephone number so she would be available to make a quick sprint back to Upper Marlboro from her mini-vacation if she was needed.

Woodall and Assistant State's Attorney Deborah Johnston were representing the prosecution when the jurors returned Monday morning and court officers learned almost immediately of an unexpected problem.

One of the jurors had peered in a copy of the fourth edition of *Black's Law Dictionary* to look up the definition of the word, "premeditation." And before the jury was called into the courtroom, she had shared the information with other members of the panel. During questioning by the judge, juror Phylis Chen disclosed she also looked up the word "deliberate" in the same dictionary. Ms. Chen said she was beginning to read the fine print when the jury was summoned. Trainor asked for a mistrial.

After considerable discussion, and polling the jury to obtain individual assurances that their verdicts would not be affected by what was read to them from the dictionary, Judge Salmon ruled that deliberations could continue. Trainor's motion for mistrial was denied.

About ninety minutes after deliberations were resumed, the jury notified Judge Salmon they had reached verdicts. The attorneys and Lisa were quickly summoned to the courtroom. The defendant was dressed in a flowered skirt and dark jacket, and her face was expressionless as she sat between her lawyers to await the verdict.

Forewoman Linda Thompson reported the jury had found the defendant guilty of first-degree murder, and guilty of use of a handgun in commission of a felony. The verdicts were unanimous. The prosecution had scored a total victory, a clean sweep.

Lisa's head seemed to slump into her shoulders at the defense table, but there were no screams or emotional displays.

Shortly after the convicted murderess was led out of the courtroom, one of the jurors told a reporter for the *Journal* that Lisa lost her credibility after she was called as a witness, and it was difficult to believe anything she said. In the same news story Trainor was quoted as declaring that the prosecutor's tactic of attacking his client's credibility and past rather than what happened at the apartment had clearly worked.

Speaking anonymously, jurors also indicated they were impressed by Astheimer's testimony about the sequence of shots. And they said they were suspicious of Lisa's story of returning to the apartment after Roger stuck a gun in her face.

Woodall described Lisa to another reporter as a cold woman and said she and her colleagues were pleased that jurors "saw through her con."

Friday morning, October 2, was scheduled for sentencing. But delays added nearly six weeks more before Lisa finally appeared before Judge Salmon on Thursday, November 12, to be sentenced for Roger's murder.

At the sentencing, Gwinn continued her strong argument that Roger's shooting was premeditated and Lisa should be sent to prison for a life term without parole. "The motive for this was revenge because Roger Paulson had testified against her in federal court," the prosecutor declared.

Trainor responded in his presentencing statement that it wasn't clear who loaded the pistol and who initiated the confrontation. In his forceful plea for a lenient sentence, the defense attorney also pointed out his client's troubled family background of alcoholism and abuse, including her sister's suicide.

Given an opportunity to speak before sentencing, Lisa told Judge Salmon she never meant to hurt Roger. "I still can't believe he's dead. Every night when I go to sleep I don't want to go to sleep because I still see his body lying there," she said as tears welled in her eyes and streamed down her cheeks. "During the day I can put it out of my mind with other things, but at night I can't."

The judge imposed the mandatory life term in prison on the murder conviction, and another twenty-year term for using a handgun in the commission of a felony. But the sentences weren't as harsh as they sounded.

Judge Salmon directed that the life sentence be served with the possibility of parole, not without the possibility of parole, as the prosecution asked. He said he didn't believe Roger was killed in retaliation for testifying against Lisa, but because he was throwing her out of his apartment. Based on the criminal statutes and established sentencing guidelines, it was the most lenient sentence available to him.

On a Maryland Sentencing Guidelines Worksheet, used to help compute sentences based on a system of points, it was noted that Lisa had no prior criminal record in any jurisdiction as a juvenile or adult under her own name or under any of her known aliases.

Judge Salmon also directed that the sentence for use of a handgun be served concurrently with the murder sentence. The defendant was credited for 372 days already spent behind bars since her arrest. She is expected to become eligible for consideration for parole twelve and a half years after sentencing, just about the time of her forty-second birthday in the year 2004.

Soon after sentencing, Lisa was driven by guards to the Maryland Correctional Institute for Women at Jessup. The only state prison for women in Maryland, the institution is a few miles south of Baltimore on the Howard and Arundel county line. Roger could have driven there from his home in Beltsville in about thirty minutes.

Epilogue

Since sentencing, Lisa Ann Rohn has kept busy at the Maryland Correctional Institution for Women with her own education and helping other inmates prepare to take General Educational Development examinations.

She is studying college courses and for a while attended a sewing class. She has taken advantage of various rehabilitation programs available to her, and continues to be a voracious reader. Her literary tastes run to the classics. In accordance with normal practice for dealing with convicted murderers at the institution, she is housed in maximum security.

Lisa has also maintained weekly contact through letters and telephone calls with her attorney, who continues to believe strongly in her contention that Roger was shot in self-defense.

As this book was being written, Trainor said the outcome of Lisa's murder trial continued to haunt him. And he claimed it is one of only a few cases he has handled over the years in which he genuinely believes in the innocence of a client despite a guilty verdict.

Soon after Lisa's conviction, her lawyer filed a motion for a new trial. As grounds, Trainor cited jury misconduct based on juror Chen's independent legal research and sharing of her information with other members of the panel; and on the admission into testimony of information about his client's federal conviction, even though it had already been overturned at the time of the murder trial.

The petition is still pending in Annapolis before the Maryland Court of Special Appeals, which is the intermediate appellate level in the state.

Trainor also filed a petition asking for modification of sentence, requesting his client's prison term be reduced. Documents opposing the petition were filed by the Prince Georges County State's Attorney's office. In the state's answer to the petition, Gwinn pointed out that the judge had the benefit of a presentence report at the time of sentencing. And nothing had occurred since sentencing that would warrant a reduction in the prison term. Early in March 1993, Judge Salmon issued an order that the sentence would be held in abeyance. The matter was still to be settled.

In Arlington the charges of credit card fraud were still pending against Lisa.

When Gwinn returned to the Prince Georges County Courthouse after her brief respite at the shore, she immediately plunged headlong into another challenging homicide trial. A few days later the two defendants, members of the Phantoms motorcycle gang, were convicted of first-degree murder for killing a man whom the prosecutor said they believed was a federal informant against them.

The back-to-back cases were instrumental in a decision by Gwinn's boss, State's Attorney Alexander Williams, Jr., to arrange for a bill to be introduced into the Maryland State Legislature seeking to expand the death penalty statute to include killers convicted of murdering witnesses. The proposed legislation was defeated.

Gwinn and Trainor were expecting to face off against each other in another murder case scheduled for trial in the Prince Georges County Circuit Court early in October 1993. Trainor's wife and law partner, Leslie Billman, was expected to try the case with him, marking the first time they would work together in a courtroom.

At the federal courthouse in Baltimore, Barbara Sale was promoted to Chief of Criminal Appeals, and keeps busy with research, and attempts to keep up with mounds of paperwork.

Bill Cowell retired in March 1993, after twenty-nine years and two months with the Arlington County Police Department. During baseball season, Cowell regularly drives to Norfolk, where his son, Michael Robert Cowell, has a baseball scholarship at Old Dominion College University.

He also frequently plays golf with his friend, Frank Soulier, who was the prosecutor for Huberts in Arlington. Soulier later moved to Richmond and the State Attorney General's office there, then left public service and went into private practice in Arlington.

Shortly before retiring, Cowell received a letter from a prisoner in Ohio who read a news story about the murder case and wanted to get in touch with Lisa. He said he met her in Dayton when he was playing with a band, and wanted to renew the acquaintance. Cowell did not provide him with Lisa's address.

High-tech criminals who prey on ATMs didn't take a vacation to celebrate Cowell's retirement, they simply continued to develop their skills and sharpen their techniques to keep up with the times. In May 1993 at a shopping mall on the outskirts of Manchester, Connecticut, thieves installed a bogus ATM and looted $50,000 from the accounts of legitimate customers. In the process, the ingenious thieves lifted the computer codes of two to three thousand bank cards.

Astounded Secret Service agents told news reporters they had never before run into such a sophisticated electronic rip-off. "This stuff we're seeing today, white-collar crime, is the crime of the century," Cowell says.

A few weeks after Lisa was processed into the women's prison at Jessup, authorities established the Girl Scouts Behind Bars program for the young daughters of inmates. Twice a month the girls, members of three troops, are bussed through the gates of the institution to spend a couple of hours with their mothers talking about everything from sex and drug abuse to self-esteem.

Lisa's own daughters do not participate in the program, and are believed to be with their father and his wife. Lisa also does not see her boys, who have been raised by her mother in California.

On March 16, 1993, CBS broadcast a made-for-television movie filmed by Longbow Productions called "Dying to Love You." Promoted as being based on a true story, the film deals with a tragic romance that began with a lonely man's personals ad and ends when his lover traces a murderous epilogue to their romance with a pistol. Tracy Pollan played the woman with multiple IDs. Tim Matheson played the lover who found the documents in her briefcase.

Interviewed by the *Los Angeles Times* about her role, Pollan told the writer it would make people "think twice" before replying to personals.